INSTRUCTOR'S MANUAL AND TEST BANK
TO ACCOMPANY

BUILDING VOCABULARY SKILLS, 3/e
SHORT VERSION

IMPROVING VOCABULARY SKILLS, 3/e
SHORT VERSION

ADVANCING VOCABULARY SKILLS, 3/e
SHORT VERSION

Janet M. Goldstein

TOWNSEND PRESS

Copyright © 2002 by Townsend Press, Inc.
Printed in the United States of America
ISBN 0-944210-19-8
9 8 7 6 5 4 3 2

Send book orders to:
Townsend Press
1038 Industrial Drive
West Berlin, New Jersey 08091

For even faster service, call us at our toll-free number:
1-800-772-6410

Or FAX your request to:
1-800-225-8894

Or send us e-mail at:
townsendcs@aol.com

Instructor's Manual and Test Bank to Accompany
BUILDING VOCABULARY SKILLS, SHORT VERSION, 3/e
IMPROVING VOCABULARY SKILLS, SHORT VERSION, 3/e
ADVANCING VOCABULARY SKILLS, SHORT VERSION, 3/e

Copyright © 2002 by Townsend Press

Contents

Introduction

BRIEF GUIDELINES FOR USING THE VOCABULARY BOOKS

1. As you probably know, each of the three vocabulary books has a recommended reading level:

   Building Vocabulary Skills, Short Version: reading level 7–9
   Improving Vocabulary Skills, Short Version: reading level 9–11
   Advancing Vocabulary Skills, Short Version: reading level 11–13

Be careful not to choose a book on too high an instructional level. Ideally, most of your students should have a sense of *some* of the words in the book you choose. As they work through the chapters, they can then strengthen the words they already know, as well as master the words they're only half sure of, or don't know at all. For most remedial and developmental courses, we recommend the first two books.

A given level is likely to be too difficult if students know almost none of the words. You run the risk of operating on a level of frustration rather than instruction. *To repeat, then: Please take very special care that you choose a book that will not be too difficult for the majority of your students.*

2. Don't feel you must cover every single chapter in a book. Each book is packed with activities—ones that will take a fair amount of time for students to work on at home, or for you to cover with them in class. The activities are necessary, for the simple truth is that the more students work with words, the better they will understand them. *It is better to cover fewer words more thoroughly than to try to cover too many too lightly.*

3. The "Final Check" passage in each chapter poses a more difficult challenge for students than the sentence-level activities that precede it. To handle the passages, students must have done their homework with the earlier activities. The passage will be an excellent final opportunity for them to deepen their knowledge of the words in the chapter.

Because the final check is such a challenge, as well as an opportunity to solidify learning, we recommend that you *not* use it as a mastery test. Instead, we suggest that you use the appropriate mastery test in this book.

4. The pages in the student book (though not in the instructor's edition) are perforated and so can be easily torn out and removed. In particular, you may want students to hand in the unit tests, which are on the front and back sides of a page.

5. Pretests are available for each book as well as each vocabulary unit in each book. The pretests start on page 7 of this *Instructor's Manual*. You have permission to make as many copies as you want of these pretests (and the other materials in this book) if you are currently using one of the vocabulary texts in a course. The pretests can be used at the start of a unit, and the posttests at the end of a unit, as an accurate way to measure vocabulary progress and mastery.

A SUGGESTED INSTRUCTIONAL APPROACH

Here is a suggested classroom approach that we think will maintain interest and keep students active in learning the words. You may want to use all or part of it—or you may find that it helps you decide the special way you want to teach the words to your students.

First of all, have students work through the introduction to the book (on pages 1 to 6). Don't teach it; have them *read* it (they need the reading practice!), follow directions, and insert all the answers needed. Then spend a few minutes reviewing their answers and checking their understanding of the material.

Next, give students the pretest for the unit you will be covering. Explain that at the end of the unit, they will be given a posttest on the same words, so you and they will be able to measure what they have learned. Then proceed as follows:

1. Preview each of the ten words in a chapter by printing the words, one at a time, on the board. Ask students if they can pronounce each word. As needed, write some of the pronunciations on the board. You may also want to use, or ask students to use, some of the words in a sentence. And it's OK to ask for or to give short meanings of some of the words. Don't go into a lot of detail, but make this a good general introduction to the words.

Then, based on the verbal preview, ask students to turn to the first page of the chapter. Explain that in each case the two sentences in "Ten Words in Context" will give clues to the meaning of the boldfaced word. You can say, "OK, take five minutes or so and read the sentences in "Ten Words in Context." Or you can proceed immediately to Step 2.

2. Put students in groups of two or three. (It is hard to overstate the value that small group work can have: if managed successfully, it uses peer pressure to keep everyone involved in the work of the class.) Explain, "Here's what I want you to do. One of you read the first word and the two sentences that contain the word. Make sure it's being pronounced correctly. Always help each other out with the pronunciation. Then think about the context very carefully. The context will give you very strong clues as to what the word means. Your ability to use the context surrounding an unfamiliar word is an excellent skill to have whenever you're reading something and you come upon a word you don't know. Then I'd like all of you to see if you can pick out the right meaning from the three answer choices that follow that first word.

"After you do that, have someone else in your group pronounce the second word and read the two sentences for that word. Then work together again and pick out the right answer choice. And so on, until you've done all ten words. Look up at me when you've done all the words."

3. Of course, not every group will finish the words at exactly the same time. We suggest you take a middle-ground approach to the challenging fact that every group will move at a different speed. When a couple of the groups are finished (and starting to get restless), and others are still working, say, "OK—even if you're not quite finished yet, we're going to go over the ten words as a class. Somebody please volunteer to pronounce the first word and give us its meaning."

4. After reviewing the pronunciations and meanings of the words, say, "Now I want you to work as a group in adding the words needed in Sentence Check 1 and Sentence Check 2. Again, you want to practice *looking at context* very carefully. Context will give you clues you need to figure out the meanings of words."

5. When several groups are finished, say, "OK, not everyone is quite finished, but we're going to go over the sentences you've been working with. Will someone volunteer to read the first sentence and insert the word needed?"

6. Next, say, "The last activity here is the most challenging. Why don't you all work on this individually. Read over the passage once. Then go back and start reading more carefully and slowly and try to put in some of the words. Then go back a third time to get the remaining words. You may not be able to get all the words at first. Try to get some of them. That will help you do the rest. Pay close attention to the context. Remember you're building up your skill at using context to figure out the meaning of a word."

7. When some people are done, say, "All right—let's review the passage. Would someone read the first couple of sentences and insert the missing words?"

8. Finally, tell students to review and study the ten words at home. Then, at the start of the next class, say, "Spend about two minutes reviewing the words. I'll then pass out a mastery test for the ten words. I will grade this test, so you want to do your best to remember the words." (Knowing that a grade is going to be involved always provides students with an extra boost of incentive.)

An alternative instructional approach is to proceed as described above for steps 1 to 3. Then, instead of having students work in small groups, ask them to work individually on Sentence Check 1 and Sentence Check 2. After they are finished, have them come individually to your desk so that you can quickly check their answers, clarify any confusion, and move them on to the Final Check. In this individualized scenario, everyone is working at his or her own pace, and you are working at a *very* steady pace. When students finish the Final Check, you can either have them work with people who are not done, or get a head start on another chapter that you plan to assign for homework.

ADDITIONAL ACTIVITIES

Let us repeat a point stated earlier: *The more students work with words, the more they can learn.* Here are other activities you can use, in addition to the many in the book. Choose whichever combination of activities goes best with your teaching style and the learning styles of your students.

1. Word cards. Students can use 3 × 5 or 4 × 6 index cards to create a bank of words. Word cards can help students master words in the book; the cards are also a helpful tool for learning unknown words that students come across in reading. Students simply jot down an unfamiliar word on the front of the card. Then, when they have finished their reading, they can complete the front and back of a card. Here is a suggested format:

Front of Card	*Back of Card*
p. 9, BVS　　　　　　　　　　*Verb*　　　　　　comply　　　　　　Synonym: obey　　　Antonym: disobey	1) To do as commanded or asked.　　2) "My wife is so used to being the boss at work," Martin said, "that she is annoyed when I don't <u>comply</u> with her every request at home."　　3) Our teacher expects us to <u>comply</u> with his instructions without asking questions.

Note that the front of the card has the target word, the page number and source where the word can be located, the part of speech, a synonym, and an antonym. The back of the card has three entries: 1) the *definition*, based on the way the word is used in context; 2) a *phrase or sentence* showing the word in context (this can be taken from the source where the student has come upon the word); and 3) a *student-created sentence* which shows an understanding of the word. Students can use this same format when they encounter unfamiliar words in their textbooks and other reading.

2. Identifying words. Present lists of words written with diacritical marks and ask students to identify the words. For example:

tăk′tĭk _____

rĭ-kûr′ _____

ĭ-kwāt′ _____

mă-lĭsh′əs _____

rĭ-sĭp′rə-kāt _____

3. Analogies. Using analogies is another way to encourage students to think about words. Students should first be taught the format of analogies, and instructors should begin with the simpler types of analogies: synonyms and antonyms. For example:

> Choose the italicized word needed to complete each analogy:
> acknowledge : admit = avert : *cure, prevent, accept*
> candid : dishonest = concise : *wordy, brief, funny*
> precise : methodical = stop : *terminate, speculate, nurture*
> modern : obsolete = pacify : *mediate, hamper, infuriate*

Keep in mind that analogies are difficult for students, especially at-risk students. But if instructor guidance is provided, analogies can help even at-risk students think about words conceptually.

Note that Unit Test 4 in each unit contains twenty word analogies—an activity that is new to the third edition.

4. Imaging. The use of imagery as a way of remembering vocabulary words has been researched rather extensively. Results typically indicate that students who are trained to use imagery techniques—or in simple terms, told to "form pictures in their minds"—remember the meanings of words better than those who do not employ such techniques.

Here's an example: Think of a mugger facing you, his hands clutching a long, heavy piece of gray pipe. On the pipe are written in dripping red paint the letters C-O-M-P-L-Y. You are handing over your wallet.

We suggest taking five or ten minutes every once in a while to have students get a piece of paper and write up their images—the more vivid the better—for remembering a given word in a chapter. Then ask students to hand in the paper (signing their names to the paper is optional). Quickly flip through the papers, reading the most effective ones aloud to the class.

5. Generating sentences. Have students generate their own sentences using the words, or as a more advanced activity, have them write a story using five of the words. (You may want to have a paraprofessional working with you for these activities, which require individual checking and detailed feedback.)

6. Group-Label. This more abstract activity is best used after students have a larger word bank from which to work. It might be used at the end of a unit of five vocabulary chapters. Students are asked to classify words into groups and to give each group a label that would be common somehow to all words in that group. Here are examples:

Words related to honesty
   (BVS, Unit One)
   acknowledge
   candid
   hypocrite
   impartial
   legitimate

Words relating to conflict
   (IVS, Unit One)
   antagonist
   animosity
   malign
   exploit
   assail

SUGGESTED SYLLABI

Suggested Syllabus for Using the Book as a Core Text

Since each book consists of 20 chapters packed with activities, it can easily serve as a core text for a vocabulary course—especially when supplemented by the test bank and the computer software. In a 15-week class that meets three hours a week, you can cover slightly more than one chapter a week. The remaining time can be used for the unit tests that close each of the four units in each book, as well as for the pretests, posttests, mastery tests, and additional material on the computer disks.

We recommend strongly that students be encouraged to do a lot of reading at the same time that they are learning vocabulary words. For remedial and developmental students, widespread reading, in addition to continuing, intensive work on vocabulary, is the best way to develop vocabulary skills.

Suggested Syllabus for Using the Book as a Supplement in a Reading Course

In many courses, the vocabulary book will serve as a supplementary text. In such cases, and assuming a 15-week semester with three hours of class a week, one hour a week can be devoted to vocabulary. In part of that hour, go over the first three pages in class, using a method similar to the one we have described on pages 2-3. Assign the last part of the chapter (Sentence Check 2 and the Final Check) for homework. Then, as the first item of business in the next class, review that material. Follow up the review with the appropriate mastery test from this booklet. In this manner, 14 or 15 chapters can be covered in class.

Assign as homework the remaining five or six chapters, one or two per unit. Then, at the end of each unit of five vocabulary chapters, give students one of the four vocabulary unit tests in the book. The unit test will enable you to hold students responsible for the outside-of-class vocabulary chapters as well.

You might want to tell students in advance that you will give them one of the unit tests. However, don't tell them *which* of the four tests you will give. Encourage them, in other words, to review all of the words in the unit test materials. You might want to tell students in advance that you will give them one of the unit tests. However, don't tell them *which* of the three tests you will give. Encourage them, in other words, to review all of the words in the unit test materials.

If there is not enough time in class to give the unit tests, you can ask students to do all four of the unit tests at home. Then, in class, collect and grade *one* of the four. (Again, students should not know which of the four you will collect. That way, they will have to assume responsibility for working with all of the words.)

ABOUT THE COMPUTER SOFTWARE

After students complete a vocabulary chapter in the book, they can deepen their learning by turning to the computer. Two main tests are provided for each chapter in each Townsend Press vocabulary book: one testing *words in context*, the other (more advanced) testing the *meanings of the words without context*.

The tests, available in either Windows or Macintosh format, include a number of user- and instructor-friendly features: a sound option, mouse support, icons, color, dialog balloons, a record-keeping file, and actual, audible pronunciations of each word. Students can access their scores at any time; instructors can access student scores by selecting Administrator mode and entering the appropriate password.

Here are other features of this powerful computer program:

- Frequent use is made of the user's first name—a highly motivational word to any student!

- Every answer is followed by a brief explanation of that answer. Such explanations help ensure learning. Thus the software *teaches* as well as tests.

- A running score appears at the bottom of each screen, so the user always knows how well he or she is doing.

- A score file shows or prints out the user's final scores.

ABOUT THE WORD LISTS

As stated in the preface, word frequency lists were consulted in selecting the vocabulary words used in each book. Two sources in particular should be noted:

Word Frequency Book—John B. Carroll, Peter Davies, and Barry Richman.
The American Heritage Publishing Company, Inc., 1971.

The Living Word Vocabulary—Edgar Dale and Joseph O'Rourke.
World Book–Childcraft International, Inc., 1981.

Also consulted were lists in a wide number of vocabulary books as well as words in standardized reading tests. In addition, the authors and editors prepared their own lists. A computer was used to help in the consolidation of the many word lists. Group discussion then led to final decisions about the words that would be most appropriate for students on each reading level.

RESEARCH AND VOCABULARY INSTRUCTION

Sherrie Nist has prepared an article offering suggestions on vocabulary instruction in the context of current research on vocabulary development. Some of the article has been incorporated into this introduction. The article, which includes an extensive bibliography, is available at no charge by writing to Townsend Press.

A FINAL NOTE

We invite you to write or otherwise communicate to us about your experiences in using the vocabulary books. This series is not a static project; we intend to revise it on a regular basis, responding to your suggestions and comments as well as our own continuing classroom experiences with the texts. To contact us, write to the Vocabulary Series Editor, Townsend Press, 1038 Industrial Drive, West Berlin, NJ 08091; or email us at <townsendcs@aol.com>. By learning the reactions of you and your students, we can work at making what we feel are very good books even better.

Pretest

> This test contains 100 items. In the space provided, write the letter of the choice that is closest in meaning to the **boldfaced** word.
>
> *Important:* Keep in mind that this test is for diagnostic purposes only. **If you do not know a word, leave the space blank rather than guess at it.**

____ 1. **compel**　　**a)** avoid　　**b)** delight　　**c)** force　　**d)** finish

____ 2. **drastic**　　**a)** dirty　　**b)** suitable　　**c)** extreme　　**d)** sticky

____ 3. **comply**　　**a)** choose　　**b)** forget　　**c)** run into　　**d)** do as asked

____ 4. **acknowledge**　　**a)** prevent　　**b)** admit　　**c)** study　　**d)** deny

____ 5. **concise**　　**a)** peaceful　　**b)** clear and brief　　**c)** proper　　**d)** wordy

____ 6. **isolate**　　**a)** combine　　**b)** heat up　　**c)** separate　　**d)** freeze

____ 7. **fortify**　　**a)** suggest　　**b)** strengthen　　**c)** avoid　　**d)** approve of

____ 8. **extensive**　　**a)** bold　　**b)** separated　　**c)** outside　　**d)** large in space or amount

____ 9. **refuge**　　**a)** shelter　　**b)** rejection　　**c)** building　　**d)** garbage

____ 10. **erratic**　　**a)** inconsistent　　**b)** mistaken　　**c)** in a city　　**d)** noisy

____ 11. **morale**　　**a)** spirit　　**b)** principle　　**c)** threat　　**d)** majority

____ 12. **lenient**　　**a)** heavy　　**b)** not strict　　**c)** delayed　　**d)** not biased

____ 13. **undermine**　　**a)** weaken　　**b)** cross out　　**c)** reach　　**d)** dig up

____ 14. **menace**　　**a)** character　　**b)** threat　　**c)** assistance　　**d)** puzzle

____ 15. **impartial**　　**a)** without prejudice　　**b)** not whole　　**c)** hidden　　**d)** strict

____ 16. **endorse**　　**a)** suggest　　**b)** stop　　**c)** support　　**d)** start

____ 17. **imply**　　**a)** approve of　　**b)** interfere　　**c)** do mischief　　**d)** suggest

____ 18. **obstacle**　　**a)** barrier　　**b)** remedy　　**c)** list　　**d)** answer

____ 19. **novice**　　**a)** book　　**b)** false impression　　**c)** beginner　　**d)** servant

____ 20. **hypocrite**　　**a)** interference　　**b)** insincere person　　**c)** injection　　**d)** threat

____ 21. **superficial**　　**a)** lacking depth　　**b)** perfect　　**c)** very deep　　**d)** faulty

____ 22. **denounce**　　**a)** introduce　　**b)** condemn　　**c)** change　　**d)** compliment

____ 23. **transition**　　**a)** purchase　　**b)** invention　　**c)** repetition　　**d)** change

____ 24. **sustain**　　**a)** keep going　　**b)** approve of　　**c)** avoid　　**d)** wait for

____ 25. **conservative**　　**a)** not definite　　**b)** opinionated　　**c)** resisting change　　**d)** understanding

(Continues on next page)

_____	26. **compensate**	a) change	b) win out	c) receive	d) repay
_____	27. **verify**	a) imagine	b) prove	c) keep going	d) cancel
_____	28. **surpass**	a) go beyond	b) reverse	c) take	d) prove wrong
_____	29. **tentative**	a) suitable	b) not final	c) outside	d) unclear
_____	30. **diversity**	a) separation	b) conclusion	c) enthusiasm	d) variety
_____	31. **prudent**	a) rudely brief	b) careful	c) obvious	d) delicate
_____	32. **apprehensive**	a) uneasy	b) thoughtful	c) relaxed	d) opinionated
_____	33. **acute**	a) mild	b) dull	c) severe	d) nervous
_____	34. **prominent**	a) clean	b) obvious	c) dangerous	d) reasonable
_____	35. **arrogant**	a) wealthy	b) ridiculous	c) average	d) overly proud
_____	36. **cite**	a) repeat	b) mention in support	c) look for	d) read
_____	37. **retort**	a) great respect	b) sharp reply	c) false idea	d) court order
_____	38. **exempt**	a) needed badly	b) attacked	c) unconcerned	d) free of a duty
_____	39. **accessible**	a) easily reached	b) itchy	c) difficult	d) folded
_____	40. **prevail**	a) climb	b) win out	c) lose	d) enroll early
_____	41. **evasive**	a) talkative	b) deliberately unclear	c) friendly	d) overly forceful
_____	42. **elapse**	a) flow	b) pass by	c) measure	d) record
_____	43. **lethal**	a) sweet-smelling	b) ancient	c) deadly	d) healthy
_____	44. **ordeal**	a) change	b) painful experience	c) good time	d) office
_____	45. **infer**	a) offer	b) conclude	c) reject	d) answer
_____	46. **unique**	a) common	b) pure	c) one-of-a-kind	d) well-known
_____	47. **subtle**	a) early	b) direct	c) not obvious	d) surprising
_____	48. **devise**	a) steal	b) escape	c) think up	d) redo
_____	49. **stimulate**	a) arouse	b) anger	c) make tired	d) confuse
_____	50. **convey**	a) communicate	b) allow	c) invent	d) approve

(Continues on next page)

_____ 51. **inevitable**   a) unavoidable   b) dangerous   c) spiteful   d) doubtful

_____ 52. **equate**   a) adjust   b) consider equal   c) attack   d) overcome

_____ 53. **patron**   a) father   b) enemy   c) steady customer   d) one with a hopeless view

_____ 54. **option**   a) problem   b) requirement   c) attitude   d) choice

_____ 55. **endeavor**   a) meet   b) state   c) try   d) avoid

_____ 56. **refute**   a) prove wrong   b) replay   c) appeal   d) walk

_____ 57. **dismay**   a) thrill   b) lift   c) return   d) discourage

_____ 58. **reciprocate**   a) pay back   b) frown   c) slip   d) step

_____ 59. **retain**   a) return   b) keep   c) redo   d) come forth

_____ 60. **adapt**   a) stick to something   b) adjust to a situation   c) avoid   d) strike

_____ 61. **indifferent**   a) similar   b) calm   c) well-adjusted   d) unconcerned

_____ 62. **elaborate**   a) large   b) complex   c) expensive   d) boring

_____ 63. **liberal**   a) generous   b) thrifty   c) famous   d) short

_____ 64. **mediocre**   a) outstanding   b) ordinary   c) bad-tasting   d) believable

_____ 65. **emerge**   a) go under water   b) come forth   c) lie   d) draw back

_____ 66. **elite**   a) free   b) underprivileged   c) superior   d) proud

_____ 67. **essence**   a) fundamental characteristic   b) tiny part   c) much later   d) rule

_____ 68. **allude**   a) refer indirectly   b) damage   c) protest   d) pay back

_____ 69. **impair**   a) fix   b) write down   c) employ   d) damage

_____ 70. **coerce**   a) attract   b) refuse   c) remove   d) force

_____ 71. **plausible**   a) boring   b) unbearable   c) believable   d) misspelled

_____ 72. **recur**   a) prevent   b) remember   c) forget   d) occur again

_____ 73. **revoke**   a) annoy   b) protest   c) cancel   d) adjust

_____ 74. **stereotype**   a) oversimplified image   b) two channels   c) plan   d) photograph

_____ 75. **reprimand**   a) harsh criticism   b) business deal   c) ruling   d) answer

(Continues on next page)

_____ 76. **destiny**   **a)** freedom   **b)** fate   **c)** generosity   **d)** boredom

_____ 77. **tedious**   **a)** difficult   **b)** heavy   **c)** ridiculous   **d)** boring

_____ 78. **detain**   **a)** care for   **b)** attract   **c)** delay   **d)** describe

_____ 79. **consequence**   **a)** falsehood   **b)** result   **c)** method   **d)** series

_____ 80. **diminish**   **a)** lessen   **b)** make darker   **c)** enlarge   **d)** move upward

_____ 81. **site**   **a)** silence   **b)** location   **c)** time   **d)** vision

_____ 82. **discriminate**   **a)** arrest   **b)** delay   **c)** distinguish   **d)** discuss

_____ 83. **profound**   **a)** kind   **b)** deeply felt   **c)** cautious   **d)** logical

_____ 84. **vocation**   **a)** hobby   **b)** trip   **c)** report   **d)** profession

_____ 85. **subside**   **a)** calm down   **b)** insult   **c)** arouse   **d)** tire easily

_____ 86. **intervene**   **a)** come between   **b)** arrest   **c)** resist   **d)** send for

_____ 87. **sedate**   **a)** bold   **b)** plain   **c)** calm   **d)** pure

_____ 88. **perceptive**   **a)** brave   **b)** available   **c)** aware   **d)** careless

_____ 89. **innate**   **a)** learned   **b)** underneath   **c)** inborn   **d)** clever

_____ 90. **obstinate**   **a)** friendly   **b)** frightful   **c)** stubborn   **d)** cautious

_____ 91. **susceptible**   **a)** easily affected   **b)** greedy   **c)** lazy   **d)** easily noticed

_____ 92. **defy**   **a)** send for   **b)** approve   **c)** improve   **d)** resist

_____ 93. **valid**   **a)** logical   **b)** pure   **c)** clever   **d)** gloomy

_____ 94. **confirm**   **a)** follow   **b)** reject   **c)** support the truth of something   **d)** speed up

_____ 95. **vigorous**   **a)** harsh   **b)** energetic   **c)** kind   **d)** rushed

_____ 96. **adverse**   **a)** strict   **b)** profitable   **c)** rhyming   **d)** harmful

_____ 97. **coherent**   **a)** necessary   **b)** lively   **c)** wordy   **d)** logical and orderly

_____ 98. **deteriorate**   **a)** worsen   **b)** speed up   **c)** age   **d)** take advantage of

_____ 99. **comparable**   **a)** odd   **b)** similar   **c)** unavoidable   **d)** lacking

_____ 100. **audible**   **a)** nearby   **b)** believable   **c)** willing   **d)** able to be heard

---

STOP. This is the end of the test. If there is time remaining, you may go back and recheck your answers. When the time is up, hand in both your answer sheet and this test booklet to your instructor.

NAME: _____

SECTION: _____ DATE: _____

Posttest

SCORE: _____

This test contains 100 items. In the space provided, write the letter of the choice that is closest in meaning to the **boldfaced** word.

____ 1. **compel** a) finish b) delight c) force d) avoid

____ 2. **isolate** a) separate b) heat up c) combine d) freeze

____ 3. **endorse** a) suggest b) stop c) support d) start

____ 4. **refuge** a) garbage b) building c) rejection d) shelter

____ 5. **menace** a) character b) threat c) assistance d) puzzle

____ 6. **transition** a) invention b) purchase c) repetition d) change

____ 7. **acknowledge** a) prevent b) study c) admit d) deny

____ 8. **superficial** a) lacking depth b) perfect c) very deep d) faulty

____ 9. **extensive** a) outside b) large in space or amount c) bold d) separated

____ 10. **denounce** a) introduce b) condemn c) change d) compliment

____ 11. **morale** a) spirit b) majority c) threat d) principle

____ 12. **undermine** a) cross out b) weaken c) reach d) dig up

____ 13. **drastic** a) dirty b) extreme c) suitable d) sticky

____ 14. **impartial** a) strict b) not whole c) hidden d) without prejudice

____ 15. **imply** a) approve of b) interfere c) do mischief d) suggest

____ 16. **fortify** a) avoid b) strengthen c) approve of d) suggest

____ 17. **concise** a) wordy b) clear and brief c) peaceful d) proper

____ 18. **conservative** a) not definite b) opinionated c) resisting change d) understanding

____ 19. **novice** a) false impression b) book c) beginner d) servant

____ 20. **erratic** a) inconsistent b) mistaken c) in a city d) noisy

____ 21. **hypocrite** a) injection b) insincere person c) interference d) threat

____ 22. **lenient** a) not biased b) not strict c) delayed d) heavy

____ 23. **sustain** a) avoid b) approve of c) wait for d) keep going

____ 24. **obstacle** a) remedy b) list c) answer d) barrier

____ 25. **comply** a) choose b) run into c) forget d) do as asked

(Continues on next page)

____ 26. **arrogant**   a) average   b) wealthy   c) ridiculous   d) overly proud

____ 27. **infer**   a) offer   b) conclude   c) reject   d) answer

____ 28. **verify**   a) cancel   b) prove   c) keep going   d) improve

____ 29. **prudent**   a) rudely brief   b) careful   c) obvious   d) delicate

____ 30. **evasive**   a) talkative   b) deliberately unclear   c) friendly   d) overly forceful

____ 31. **apprehensive**   a) relaxed   b) thoughtful   c) opinionated   d) uneasy

____ 32. **accessible**   a) easily reached   b) folded   c) difficult   d) itchy

____ 33. **unique**   a) pure   b) common   c) one-of-a-kind   d) well-known

____ 34. **acute**   a) dull   b) mild   c) nervous   d) severe

____ 35. **subtle**   a) surprising   b) direct   c) not obvious   d) early

____ 36. **retort**   a) great respect   b) sharp reply   c) false idea   d) court order

____ 37. **diversity**   a) variety   b) enthusiasm   c) conclusion   d) separation

____ 38. **exempt**   a) needed badly   b) attacked   c) unconcerned   d) free of a duty

____ 39. **devise**   a) escape   b) think up   c) steal   d) redo

____ 40. **compensate**   a) receive   b) win out   c) change   d) repay

____ 41. **cite**   a) read   b) mention in support   c) look for   d) repeat

____ 42. **convey**   a) invent   b) allow   c) communicate   d) approve

____ 43. **lethal**   a) sweet-smelling   b) healthy   c) ancient   d) deadly

____ 44. **surpass**   a) go beyond   b) reverse   c) take   d) prove wrong

____ 45. **ordeal**   a) office   b) painful experience   c) good time   d) change

____ 46. **prevail**   a) lose   b) enroll early   c) climb   d) win out

____ 47. **stimulate**   a) arouse   b) anger   c) make tired   d) confuse

____ 48. **tentative**   a) unclear   b) not final   c) outside   d) suitable

____ 49. **elapse**   a) pass by   b) record   c) measure   d) flow

____ 50. **prominent**   a) dangerous   b) clean   c) obvious   d) reasonable

(Continues on next page)

_____ 51. **option**   a) attitude   b) requirement   c) problem   d) choice

_____ 52. **reprimand**   a) business deal   b) harsh criticism   c) answer   d) ruling

_____ 53. **adapt**   a) adjust to a situation   b) stick to something   c) avoid   d) strike

_____ 54. **refute**   a) prove wrong   b) replay   c) appeal   d) walk

_____ 55. **plausible**   a) boring   b) unbearable   c) believable   d) misspelled

_____ 56. **reciprocate**   a) pay back   b) step   c) frown   d) slip

_____ 57. **essence**   a) rule   b) tiny part   c) much later   d) fundamental characteristic

_____ 58. **revoke**   a) adjust   b) annoy   c) protect   d) cancel

_____ 59. **retain**   a) redo   b) keep   c) return   d) come forth

_____ 60. **inevitable**   a) unavoidable   b) dangerous   c) spiteful   d) doubtful

_____ 61. **emerge**   a) draw back   b) come forth   c) lie   d) go under water

_____ 62. **impair**   a) damage   b) employ   c) write down   d) fix

_____ 63. **equate**   a) overcome   b) consider equal   c) attack   d) adjust

_____ 64. **coerce**   a) attract   b) refuse   c) remove   d) force

_____ 65. **patron**   a) steady customer   b) enemy   c) father   d) one with a hopeless view

_____ 66. **liberal**   a) thrifty   b) generous   c) short   d) famous

_____ 67. **dismay**   a) thrill   b) lift   c) return   d) discourage

_____ 68. **elite**   a) underprivileged   b) free   c) proud   d) superior

_____ 69. **endeavor**   a) state   b) meet   c) avoid   d) try

_____ 70. **allude**   a) pay back   b) damage   c) protest   d) refer indirectly

_____ 71. **recur**   a) occur again   b) remember   c) forget   d) prevent

_____ 72. **indifferent**   a) similar   b) calm   c) well-adjusted   d) unconcerned

_____ 73. **mediocre**   a) believable   b) outstanding   c) bad-tasting   d) ordinary

_____ 74. **stereotype**   a) photograph   b) oversimplified image   c) plan   d) two channels

_____ 75. **elaborate**   a) large   b) complex   c) expensive   d) boring

(Continues on next page)

_____ 76. **destiny** a) fate b) freedom c) generosity d) boredom

_____ 77. **deteriorate** a) worsen b) speed up c) age d) take advantage of

_____ 78. **perceptive** a) careless b) available c) aware d) brave

_____ 79. **sedate** a) plain b) bold c) pure d) calm

_____ 80. **vocation** a) profession b) hobby c) trip d) report

_____ 81. **innate** a) learned b) underneath c) inborn d) clever

_____ 82. **detain** a) care for b) delay c) describe d) attract

_____ 83. **diminish** a) move upward b) make darker c) enlarge d) lessen

_____ 84. **coherent** a) necessary b) lively c) wordy d) logical and orderly

_____ 85. **intervene** a) send for b) come between c) arrest d) resist

_____ 86. **profound** a) cautious b) deeply felt c) kind d) logical

_____ 87. **obstinate** a) frightful b) stubborn c) friendly d) cautious

_____ 88. **comparable** a) similar b) odd c) unavoidable d) lacking

_____ 89. **susceptible** a) easily affected b) greedy c) lazy d) easily noticed

_____ 90. **consequence** a) series b) falsehood c) result d) method

_____ 91. **valid** a) clever b) pure c) logical d) gloomy

_____ 92. **confirm** a) follow b) reject c) support the truth of something d) speed up

_____ 93. **site** a) silence b) time c) location d) vision

_____ 94. **vigorous** a) kind b) rushed c) harsh d) energetic

_____ 95. **discriminate** a) arrest b) delay c) distinguish d) harm

_____ 96. **tedious** a) difficult b) boring c) ridiculous d) heavy

_____ 97. **adverse** a) harmful b) profitable c) rhyming d) strict

_____ 98. **defy** a) send for b) approve c) improve d) resist

_____ 99. **subside** a) tire easily b) arouse c) insult d) calm down

_____ 100. **audible** a) willing b) believable c) nearby d) able to be heard

---

STOP. This is the end of the test. If there is time remaining, you may go back and recheck your answers. When the time is up, hand in both your answer sheet and this test booklet to your instructor.

Name: _____

Unit One: *Pretest*

In the space provided, write the letter of the choice that is closest in meaning to the **boldfaced** word.

_____ 1. **compel**   **a)** avoid   **b)** delight   **c)** force   **d)** finish

_____ 2. **drastic**   **a)** dirty   **b)** suitable   **c)** extreme   **d)** sticky

_____ 3. **comply**   **a)** choose   **b)** forget   **c)** run into   **d)** do as asked

_____ 4. **alternative**   **a)** command   **b)** design   **c)** assignment   **d)** choice

_____ 5. **acknowledge**   **a)** prevent   **b)** admit   **c)** study   **d)** deny

_____ 6. **candid**   **a)** honest   **b)** intense   **c)** long   **d)** improper

_____ 7. **concise**   **a)** peaceful   **b)** clear and brief   **c)** proper   **d)** wordy

_____ 8. **appropriate**   **a)** illegal   **b)** proper   **c)** extreme   **d)** well-dressed

_____ 9. **illuminate**   **a)** lose   **b)** become sick   **c)** light up   **d)** desire greatly

_____ 10. **urban**   **a)** of a city   **b)** circular   **c)** not allowed   **d)** large

_____ 11. **reminisce**   **a)** gather   **b)** remember   **c)** travel   **d)** strengthen

_____ 12. **isolate**   **a)** combine   **b)** heat up   **c)** separate   **d)** freeze

_____ 13. **fortify**   **a)** suggest   **b)** strengthen   **c)** avoid   **d)** approve of

_____ 14. **extensive**   **a)** bold   **b)** separated   **c)** outside   **d)** large in space or amount

_____ 15. **refuge**   **a)** shelter   **b)** rejection   **c)** building   **d)** garbage

_____ 16. **erratic**   **a)** inconsistent   **b)** mistaken   **c)** in a city   **d)** noisy

_____ 17. **legitimate**   **a)** threatening   **b)** profitable   **c)** obvious   **d)** lawful

_____ 18. **overt**   **a)** proper   **b)** obvious   **c)** completed   **d)** fair

_____ 19. **morale**   **a)** spirit   **b)** principle   **c)** threat   **d)** majority

_____ 20. **lenient**   **a)** heavy   **b)** not strict   **c)** delayed   **d)** not biased

_____ 21. **naive**   **a)** clever   **b)** fair   **c)** unsuspecting   **d)** merciful

_____ 22. **undermine**   **a)** weaken   **b)** cross out   **c)** reach   **d)** dig up

_____ 23. **menace**   **a)** character   **b)** threat   **c)** assistance   **d)** puzzle

_____ 24. **impartial**   **a)** without prejudice   **b)** not whole   **c)** hidden   **d)** strict

_____ 25. **endorse**   **a)** suggest   **b)** stop   **c)** support   **d)** start

(Continues on next page)

_____ 26. **illusion**   **a)** mistaken view   **b)** bad health   **c)** new idea   **d)** power

_____ 27. **imply**   **a)** approve of   **b)** interfere   **c)** do mischief   **d)** suggest

_____ 28. **obstacle**   **a)** barrier   **b)** remedy   **c)** list   **d)** answer

_____ 29. **novice**   **a)** book   **b)** false impression   **c)** beginner   **d)** servant

_____ 30. **impact**   **a)** force   **b)** inside   **c)** remedy   **d)** agreement

_____ 31. **hypocrite**   **a)** interference   **b)** insincere person   **c)** injection   **d)** threat

_____ 32. **idealistic**   **a)** full of ideas   **b)** searching   **c)** emphasizing ideals   **d)** necessary

_____ 33. **superficial**   **a)** lacking depth   **b)** perfect   **c)** very deep   **d)** faulty

_____ 34. **concede**   **a)** go beyond   **b)** reveal   **c)** dislike   **d)** admit

_____ 35. **deter**   **a)** refuse   **b)** make last longer   **c)** prevent   **d)** damage

_____ 36. **denounce**   **a)** introduce   **b)** condemn   **c)** change   **d)** compliment

_____ 37. **transition**   **a)** purchase   **b)** invention   **c)** repetition   **d)** change

_____ 38. **sustain**   **a)** keep going   **b)** approve of   **c)** avoid   **d)** wait for

_____ 39. **conservative**   **a)** not definite   **b)** opinionated   **c)** resisting change   **d)** understanding

_____ 40. **scapegoat**   **a)** example   **b)** one blamed for another's mistake   **c)** winner
     d) one who takes

_____ 41. **avert**   **a)** begin   **b)** travel   **c)** prevent   **d)** do too late

_____ 42. **anecdote**   **a)** brief story   **b)** reply   **c)** cure   **d)** confession

_____ 43. **dialog**   **a)** answer   **b)** story   **c)** a passage of conversation   **d)** belief

_____ 44. **forfeit**   **a)** lose   **b)** draw   **c)** give   **d)** recall

_____ 45. **delete**   **a)** obey   **b)** go away   **c)** erase   **d)** damage

_____ 46. **integrity**   **a)** threat   **b)** inside   **c)** complication   **d)** honesty

_____ 47. **erode**   **a)** drive   **b)** wear away   **c)** include   **d)** express indirectly

_____ 48. **gruesome**   **a)** taller   **b)** illegal   **c)** frightful   **d)** not practical

_____ 49. **contrary**   **a)** easily reached   **b)** hard   **c)** disrespectful   **d)** opposite

_____ 50. **disclose**   **a)** reveal   **b)** close   **c)** hide   **d)** continue

SCORE: (Number correct) _____ × 2 = _____ %

16

Unit One: *Posttest*

In the space provided, write the letter of the choice that is closest in meaning to the **boldfaced** word.

_____ 1. **compel**   **a)** finish   **b)** delight   **c)** force   **d)** avoid

_____ 2. **concede**   **a)** go beyond   **b)** reveal   **c)** dislike   **d)** admit

_____ 3. **isolate**   **a)** separate   **b)** heat up   **c)** combine   **d)** freeze

_____ 4. **endorse**   **a)** suggest   **b)** stop   **c)** support   **d)** start

_____ 5. **overt**   **a)** proper   **b)** fair   **c)** completed   **d)** obvious

_____ 6. **deter**   **a)** prevent   **b)** make last longer   **c)** refuse   **d)** damage

_____ 7. **reminisce**   **a)** gather   **b)** remember   **c)** travel   **d)** strengthen

_____ 8. **comply**   **a)** choose   **b)** run into   **c)** forget   **d)** do as asked

_____ 9. **alternative**   **a)** command   **b)** design   **c)** assignment   **d)** choice

_____ 10. **refuge**   **a)** garbage   **b)** building   **c)** rejection   **d)** shelter

_____ 11. **menace**   **a)** character   **b)** threat   **c)** assistance   **d)** puzzle

_____ 12. **candid**   **a)** improper   **b)** long   **c)** intense   **d)** honest

_____ 13. **transition**   **a)** invention   **b)** purchase   **c)** repetition   **d)** change

_____ 14. **illuminate**   **a)** lose   **b)** desire greatly   **c)** light up   **d)** become sick

_____ 15. **legitimate**   **a)** threatening   **b)** lawful   **c)** obvious   **d)** profitable

_____ 16. **illusion**   **a)** new idea   **b)** bad health   **c)** mistaken view   **d)** power

_____ 17. **acknowledge**   **a)** prevent   **b)** study   **c)** admit   **d)** deny

_____ 18. **superficial**   **a)** lacking depth   **b)** perfect   **c)** very deep   **d)** faulty

_____ 19. **extensive**   **a)** outside   **b)** large in space or amount   **c)** bold   **d)** separated

_____ 20. **urban**   **a)** not allowed   **b)** circular   **c)** of a city   **d)** large

_____ 21. **denounce**   **a)** introduce   **b)** condemn   **c)** change   **d)** compliment

_____ 22. **morale**   **a)** spirit   **b)** majority   **c)** threat   **d)** principle

_____ 23. **undermine**   **a)** cross out   **b)** weaken   **c)** reach   **d)** dig up

_____ 24. **drastic**   **a)** dirty   **b)** extreme   **c)** suitable   **d)** sticky

_____ 25. **impartial**   **a)** strict   **b)** not whole   **c)** hidden   **d)** without prejudice

(Continues on next page)

_____ 26. **imply**   **a)** approve of   **b)** interfere   **c)** do mischief   **d)** suggest

_____ 27. **fortify**   **a)** avoid   **b)** strengthen   **c)** approve of   **d)** suggest

_____ 28. **concise**   **a)** wordy   **b)** clear and brief   **c)** peaceful   **d)** proper

_____ 29. **conservative**   **a)** not definite   **b)** opinionated   **c)** resisting change   **d)** understanding

_____ 30. **novice**   **a)** false impression   **b)** book   **c)** beginner   **d)** servant

_____ 31. **scapegoat**   **a)** example   **b)** one who takes   **c)** winner
d) one blamed for another's mistake

_____ 32. **impact**   **a)** force   **b)** inside   **c)** remedy   **d)** agreement

_____ 33. **erratic**   **a)** inconsistent   **b)** mistaken   **c)** in a city   **d)** noisy

_____ 34. **naive**   **a)** clever   **b)** merciful   **c)** unsuspecting   **d)** fair

_____ 35. **appropriate**   **a)** illegal   **b)** proper   **c)** extreme   **d)** well-dressed

_____ 36. **hypocrite**   **a)** injection   **b)** insincere person   **c)** interference   **d)** threat

_____ 37. **lenient**   **a)** heavy   **b)** not strict   **c)** delayed   **d)** not biased

_____ 38. **sustain**   **a)** avoid   **b)** approve of   **c)** wait for   **d)** keep going

_____ 39. **idealistic**   **a)** full of ideas   **b)** searching   **c)** emphasizing ideals   **d)** necessary

_____ 40. **obstacle**   **a)** remedy   **b)** list   **c)** answer   **d)** barrier

_____ 41. **forfeit**   **a)** lose   **b)** recall   **c)** give   **d)** draw

_____ 42. **dialog**   **a)** a passage of conversation   **b)** short story   **c)** answer   **d)** belief

_____ 43. **anecdote**   **a)** cure   **b)** brief story   **c)** confession   **d)** reply

_____ 44. **integrity**   **a)** honesty   **b)** threat   **c)** complication   **d)** inside

_____ 45. **contrary**   **a)** hard   **b)** disrespectful   **c)** opposite   **d)** easily reached

_____ 46. **avert**   **a)** prevent   **b)** begin   **c)** travel   **d)** do too late

_____ 47. **gruesome**   **a)** frightful   **b)** not practical   **c)** taller   **d)** illegal

_____ 48. **erode**   **a)** include   **b)** drive   **c)** express indirectly   **d)** wear away

_____ 49. **delete**   **a)** go away   **b)** obey   **c)** damage   **d)** erase

_____ 50. **disclose**   **a)** continue   **b)** close   **c)** reveal   **d)** hide

SCORE: (Number correct) _____ × 2 = _____ %

Unit Two: *Pretest*

In the space provided, write the letter of the choice that is closest in meaning to the **boldfaced** word.

_____ 1. **derive** a) make known   b) get   c) hold back from   d) give in

_____ 2. **supplement** a) add to   b) prevent   c) support   d) lower

_____ 3. **compensate** a) change   b) win out   c) receive   d) repay

_____ 4. **verify** a) imagine   b) prove   c) keep going   d) cancel

_____ 5. **surpass** a) go beyond   b) reverse   c) take   d) prove wrong

_____ 6. **moderate** a) generous   b) not final   c) medium   d) bright

_____ 7. **tentative** a) suitable   b) not final   c) outside   d) unclear

_____ 8. **diversity** a) separation   b) conclusion   c) enthusiasm   d) variety

_____ 9. **prudent** a) rudely brief   b) careful   c) obvious   d) delicate

_____ 10. **apprehensive** a) uneasy   b) thoughtful   c) relaxed   d) opinionated

_____ 11. **acute** a) mild   b) dull   c) severe   d) nervous

_____ 12. **prominent** a) clean   b) obvious   c) dangerous   d) reasonable

_____ 13. **donor** a) one who gives   b) gift   c) one who receives   d) loan

_____ 14. **recipient** a) one who receives   b) steady customer   c) contributor   d) list

_____ 15. **anonymous** a) famous   b) common   c) by an unknown author   d) more than enough

_____ 16. **arrogant** a) wealthy   b) ridiculous   c) average   d) overly proud

_____ 17. **cite** a) repeat   b) mention in support   c) look for   d) read

_____ 18. **rational** a) limited   b) of poor quality   c) logical   d) patriotic

_____ 19. **retort** a) great respect   b) sharp reply   c) false idea   d) court order

_____ 20. **exempt** a) needed badly   b) attacked   c) unconcerned   d) free of a duty

_____ 21. **accessible** a) easily reached   b) itchy   c) difficult   d) folded

_____ 22. **prevail** a) climb   b) win out   c) lose   d) enroll early

_____ 23. **awe** a) jealousy   b) great respect   c) pride   d) great courage

_____ 24. **retrieve** a) get back   b) lose   c) distribute   d) announce

_____ 25. **obsession** a) possession   b) something pleasant   c) something one is overly concerned about   d) guilt

(Continues on next page)

_____ 26. **evasive**   a) talkative   b) deliberately unclear   c) friendly   d) overly forceful

_____ 27. **fluent**   a) speaking smoothly   b) full   c) overflowing   d) polluted

_____ 28. **elapse**   a) flow   b) pass by   c) measure   d) record

_____ 29. **lethal**   a) sweet-smelling   b) ancient   c) deadly   d) healthy

_____ 30. **ordeal**   a) change   b) painful experience   c) good time   d) office

_____ 31. **infer**   a) offer   b) conclude   c) reject   d) answer

_____ 32. **persistent**   a) not brave   b) rude   c) stubbornly continuing   d) bad-smelling

_____ 33. **unique**   a) common   b) pure   c) one-of-a-kind   d) well-known

_____ 34. **savor**   a) enjoy   b) disapprove   c) dread   d) approve

_____ 35. **vivid**   a) brightly colored   b) loud   c) large   d) very talkative

_____ 36. **subtle**   a) early   b) direct   c) not obvious   d) surprising

_____ 37. **devise**   a) steal   b) escape   c) think up   d) redo

_____ 38. **stimulate**   a) arouse   b) anger   c) make tired   d) confuse

_____ 39. **versatile**   a) rich   b) unclear   c) lucky   d) able to do many things well

_____ 40. **convey**   a) communicate   b) allow   c) invent   d) approve

_____ 41. **conceive**   a) prevent   b) make last longer   c) enjoy   d) think up

_____ 42. **inhibit**   a) forbid   b) hold back   c) live in   d) provide

_____ 43. **bestow**   a) take advantage of   b) try   c) frighten   d) give

_____ 44. **phobia**   a) difficult experience   b) fear   c) disease   d) attraction

_____ 45. **compatible**   a) capable   b) able to get along well   c) proud   d) friendly

_____ 46. **propel**   a) discourage   b) attract   c) push   d) reject

_____ 47. **futile**   a) without prejudice   b) useless   c) old-fashioned   d) kind

_____ 48. **harass**   a) compliment   b) bother   c) stock up   d) encourage

_____ 49. **delusion**   a) escape   b) announcement   c) false belief   d) example

_____ 50. **universal**   a) doubting   b) easily understood   c) including everyone   d) local

---

SCORE: (Number correct) _____ × 2 = _____ %

Unit Two: *Posttest*

In the space provided, write the letter of the choice that is closest in meaning to the **boldfaced** word.

_____ 1. **arrogant**   a) average   b) wealthy   c) ridiculous   d) overly proud

_____ 2. **persistent**   a) not brave   b) rude   c) stubbornly continuing   d) bad-smelling

_____ 3. **awe**   a) jealousy   b) pride   c) great respect   d) great courage

_____ 4. **infer**   a) offer   b) conclude   c) reject   d) answer

_____ 5. **verify**   a) cancel   b) prove   c) keep going   d) improve

_____ 6. **prudent**   a) rudely brief   b) careful   c) obvious   d) delicate

_____ 7. **rational**   a) logical   b) of poor quality   c) patriotic   d) limited

_____ 8. **evasive**   a) talkative   b) deliberately unclear   c) friendly   d) overly forceful

_____ 9. **vivid**   a) brightly colored   b) large   c) loud   d) very talkative

_____ 10. **apprehensive**   a) relaxed   b) thoughtful   c) opinionated   d) uneasy

_____ 11. **derive**   a) make known   b) get   c) hold back from   d) give in

_____ 12. **accessible**   a) easily reached   b) folded   c) difficult   d) itchy

_____ 13. **prominent**   a) dangerous   b) clean   c) obvious   d) reasonable

_____ 14. **donor**   a) one who receives   b) gift   c) one who gives   d) loan

_____ 15. **unique**   a) pure   b) common   c) one-of-a-kind   d) well-known

_____ 16. **acute**   a) dull   b) mild   c) nervous   d) severe

_____ 17. **anonymous**   a) famous   b) common   c) by an unknown author   d) more than enough

_____ 18. **subtle**   a) surprising   b) direct   c) not obvious   d) early

_____ 19. **retort**   a) great respect   b) sharp reply   c) false idea   d) court order

_____ 20. **diversity**   a) variety   b) enthusiasm   c) conclusion   d) separation

_____ 21. **exempt**   a) needed badly   b) attacked   c) unconcerned   d) free of a duty

_____ 22. **supplement**   a) lower   b) prevent   c) support   d) add to

_____ 23. **devise**   a) escape   b) think up   c) steal   d) redo

_____ 24. **retrieve**   a) get back   b) lose   c) distribute   d) announce

_____ 25. **compensate**   a) receive   b) win out   c) change   d) repay

(Continues on next page)

_____ 26. **cite** a) read b) mention in support c) look for d) repeat

_____ 27. **obsession** a) guilt b) something pleasant c) something one is overly concerned about d) possession

_____ 28. **recipient** a) list b) steady customer c) contributor d) one who receives

_____ 29. **convey** a) invent b) allow c) communicate d) approve

_____ 30. **fluent** a) speaking smoothly b) polluted c) overflowing d) full

_____ 31. **savor** a) enjoy b) disapprove c) dread d) approve

_____ 32. **lethal** a) sweet-smelling b) healthy c) ancient d) deadly

_____ 33. **surpass** a) go beyond b) reverse c) take d) prove wrong

_____ 34. **ordeal** a) office b) painful experience c) good time d) change

_____ 35. **moderate** a) generous b) not final c) medium d) bright

_____ 36. **prevail** a) lose b) enroll early c) climb d) win out

_____ 37. **stimulate** a) arouse b) anger c) make tired d) confuse

_____ 38. **tentative** a) unclear b) not final c) outside d) suitable

_____ 39. **versatile** a) lucky b) rich c) unclear d) able to do many things well

_____ 40. **elapse** a) pass by b) record c) measure d) flow

_____ 41. **propel** a) discourage b) attract c) reject d) push

_____ 42. **universal** a) including everyone b) easily understood c) local d) doubting

_____ 43. **futile** a) old-fashioned b) useless c) old d) without prejudice

_____ 44. **delusion** a) announcement b) example c) false belief d) escape

_____ 45. **bestow** a) try b) frighten c) give d) take advantage of

_____ 46. **harass** a) bother b) stock up c) encourage d) compliment

_____ 47. **inhibit** a) provide b) hold back c) live in d) forbid

_____ 48. **phobia** a) attraction b) fear c) difficult experience d) disease

_____ 49. **conceive** a) prevent b) think up c) enjoy d) make last longer

_____ 50. **compatible** a) friendly b) proud c) able to get along well d) capable

---

SCORE: (Number correct) _____ × 2 = _____ %

Name: _____

Unit Three: *Pretest*

In the space provided, write the letter of the choice that is closest in meaning to the **boldfaced** word.

_____ 1. **inevitable**   a) unavoidable   b) dangerous   c) spiteful   d) doubtful

_____ 2. **equate**   a) adjust   b) consider equal   c) attack   d) overcome

_____ 3. **passive**   a) not active but acted upon   b) joyful   c) quiet   d) moody

_____ 4. **patron**   a) father   b) enemy   c) steady customer   d) one with a hopeless view

_____ 5. **option**   a) problem   b) requirement   c) attitude   d) choice

_____ 6. **indignant**   a) impressed   b) angry   c) curious   d) afraid

_____ 7. **endeavor**   a) meet   b) state   c) try   d) avoid

_____ 8. **impose on**   a) arrest   b) confuse   c) disguise as   d) take advantage of

_____ 9. **refute**   a) prove wrong   b) replay   c) appeal   d) walk

_____ 10. **dismay**   a) thrill   b) lift   c) return   d) discourage

_____ 11. **gesture**   a) guess   b) thunder   c) sign   d) meal

_____ 12. **reciprocate**   a) pay back   b) frown   c) slip   d) step

_____ 13. **exile**   a) formal criticism   b) exit   c) axe   d) separation from native country

_____ 14. **ritual**   a) business deal   b) war   c) ceremony   d) show

_____ 15. **retain**   a) return   b) keep   c) redo   d) come forth

_____ 16. **adapt**   a) stick to something   b) adjust to a situation   c) avoid   d) strike

_____ 17. **indifferent**   a) similar   b) calm   c) well-adjusted   d) unconcerned

_____ 18. **exotic**   a) out   b) infected   c) local   d) foreign

_____ 19. **notable**   a) well-known   b) written   c) unable   d) odd

_____ 20. **elaborate**   a) large   b) complex   c) expensive   d) boring

_____ 21. **liberal**   a) generous   b) thrifty   c) famous   d) short

_____ 22. **frugal**   a) appealing   b) illegal   c) thrifty   d) hasty

_____ 23. **mediocre**   a) outstanding   b) ordinary   c) bad-tasting   d) believable

_____ 24. **emerge**   a) go under water   b) come forth   c) lie   d) draw back

_____ 25. **elite**   a) free   b) underprivileged   c) superior   d) proud

(Continues on next page)

_____ 26. **query**   **a)** answer   **b)** argue   **c)** question   **d)** make strange

_____ 27. **affirm**   **a)** support   **b)** reverse   **c)** indicate to be true   **d)** exercise

_____ 28. **essence**   **a)** fundamental characteristic   **b)** tiny part   **c)** much later   **d)** rule

_____ 29. **allude**   **a)** refer indirectly   **b)** damage   **c)** protest   **d)** pay back

_____ 30. **impair**   **a)** fix   **b)** write down   **c)** employ   **d)** damage

_____ 31. **sadistic**   **a)** depressed   **b)** infected   **c)** taking pleasure in cruelty   **d)** clever

_____ 32. **coerce**   **a)** attract   **b)** refuse   **c)** remove   **d)** force

_____ 33. **plausible**   **a)** boring   **b)** unbearable   **c)** believable   **d)** misspelled

_____ 34. **recur**   **a)** prevent   **b)** remember   **c)** forget   **d)** occur again

_____ 35. **shrewd**   **a)** kind   **b)** annoying   **c)** tricky   **d)** mad

_____ 36. **tactic**   **a)** result   **b)** surrender   **c)** method   **d)** ceremony

_____ 37. **revoke**   **a)** annoy   **b)** protest   **c)** cancel   **d)** adjust

_____ 38. **stereotype**   **a)** oversimplified image   **b)** two channels   **c)** plan   **d)** photograph

_____ 39. **reprimand**   **a)** harsh criticism   **b)** business deal   **c)** ruling   **d)** answer

_____ 40. **skeptical**   **a)** stubborn   **b)** forceful   **c)** generous   **d)** doubting

_____ 41. **defer**   **a)** entertain   **b)** intrude   **c)** yield   **d)** annoy

_____ 42. **malicious**   **a)** bright   **b)** mean   **c)** sweet   **d)** clever

_____ 43. **revert**   **a)** claim   **b)** return to former condition   **c)** pay back   **d)** answer

_____ 44. **recede**   **a)** remove   **b)** move back   **c)** hide   **d)** flow over

_____ 45. **indulgent**   **a)** interesting   **b)** giving in to someone's wishes   **c)** generous
d) uninteresting

_____ 46. **impulsive**   **a)** ugly   **b)** prompt   **c)** acting on sudden urges   **d)** important

_____ 47. **immunity**   **a)** freedom from something required   **b)** infection   **c)** plenty   **d)** thrift

_____ 48. **alleged**   **a)** supposed to be true   **b)** factual   **c)** trustworthy   **d)** logical

_____ 49. **provoke**   **a)** make angry   **b)** take back   **c)** rise up   **d)** prove wrong

_____ 50. **ridicule**   **a)** pay back   **b)** compliment   **c)** mock   **d)** shrink

SCORE: (Number correct) _____ × 2 = _____ %

Name: _____

Unit Three: *Posttest*

In the space provided, write the letter of the choice that is closest in meaning to the **boldfaced** word.

_____ 1. **option** a) attitude b) requirement c) problem d) choice

_____ 2. **ritual** a) business deal b) ceremony c) war d) show

_____ 3. **frugal** a) appealing b) illegal c) thrifty d) hasty

_____ 4. **indignant** a) afraid b) curious c) angry d) impressed

_____ 5. **reprimand** a) business deal b) harsh criticism c) answer d) ruling

_____ 6. **impose on** a) confuse b) arrest c) disguise as d) take advantage of

_____ 7. **query** a) answer b) argue c) question d) make strange

_____ 8. **adapt** a) adjust to a situation b) stick to something c) avoid d) strike

_____ 9. **sadistic** a) clever b) taking pleasure in cruelty c) infected d) depressed

_____ 10. **refute** a) prove wrong b) replay c) appeal d) walk

_____ 11. **gesture** a) sign b) meal c) guess d) thunder

_____ 12. **plausible** a) boring b) unbearable c) believable d) misspelled

_____ 13. **reciprocate** a) pay back b) step c) frown d) slip

_____ 14. **exile** a) formal criticism b) exit c) axe d) separation from native country

15. **essence** a) rule b) tiny part c) much later d) fundamental characteristic

_____ 16. **revoke** a) adjust b) annoy c) protect d) cancel

_____ 17. **retain** a) redo b) keep c) return d) come forth

_____ 18. **inevitable** a) unavoidable b) dangerous c) spiteful d) doubtful

_____ 19. **emerge** a) draw back b) come forth c) lie d) go under water

_____ 20. **impair** a) damage b) employ c) write down d) fix

_____ 21. **shrewd** a) kind b) annoying c) tricky d) mad

_____ 22. **exotic** a) foreign b) out c) infected d) local

_____ 23. **elaborate** a) large b) complex c) expensive d) boring

_____ 24. **equate** a) overcome b) consider equal c) attack d) adjust

_____ 25. **coerce** a) attract b) refuse c) remove d) force

(Continues on next page)

_____ 26. **patron** a) steady customer b) enemy c) father d) one with a hopeless view

_____ 27. **liberal** a) thrifty b) generous c) short d) famous

_____ 28. **dismay** a) thrill b) lift c) return d) discourage

_____ 29. **skeptical** a) doubting b) forceful c) generous d) stubborn

_____ 30. **elite** a) underprivileged b) free c) proud d) superior

_____ 31. **passive** a) not active but acted upon b) joyful c) quiet d) moody

_____ 32. **notable** a) odd b) unable c) written d) well-known

_____ 33. **endeavor** a) state b) meet c) avoid d) try

_____ 34. **affirm** a) exercise b) reverse c) indicate to be true d) support

_____ 35. **allude** a) pay back b) damage c) protest d) refer indirectly

_____ 36. **recur** a) occur again b) remember c) forget d) prevent

_____ 37. **tactic** a) surrender b) method c) result d) ceremony

_____ 38. **indifferent** a) similar b) calm c) well-adjusted d) unconcerned

_____ 39. **mediocre** a) believable b) outstanding c) bad-tasting d) ordinary

_____ 40. **stereotype** a) photograph b) oversimplified image c) plan d) two channels

_____ 41. **alleged** a) logical b) factual c) supposed to be true d) trustworthy

_____ 42. **indulgent** a) interesting b) uninteresting c) generous d) giving in to someone's wishes

_____ 43. **malicious** a) clever b) mean c) sweet d) bright

_____ 44. **defer** a) annoy b) intrude c) yield d) entertain

_____ 45. **impulsive** a) prompt b) important c) acting on sudden urges d) ugly

_____ 46. **revert** a) claim b) answer c) pay back d) return to former condition

_____ 47. **immunity** a) infection b) plenty c) freedom from something required d) thrift

_____ 48. **recede** a) move back b) flow over c) hide d) remove

_____ 49. **ridicule** a) shrink b) mock c) compliment d) pay back

_____ 50. **provoke** a) take back b) prove wrong c) rise up d) make angry

SCORE: (Number correct) _____ × 2 = _____ %

Unit Four: *Pretest*

In the space provided, write the letter of the choice that is closest in meaning to the **boldfaced** word.

_____ 1. **vital**   **a)** weak   **b)** stiff   **c)** necessary   **d)** unimportant

_____ 2. **destiny**   **a)** freedom   **b)** fate   **c)** generosity   **d)** boredom

_____ 3. **tedious**   **a)** difficult   **b)** heavy   **c)** ridiculous   **d)** boring

_____ 4. **detain**   **a)** care for   **b)** attract   **c)** delay   **d)** describe

_____ 5. **transaction**   **a)** trip   **b)** business deal   **c)** detour   **d)** ceremony

_____ 6. **procrastinate**   **a)** remember   **b)** put off doing something   **c)** misbehave   **d)** make angry

_____ 7. **consequence**   **a)** falsehood   **b)** result   **c)** method   **d)** series

_____ 8. **diminish**   **a)** lessen   **b)** make darker   **c)** enlarge   **d)** move upward

_____ 9. **severity**   **a)** rudeness   **b)** generosity   **c)** harshness   **d)** calm

_____ 10. **site**   **a)** silence   **b)** location   **c)** time   **d)** vision

_____ 11. **discriminate**   **a)** arrest   **b)** delay   **c)** distinguish   **d)** discuss

_____ 12. **profound**   **a)** kind   **b)** deeply felt   **c)** cautious   **d)** logical

_____ 13. **vocation**   **a)** hobby   **b)** trip   **c)** report   **d)** profession

_____ 14. **dispense**   **a)** stop   **b)** delay   **c)** encourage   **d)** distribute

_____ 15. **dismal**   **a)** unknown   **b)** round   **c)** tired   **d)** gloomy

_____ 16. **subside**   **a)** calm down   **b)** insult   **c)** arouse   **d)** tire easily

_____ 17. **data**   **a)** test   **b)** information   **c)** rumors   **d)** conversation

_____ 18. **intervene**   **a)** come between   **b)** arrest   **c)** resist   **d)** send for

_____ 19. **sedate**   **a)** bold   **b)** plain   **c)** calm   **d)** pure

_____ 20. **morbid**   **a)** limited   **b)** causing horror   **c)** causing respect   **d)** pleasurable

_____ 21. **parallel**   **a)** at a constant distance apart   **b)** nearsighted   **c)** farsighted   **d)** far

_____ 22. **perceptive**   **a)** brave   **b)** available   **c)** aware   **d)** careless

_____ 23. **innate**   **a)** learned   **b)** underneath   **c)** inborn   **d)** clever

_____ 24. **obstinate**   **a)** friendly   **b)** frightful   **c)** stubborn   **d)** cautious

_____ 25. **susceptible**   **a)** easily affected   **b)** greedy   **c)** lazy   **d)** easily noticed

(Continues on next page)

_____ 26. **defy** **a)** send for **b)** approve **c)** improve **d)** resist

_____ 27. **valid** **a)** logical **b)** pure **c)** clever **d)** gloomy

_____ 28. **deceptive** **a)** constant **b)** well-spoken **c)** misleading **d)** changing

_____ 29. **confirm** **a)** follow **b)** reject **c)** support the truth of something **d)** speed up

_____ 30. **vigorous** **a)** harsh **b)** energetic **c)** kind **d)** rushed

_____ 31. **submit** **a)** make fun of **b)** arrest **c)** give in **d)** refuse

_____ 32. **restrain** **a)** struggle **b)** hold back **c)** refuse **d)** order to come

_____ 33. **adverse** **a)** strict **b)** profitable **c)** rhyming **d)** harmful

_____ 34. **coherent** **a)** necessary **b)** lively **c)** wordy **d)** logical and orderly

_____ 35. **competent** **a)** unavoidable **b)** able **c)** honest **d)** depressing

_____ 36. **deteriorate** **a)** worsen **b)** speed up **c)** age **d)** take advantage of

_____ 37. **consecutive** **a)** late **b)** following one after another **c)** able **d)** at the same time

_____ 38. **comparable** **a)** odd **b)** similar **c)** unavoidable **d)** lacking

_____ 39. **audible** **a)** nearby **b)** believable **c)** willing **d)** able to be heard

_____ 40. **accelerate** **a)** quicken **b)** hold back **c)** distinguish **d)** calm down

_____ 41. **simultaneous** **a)** done at the same time **b)** recorded **c)** very important **d)** fast

_____ 42. **strategy** **a)** plan **b)** purpose **c)** discipline **d)** foundation

_____ 43. **summon** **a)** add up **b)** send for **c)** delay **d)** insult

_____ 44. **theoretical** **a)** gloomy **b)** based on theory **c)** practical **d)** pretty

_____ 45. **inept** **a)** guilty **b)** tired **c)** clumsy **d)** stubborn

_____ 46. **lament** **a)** delay **b)** rush **c)** struggle **d)** mourn

_____ 47. **seclusion** **a)** punishment **b)** pride **c)** stubbornness **d)** separation

_____ 48. **transmit** **a)** spread **b)** hold **c)** sleep **d)** grow

_____ 49. **advocate** **a)** teacher **b)** supporter **c)** player **d)** business person

_____ 50. **conspicuous** **a)** frightened **b)** stubborn **c)** obvious **d)** careful

---

SCORE: (Number correct) _____ × 2 = _____ %

28

Unit Four: *Posttest*

In the space provided, write the letter of the choice that is closest in meaning to the **boldfaced** word.

_____ 1. **destiny**   **a)** fate   **b)** freedom   **c)** generosity   **d)** boredom

_____ 2. **dismal**   **a)** unknown   **b)** tired   **c)** gloomy   **d)** round

_____ 3. **deteriorate**   **a)** worsen   **b)** speed up   **c)** age   **d)** take advantage of

_____ 4. **perceptive**   **a)** careless   **b)** available   **c)** aware   **d)** brave

_____ 5. **sedate**   **a)** plain   **b)** bold   **c)** pure   **d)** calm

_____ 6. **transaction**   **a)** trip   **b)** business deal   **c)** detour   **d)** ceremony

_____ 7. **consecutive**   **a)** able   **b)** following one after another   **c)** late   **d)** at the same time

_____ 8. **vocation**   **a)** profession   **b)** hobby   **c)** trip   **d)** report

_____ 9. **procrastinate**   **a)** make angry   **b)** put off doing something   **c)** misbehave   **d)** remember

_____ 10. **innate**   **a)** learned   **b)** underneath   **c)** inborn   **d)** clever

_____ 11. **competent**   **a)** unavoidable   **b)** depressing   **c)** honest   **d)** able

_____ 12. **detain**   **a)** care for   **b)** delay   **c)** describe   **d)** attract

_____ 13. **diminish**   **a)** move upward   **b)** make darker   **c)** enlarge   **d)** lessen

_____ 14. **severity**   **a)** rudeness   **b)** generosity   **c)** harshness   **d)** calm

_____ 15. **coherent**   **a)** necessary   **b)** lively   **c)** wordy   **d)** logical and orderly

_____ 16. **intervene**   **a)** send for   **b)** come between   **c)** arrest   **d)** resist

_____ 17. **profound**   **a)** cautious   **b)** deeply felt   **c)** kind   **d)** logical

_____ 18. **vital**   **a)** necessary   **b)** stiff   **c)** weak   **d)** unimportant

_____ 19. **obstinate**   **a)** frightful   **b)** stubborn   **c)** friendly   **d)** cautious

_____ 20. **comparable**   **a)** similar   **b)** odd   **c)** unavoidable   **d)** lacking

_____ 21. **dispense**   **a)** list   **b)** distribute   **c)** encourage   **d)** delay

_____ 22. **parallel**   **a)** nearsighted   **b)** at a constant distance apart   **c)** farsighted   **d)** far

_____ 23. **susceptible**   **a)** easily affected   **b)** greedy   **c)** lazy   **d)** easily noticed

_____ 24. **consequence**   **a)** series   **b)** falsehood   **c)** result   **d)** method

_____ 25. **valid**   **a)** clever   **b)** pure   **c)** logical   **d)** gloomy

(Continues on next page)

_____ 26. **confirm**   a) follow   b) reject   c) support the truth of something   d) speed up

_____ 27. **site**   a) silence   b) time   c) location   d) vision

_____ 28. **vigorous**   a) kind   b) rushed   c) harsh   d) energetic

_____ 29. **discriminate**   a) arrest   b) delay   c) distinguish   d) discuss

_____ 30. **submit**   a) make fun of   b) arrest   c) give in   d) refuse

_____ 31. **restrain**   a) hold back   b) struggle   c) order to come   d) refuse

_____ 32. **tedious**   a) difficult   b) boring   c) ridiculous   d) heavy

_____ 33. **adverse**   a) harmful   b) profitable   c) rhyming   d) strict

_____ 34. **defy**   a) send for   b) approve   c) improve   d) resist

_____ 35. **subside**   a) tire easily   b) arouse   c) insult   d) calm down

_____ 36. **morbid**   a) causing respect   b) pleasurable   c) limited   d) causing horror

_____ 37. **data**   a) conversation   b) rumors   c) information   d) test

_____ 38. **audible**   a) willing   b) believable   c) nearby   d) able to be heard

_____ 39. **accelerate**   a) distinguish   b) quicken   c) hold back   d) calm down

_____ 40. **deceptive**   a) changing   b) well-spoken   c) constant   d) misleading

_____ 41. **advocate**   a) teacher   b) business person   c) player   d) supporter

_____ 42. **summon**   a) delay   b) send for   c) insult   d) add up

_____ 43. **conspicuous**   a) obvious   b) stubborn   c) frightened   d) careful

_____ 44. **simultaneous**   a) recorded   b) fast   c) very important   d) done at the same time

_____ 45. **strategy**   a) plan   b) foundation   c) purpose   d) discipline

_____ 46. **lament**   a) rush   b) mourn   c) struggle   d) delay

_____ 47. **theoretical**   a) gloomy   b) pretty   c) practical   d) based on theory

_____ 48. **inept**   a) tired   b) clumsy   c) guilty   d) stubborn

_____ 49. **seclusion**   a) pride   b) separation   c) stubbornness   d) punishment

_____ 50. **transmit**   a) sleep   b) hold   c) grow   d) spread

---

SCORE: (Number correct) _____ × 2 = _____ %

Pretest / Posttest

ANSWER SHEET

1. _____	26. _____	51. _____	76. _____
2. _____	27. _____	52. _____	77. _____
3. _____	28. _____	53. _____	78. _____
4. _____	29. _____	54. _____	79. _____
5. _____	30. _____	55. _____	80. _____
6. _____	31. _____	56. _____	81. _____
7. _____	32. _____	57. _____	82. _____
8. _____	33. _____	58. _____	83. _____
9. _____	34. _____	59. _____	84. _____
10. _____	35. _____	60. _____	85. _____
11. _____	36. _____	61. _____	86. _____
12. _____	37. _____	62. _____	87. _____
13. _____	38. _____	63. _____	88. _____
14. _____	39. _____	64. _____	89. _____
15. _____	40. _____	65. _____	90. _____
16. _____	41. _____	66. _____	91. _____
17. _____	42. _____	67. _____	92. _____
18. _____	43. _____	68. _____	93. _____
19. _____	44. _____	69. _____	94. _____
20. _____	45. _____	70. _____	95. _____
21. _____	46. _____	71. _____	96. _____
22. _____	47. _____	72. _____	97. _____
23. _____	48. _____	73. _____	98. _____
24. _____	49. _____	74. _____	99. _____
25. _____	50. _____	75. _____	100. _____

Pretest

ANSWER KEY

1. c	26. d	51. a	76. b
2. c	27. b	52. b	77. d
3. d	28. a	53. c	78. c
4. b	29. b	54. d	79. b
5. b	30. d	55. c	80. a
6. c	31. b	56. a	81. b
7. b	32. a	57. d	82. c
8. d	33. c	58. a	83. b
9. a	34. b	59. b	84. d
10. a	35. d	60. b	85. a
11. a	36. b	61. d	86. a
12. b	37. b	62. b	87. c
13. a	38. d	63. a	88. c
14. b	39. a	64. b	89. c
15. a	40. b	65. b	90. c
16. c	41. b	66. c	91. a
17. d	42. b	67. a	92. d
18. a	43. c	68. a	93. a
19. c	44. b	69. d	94. c
20. b	45. b	70. d	95. b
21. a	46. c	71. c	96. d
22. b	47. c	72. d	97. d
23. d	48. c	73. c	98. a
24. a	49. a	74. a	99. b
25. c	50. a	75. a	100. d

Posttest

ANSWER KEY

1. c	26. d	51. d	76. a
2. a	27. b	52. b	77. a
3. c	28. b	53. a	78. c
4. d	29. b	54. a	79. d
5. b	30. b	55. c	80. a
6. d	31. d	56. a	81. c
7. c	32. a	57. d	82. b
8. a	33. c	58. d	83. d
9. b	34. d	59. b	84. d
10. b	35. c	60. a	85. b
11. a	36. b	61. b	86. b
12. b	37. a	62. a	87. b
13. b	38. d	63. b	88. a
14. d	39. b	64. d	89. a
15. d	40. d	65. a	90. c
16. b	41. b	66. b	91. c
17. b	42. c	67. d	92. c
18. c	43. d	68. d	93. c
19. c	44. a	69. d	94. d
20. a	45. b	70. d	95. c
21. b	46. d	71. a	96. b
22. b	47. a	72. d	97. a
23. d	48. b	73. d	98. d
24. d	49. a	74. b	99. d
25. d	50. c	75. b	100. d

Posttest

Answers to the Pretests and Posttests:

BUILDING VOCABULARY SKILLS, SHORT VERSION

Unit One		Unit Two		Unit Three		Unit Four	
Pretest	*Posttest*	*Pretest*	*Posttest*	*Pretest*	*Posttest*	*Pretest*	*Posttest*
1. c	1. c	1. b	1. d	1. a	1. d	1. c	1. a
2. c	2. d	2. a	2. c	2. b	2. b	2. b	2. c
3. d	3. a	3. d	3. c	3. a	3. c	3. d	3. a
4. d	4. c	4. b	4. b	4. c	4. c	4. c	4. c
5. b	5. d	5. a	5. b	5. d	5. b	5. b	5. d
6. a	6. a	6. c	6. b	6. b	6. d	6. b	6. b
7. b	7. b	7. b	7. a	7. c	7. c	7. b	7. b
8. b	8. d	8. d	8. b	8. d	8. a	8. a	8. a
9. c	9. d	9. b	9. a	9. a	9. b	9. c	9. b
10. a	10. d	10. a	10. d	10. d	10. a	10. b	10. c
11. b	11. b	11. c	11. b	11. c	11. a	11. c	11. d
12. c	12. d	12. b	12. a	12. a	12. c	12. b	12. b
13. b	13. d	13. a	13. c	13. d	13. a	13. d	13. d
14. d	14. c	14. a	14. c	14. c	14. d	14. d	14. c
15. a	15. b	15. c	15. c	15. b	15. d	15. d	15. d
16. a	16. c	16. d	16. d	16. b	16. d	16. a	16. b
17. d	17. c	17. b	17. c	17. d	17. b	17. b	17. b
18. b	18. a	18. c	18. c	18. d	18. a	18. a	18. a
19. a	19. b	19. b	19. b	19. a	19. b	19. c	19. b
20. b	20. c	20. d	20. a	20. b	20. a	20. b	20. a
21. c	21. b	21. a	21. d	21. a	21. c	21. a	21. b
22. a	22. a	22. b	22. d	22. c	22. a	22. c	22. b
23. b	23. b	23. b	23. b	23. b	23. b	23. c	23. a
24. a	24. b	24. a	24. a	24. b	24. b	24. c	24. c
25. c	25. d	25. c	25. d	25. c	25. d	25. a	25. c
26. a	26. d	26. b	26. b	26. c	26. a	26. d	26. c
27. d	27. b	27. a	27. c	27. c	27. b	27. a	27. c
28. a	28. b	28. b	28. d	28. a	28. d	28. c	28. d
29. c	29. c	29. c	29. c	29. a	29. a	29. c	29. c
30. a	30. c	30. b	30. a	30. d	30. d	30. b	30. c
31. b	31. d	31. b	31. a	31. c	31. a	31. c	31. a
32. c	32. a	32. c	32. d	32. d	32. d	32. b	32. b
33. a	33. a	33. c	33. a	33. c	33. d	33. d	33. a
34. d	34. c	34. a	34. b	34. d	34. c	34. d	34. d
35. c	35. b	35. a	35. c	35. c	35. d	35. b	35. d
36. b	36. b	36. c	36. d	36. c	36. a	36. a	36. d
37. d	37. b	37. c	37. a	37. c	37. b	37. b	37. c
38. a	38. d	38. a	38. b	38. a	38. d	38. b	38. d
39. c	39. c	39. d	39. d	39. a	39. d	39. d	39. b
40. b	40. d	40. a	40. a	40. d	40. b	40. a	40. d
41. c	41. a	41. d	41. d	41. c	41. c	41. a	41. d
42. a	42. a	42. b	42. a	42. b	42. d	42. a	42. b
43. c	43. b	43. d	43. b	43. b	43. b	43. b	43. a
44. a	44. a	44. b	44. c	44. b	44. c	44. b	44. d
45. c	45. c	45. b	45. c	45. b	45. c	45. c	45. a
46. d	46. a	46. c	46. a	46. c	46. d	46. d	46. b
47. b	47. a	47. b	47. b	47. a	47. c	47. d	47. d
48. c	48. d	48. b	48. b	48. a	48. a	48. a	48. b
49. d	49. d	49. c	49. b	49. a	49. b	49. b	49. b
50. a	50. c	50. c	50. c	50. c	50. d	50. c	50. d

Answers to the Activities in
BUILDING VOCABULARY SKILLS, SHORT VERSION

Chapter 1 (Taking Exams)

Ten Words in Context	Matching Words/Defs	Sentence Check 1	Sentence Check 2	Final Check
1. b 6. a	1. 8 6. 7	1. f 6. h	1–2. a, f	1. i 6. c
2. a 7. c	2. 4 7. 6	2. c 7. g	3–4. d, h	2. g 7. a
3. b 8. b	3. 2 8. 3	3. j 8. b	5–6. b, g	3. j 8. e
4. c 9. c	4. 10 9. 9	4. e 9. a	7–8. c, e	4. d 9. b
5. b 10. b	5. 1 10. 5	5. i 10. d	9–10. i, j	5. f 10. h

Chapter 2 (Nate the Woodsman)

Ten Words in Context	Matching Words/Defs	Sentence Check 1	Sentence Check 2	Final Check
1. b 6. c	1. 6 6. 7	1. b 6. i	1–2. c, h	1. j 6. b
2. c 7. b	2. 4 7. 3	2. h 7. f	3–4. i, b	2. g 7. i
3. c 8. a	3. 8 8. 5	3. e 8. a	5–6. j, f	3. h 8. c
4. a 9. a	4. 10 9. 9	4. d 9. c	7–8. g, e	4. d 9. a
5. b 10. b	5. 1 10. 2	5. g 10. j	9–10. a, d	5. f 10. e

Chapter 3 (Who's on Trial?)

Ten Words in Context	Matching Words/Defs	Sentence Check 1	Sentence Check 2	Final Check
1. c 6. c	1. 2 6. 10	1. b 6. h	1–2. i, h	1. b 6. f
2. b 7. a	2. 6 7. 9	2. j 7. a	3–4. g, d	2. h 7. g
3. a 8. a	3. 4 8. 5	3. f 8. i	5–6. c, a	3. d 8. i
4. b 9. a	4. 7 9. 8	4. g 9. e	7–8. f, j	4. c 9. e
5. b 10. c	5. 1 10. 3	5. d 10. c	9–10. b, c	5. j 10. a

Chapter 4 (Night Nurse)

Ten Words in Context	Matching Words/Defs	Sentence Check 1	Sentence Check 2	Final Check
1. b 6. c	1. 8 6. 3	1. c 6. d	1–2. h, a	1. d 6. h
2. a 7. a	2. 10 7. 9	2. b 7. a	3–4. f, g	2. a 7. i
3. c 8. c	3. 4 8. 7	3. h 8. g	5–6. e, j	3. f 8. b
4. a 9. b	4. 6 9. 2	4. i 9. j	7–8. i, d	4. j 9. c
5. b 10. c	5. 1 10. 5	5. e 10. f	9–10. b, c	5. e 10. g

Chapter 5 (Relating to Parents)

Ten Words in Context	Matching Words/Defs	Sentence Check 1	Sentence Check 2	Final Check
1. b 6. a	1. 8 6. 5	1. g 6. h	1–2. j, i	1. c 6. j
2. c 7. c	2. 3 7. 6	2. i 7. f	3–4. h, e	2. b 7. a
3. a 8. a	3. 10 8. 4	3. d 8. j	5–6. g, d	3. h 8. g
4. c 9. c	4. 7 9. 9	4. a 9. c	7–8. b, a	4. i 9. f
5. a 10. c	5. 1 10. 2	5. e 10. b	9–10. f, c	5. d 10. e

Chapter 6 (Job Choices)

Ten Words in Context	Matching Words/Defs	Sentence Check 1	Sentence Check 2	Final Check
1. b 6. b	1. 4 6. 3	1. c 6. g	1–2. b, e	1. i 6. g
2. a 7. b	2. 1 7. 9	2. j 7. e	3–4. i, j	2. j 7. e
3. b 8. a	3. 8 8. 6	3. f 8. b	5–6. a, h	3. d 8. h
4. c 9. b	4. 10 9. 2	4. i 9. d	7–8. c, g	4. a 9. b
5. a 10. c	5. 7 10. 5	5. h 10. a	9–10. d, f	5. f 10. c

Chapter 7 (Museum Pet)

Ten Words in Context	Matching Words/Defs	Sentence Check 1	Sentence Check 2	Final Check
1. a 6. b	1. 6 6. 4	1. g 6. e	1–2. d, f	1. e 6. h
2. b 7. b	2. 3 7. 8	2. b 7. i	3–4. i, a	2. b 7. j
3. a 8. c	3. 7 8. 10	3. a 8. c	5–6. c, h	3. c 8. a
4. c 9. c	4. 9 9. 2	4. d 9. f	7–8. j, b	4. f 9. i
5. c 10. b	5. 1 10. 5	5. j 10. h	9–10. e, g	5. g 10. d

Chapter 8 (Our Headstrong Baby)

Ten Words in Context	Matching Words/Defs	Sentence Check 1	Sentence Check 2	Final Check
1. b 6. a	1. 8 6. 10	1. f 6. b	1–2. b, f	1. e 6. g
2. b 7. b	2. 3 7. 4	2. g 7. d	3–4. c, e	2. d 7. c
3. b 8. c	3. 9 8. 6	3. j 8. c	5–6. d, g	3. h 8. a
4. c 9. b	4. 7 9. 2	4. e 9. h	7–8. h, j	4. b 9. j
5. a 10. c	5. 1 10. 5	5. a 10. i	9–10. a, i	5. f 10. i

Chapter 9 (A Narrow Escape)

Ten Words in Context	Matching Words/Defs	Sentence Check 1	Sentence Check 2	Final Check
1. c 6. a	1. 6 6. 7	1. c 6. g	1–2. h, g	1. h 6. b
2. b 7. b	2. 8 7. 10	2. e 7. i	3–4. b, f	2. c 7. d
3. c 8. c	3. 9 8. 1	3. h 8. d	5–6. a, i	3. f 8. g
4. a 9. c	4. 2 9. 3	4. b 9. j	7–8. j, c	4. a 9. e
5. b 10. a	5. 4 10. 5	5. a 10. f	9–10. e, d	5. j 10. i

Chapter 10 (The Power of Advertising)

Ten Words in Context	Matching Words/Defs	Sentence Check 1	Sentence Check 2	Final Check
1. c 6. c	1. 7 6. 5	1. c 6. e	1–2. a, i	1. j 6. i
2. b 7. c	2. 3 7. 8	2. h 7. a	3–4. d, g	2. f 7. h
3. a 8. b	3. 10 8. 4	3. d 8. b	5–6. c, e	3. e 8. b
4. b 9. a	4. 6 9. 2	4. f 9. g	7–8. j, f	4. d 9. c
5. a 10. b	5. 1 10. 9	5. j 10. i	9–10. h, b	5. a 10. c

Chapter 11 (Waiter)

Ten Words in Context	Matching Words/Defs	Sentence Check 1	Sentence Check 2	Final Check
1. b 6. c	1. 8 6. 2	1. f 6. g	1–2. e, c	1. e 6. c
2. a 7. a	2. 4 7. 5	2. h 7. d	3–4. j, b	2. i 7. f
3. b 8. c	3. 9 8. 10	3. c 8. e	5–6. i, d	3. j 8. h
4. a 9. b	4. 6 9. 7	4. i 9. a	7–8. f, h	4. b 9. g
5. a 10. c	5. 3 10. 1	5. j 10. b	9–10. g, a	5. d 10. a

Chapter 12 (Adjusting to a New Culture)

Ten Words in Context	Matching Words/Defs	Sentence Check 1	Sentence Check 2	Final Check
1. b 6. b	1. 9 6. 7	1. b 6. i	1–2. b, g	1. b 6. e
2. a 7. c	2. 4 7. 1	2. e 7. a	3–4. f, d	2. c 7. h
3. c 8. a	3. 6 8. 5	3. g 8. c	5–6. e, i	3. a 8. g
4. a 9. a	4. 3 9. 8	4. d 9. f	7–8. j, h	4. f 9. j
5. b 10. b	5. 10 10. 2	5. h 10. j	9–10. a, c	5. d 10. i

Chapter 13 (A Dream About Wealth)

Ten Words in Context	Matching Words/Defs	Sentence Check 1	Sentence Check 2	Final Check
1. b 6. b	1. 2 6. 9	1. i 6. a	1–2. j, i	1. j 6. g
2. a 7. b	2. 10 7. 5	2. g 7. f	3–4. b, d	2. c 7. h
3. b 8. c	3. 6 8. 3	3. b 8. d	5–6. c, a	3. a 8. f
4. c 9. a	4. 8 9. 4	4. j 9. e	7–8. f, h	4. i 9. b
5. c 10. b	5. 1 10. 7	5. h 10. c	9–10. e, g	5. e 10. d

Chapter 17 (A Change in View)

Ten Words in Context	Matching Words/Defs	Sentence Check 1	Sentence Check 2	Final Check
1. a 6. c	1. 4 6. 2	1. a 6. b	1–2. d, j	1. j 6. f
2. c 7. b	2. 1 7. 8	2. d 7. c	3–4. f, g	2. i 7. e
3. b 8. a	3. 6 8. 3	3. g 8. e	5–6. b, a	3. b 8. a
4. a 9. b	4. 10 9. 5	4. h 9. i	7–8. h, i	4. h 9. c
5. b 10. c	5. 9 10. 7	5. j 10. f	9–10. e, c	5. d 10. g

Chapter 14 (Children and Drugs)

Ten Words in Context	Matching Words/Defs	Sentence Check 1	Sentence Check 2	Final Check
1. b 6. a	1. 8 6. 1	1. d 6. a	1–2. a, e	1. j 6. b
2. a 7. b	2. 3 7. 5	2. j 7. b	3–4. i, f	2. i 7. g
3. b 8. c	3. 10 8. 4	3. h 8. e	5–6. d, c	3. d 8. a
4. c 9. a	4. 6 9. 2	4. f 9. i	7–8. j, h	4. c 9. h
5. b 10. b	5. 7 10. 9	5. g 10. c	9–10. b, g	5. e 10. f

Chapter 18 (Family Differences)

Ten Words in Context	Matching Words/Defs	Sentence Check 1	Sentence Check 2	Final Check
1. b 6. a	1. 4 6. 3	1. a 6. i	1–2. j, g	1. b 6. i
2. b 7. c	2. 10 7. 5	2. b 7. d	3–4. f, a	2. d 7. f
3. a 8. b	3. 8 8. 6	3. f 8. g	5–6. c, h	3. j 8. e
4. c 9. b	4. 9 9. 2	4. j 9. e	7–8. e, b	4. g 9. h
5. a 10. c	5. 1 10. 7	5. h 10. c	9–10. i, d	5. c 10. a

Chapter 15 (Party House)

Ten Words in Context	Matching Words/Defs	Sentence Check 1	Sentence Check 2	Final Check
1. b 6. c	1. 8 6. 10	1. f 6. j	1–2. g, j	1. b 6. h
2. c 7. c	2. 7 7. 4	2. i 7. h	3–4. i, c	2. g 7. i
3. c 8. b	3. 1 8. 6	3. a 8. d	5–6. h, a	3. a 8. j
4. b 9. a	4. 2 9. 3	4. g 9. b	7–8. d, e	4. c 9. f
5. a 10. a	5. 5 10. 9	5. c 10. e	9–10. f, b	5. d 10. e

Chapter 19 (Chicken Pox)

Ten Words in Context	Matching Words/Defs	Sentence Check 1	Sentence Check 2	Final Check
1. b 6. c	1. 5 6. 9	1. j 6. e	1–2. j, d	1. j 6. h
2. c 7. b	2. 7 7. 10	2. i 7. d	3–4. f, c	2. e 7. i
3. a 8. a	3. 2 8. 6	3. g 8. b	5–6. g, a	3. f 8. c
4. b 9. b	4. 3 9. 8	4. a 9. h	7–8. e, h	4. b 9. d
5. a 10. c	5. 1 10. 4	5. f 10. c	9–10. b, i	5. a 10. g

Chapter 16 (Procrastinator)

Ten Words in Context	Matching Words/Defs	Sentence Check 1	Sentence Check 2	Final Check
1. a 6. b	1. 6 6. 10	1. i 6. g	1–2. g, f	1. e 6. a
2. b 7. c	2. 4 7. 8	2. d 7. b	3–4. c, i	2. c 7. d
3. a 8. a	3. 7 8. 3	3. e 8. j	5–6. a, j	3. g 8. i
4. c 9. b	4. 1 9. 5	4. a 9. c	7–8. e, d	4. j 9. f
5. c 10. b	5. 9 10. 2	5. f 10. h	9–10. h, b	5. h 10. b

Chapter 20 (Walking)

Ten Words in Context	Matching Words/Defs	Sentence Check 1	Sentence Check 2	Final Check
1. b 6. b	1. 4 6. 9	1. i 6. d	1–2. j, g	1. c 6. h
2. b 7. c	2. 8 7. 5	2. g 7. j	3–4. h, d	2. f 7. i
3. c 8. c	3. 6 8. 3	3. b 8. f	5–6. b, a	3. b 8. a
4. c 9. a	4. 2 9. 10	4. c 9. e	7–8. e, f	4. g 9. e
5. a 10. c	5. 1 10. 7	5. a 10. h	9–10. c, i	5. j 10. d

Name: _____

Mastery Test: *Chapter 1 (Taking Exams)*

In the space provided, write the word from the box needed to complete each sentence. Then put the **letter** of that word in the column at the left. Use each word once.

a. **acknowledge**	b. **alternative**	c. **anecdote**	d. **appropriate**	e. **avert**
f. **candid**	g. **compel**	h. **comply**	i. **concise**	j. **drastic**

_____ 1. Fred thinks it's funny to do the opposite of what everyone else considers _____. For instance, he likes to send sympathy cards for weddings and birthdays.

_____ 2. We keep a flashlight in every room to _____ being left in the dark in the event of a power failure.

_____ 3. According to a(n) _____ a friend told me, someone once asked boxer Muhammed Ali if he were the "greatest" at golf. "Yes," Ali answered. "I just haven't played yet."

_____ 4. A really successful commercial _____s viewers to leap from their chairs and rush out to buy the advertised item.

_____ 5. All of the restaurant's desserts were fattening, so I chose another _____. I had a frozen fruit bar at home instead.

_____ 6. To get me to _____ with her demands, my sister threatens to tell my boyfriend what I said after our first date: "Bo-ring!"

_____ 7. Because they're not eager to _____ that cockroaches are among their residents, Germans refer to the "German cockroach" as the "Russian roach."

_____ 8. Most newspapers have limited space for letters to the editor, so yours will have a better chance of being published if it's _____.

_____ 9. Every day, polluters get away with dumping thousands of pounds of plastic into the sea. Clearly, we need more _____ penalties to make them stop.

_____ 10. When Flora asked Rob to be really truthful in his opinion of her new dress, he told her, "To be perfectly _____, I don't like the color, style, or material, but it fits you really well."

SCORE: (Number correct) _____ × 10 = _____ %

Mastery Test: *Chapter 2 (Nate the Woodsman)*

In the space provided, write the word from the box needed to complete each sentence. Then put the **letter** of that word in the column at the left. Use each word once.

a. **dialog**	b. **erratic**	c. **extensive**	d. **forfeit**	e. **fortify**
f. **illuminate**	g. **isolate**	h. **refuge**	i. **reminisce**	j. **urban**

_____ 1. Job opportunities are most numerous in _____ areas. Thus many people have no choice but to live surrounded by the concrete, metal, and glass of the city.

_____ 2. In the movie, the characters' British accents were so thick that I had trouble understanding some of the _____.

_____ 3. To _____ their stores against the coming hurricane, beachfront shopkeepers nailed boards over the windows.

_____ 4. The zoo had to _____ one baboon who was attacking the others. He was put in his own cage in another building.

_____ 5. At my class reunion, we _____(e)d about our years at school, including the time I broke my arm in gym and the day a piece of scenery fell during a play and hit the principal.

_____ 6. Lately the weather has been wildly _____ . This morning, for example, it was raining and 90 degrees; by the late afternoon, it was dry and in the 50's, and it rained again at night.

_____ 7. These days, candles are mainly used for decoration since most people have electric lights to _____ their homes.

_____ 8. Many homeless people cannot find a place of _____ from wintry weather.

_____ 9. The magazine printed only one paragraph on the "Save the Earth" meeting, but the local newspaper provided _____ coverage of the event—with photos and a full-page story.

_____ 10. The Olympic swimmer had to _____ his gold medal when officials discovered that he had taken illegal muscle-building drugs.

SCORE: (Number correct) _____ × 10 = _____ %

Mastery Test: *Chapter 3 (Who's on Trial?)*

In the space provided, write the word from the box needed to complete each sentence. Then put the **letter** of that word in the column at the left. Use each word once.

a. **delete**	b. **impartial**	c. **integrity**	d. **legitimate**	e. **lenient**
f. **menace**	g. **morale**	h. **naive**	i. **overt**	j. **undermine**

_____ 1. Abraham Lincoln is sometimes called "Honest Abe" because of his reputation for

_____.

_____ 2. The paperback version of the novel was a shortened one—two chapters had been

_____(e)d.

_____ 3. Violent crime is a(n) _____ to us all. In this century, nearly twice as many Americans have been murdered as have died in wars.

_____ 4. The Smiths' pleasure in their son's engagement was certainly _____. They walked around with big smiles on their faces all night.

_____ 5. When the cake collapsed, my _____ as a baker did too. I now don't even have enough confidence or desire to bake a cake mix.

_____ 6. After Joe smashed the headlights of the family car, he hoped his parents would be

_____. Instead, they grounded him until he paid for the damage.

_____ 7. During the piano contest, the players were hidden behind a curtain so that the judges would cast

_____ votes.

_____ 8. For years, termites _____(e)d the house's wooden frame until it became dangerously damaged.

_____ 9. When Lily started her job, she was _____ enough to think the other salespeople would be cooperative. However, she soon learned some people would stab her in the back for a sale.

_____ 10. In most states, a marriage is not _____ unless the bride and groom applied for a license and got blood tests before the wedding.

SCORE: (Number correct) _____ × 10 = _____ %

Mastery Test: *Chapter 4 (Night Nurse)*

In the space provided, write the word from the box needed to complete each sentence. Then put the **letter** of that word in the column at the left. Use each word once.

a. **endorse**	b. **erode**	c. **gruesome**	d. **hypocrite**	e. **idealistic**
f. **illusion**	g. **impact**	h. **imply**	i. **novice**	j. **obstacle**

_____ 1. The baseball struck the batter with such _____ that it broke his jaw.

_____ 2. Although a majority of people in the state support the death penalty, the governor does not _____ it.

_____ 3. If you blink two lights on and off in an otherwise dark room, you create the _____ that a single light is moving back and forth.

_____ 4. Cliff's question to Judy—"Wouldn't you rather grab a hamburger than bother going to a fancy restaurant?"—was meant to _____ that he was low on cash.

_____ 5. A(n) _____ at ice-skating, I can only manage to remain upright, while my experienced friends leap and twirl around me.

_____ 6. The bodies taken out of the burned car were so _____ that even the medical examiner found the sight shocking.

_____ 7. In the movie *Mr. Smith Goes to Washington*, Jimmy Stewart plays a(n) _____ senator who values honesty and public service more than riches.

_____ 8. In the fairy tale "Rapunzel," there is one great _____ to the hero and heroine's happiness: she is locked in a tall tower with no door.

_____ 9. The centuries had caused the Greek statue's colorful layer of paint to _____, leaving only the underlying white marble.

_____ 10. Roy is such a(n) _____. He disapproves of handguns for other people, but he keeps one on his night table.

SCORE: (Number correct) _____ × 10 = _____ %	

Name: _____

Mastery Test: *Chapter 5 (Relating to Parents)*

In the space provided, write the word from the box needed to complete each sentence. Then put the **letter** of that word in the column at the left. Use each word once.

a. **concede**	b. **conservative**	c. **contrary**	d. **denounce**	e. **deter**
f. **disclose**	g. **scapegoat**	h. **superficial**	i. **sustain**	j. **transition**

_____ 1. There was too little time to make the _____ from bright sunlight to the dark movie theater. So I blindly felt my way down the aisle and then sat in the lap of a total stranger.

_____ 2. Alex and Joe have _____ views of life. To Alex "life is a bowl of cherries," but to Joe "it's the pits."

_____ 3. Gordon used to favor major changes in the company's treatment of workers. As soon as he became president, however, he turned _____.

_____ 4. The car's patches of rust, lumpy seats, and moldy odor were enough to _____ me from buying it.

_____ 5. When Max cheated on the test, the teacher _____(e)d him in front of the whole class and also expressed her disapproval of Max in a letter to his parents.

_____ 6. Josie and Kate's friendship is deep, not _____. For example, they share their innermost thoughts and offer each other support in difficult times.

_____ 7. Marilyn didn't intend to _____ the cost of the tie she gave Andy, but she revealed it down to the penny: when she wrapped the gift, she forgot to remove the price tag.

_____ 8. After bragging about his skill as a carpenter, Tony was unwilling to _____ that the crooked table was his own creation and not from a junk shop.

_____ 9. Studies show that girls are more likely than boys to accept blame for their errors. Boys are more likely to look for _____s to blame instead.

_____ 10. After the first ten minutes of weightlifting, I couldn't _____ the workout without risking muscle damage, so I stopped.

SCORE: (Number correct) _____ × 10 = _____ %

Mastery Test: *Chapter 6 (Job Choices)*

In the space provided, write the word from the box needed to complete each sentence. Then put the **letter** of that word in the column at the left. Use each word once.

a. **compensate**	b. **conceive**	c. **derive**	d. **diversity**	e. **inhibit**
f. **moderate**	g. **supplement**	h. **surpass**	i. **tentative**	j. **verify**

_b___ 1. No one in town could _____ of Gail as a murderer—she seemed too gentle and sweet to take someone's life.

_____ 2. Bob had hoped to get a C in geometry, so the A he received certainly _____(e)d what he expected.

_____ 3. Clint calls himself a _____ TV watcher, but I feel he watches much more than just a few programs a day.

_____ 4. The _____ of products at outdoor markets is one of their attractions. Often they have baked goods, home decorations, fresh produce, and even clothing for sale.

_____ 5. David _____s his income from several part-time jobs: word processing, waiting on tables, and yard work.

_____ 6. Since mold grows most quickly in warm temperatures, refrigeration _____s its growth on food.

_____ 7. When people apply for jobs at a company, the personnel director calls their previous employers to _____ that they have reported their job experience truthfully.

_____ 8. Robert's supervisor gave him only _____ approval to take a day off. She had to check with her own boss to be sure.

_____ 9. Because hay doesn't give our horses full nutrition, we _____ their diet with grains.

_____ 10. Mrs. Brown promised to _____ Al for the gas he used driving her to the airport, but she hasn't paid him a penny yet.

SCORE: (Number correct) _____ × 10 = _____ %

Mastery Test: *Chapter 7 (Museum Pet)*

In the space provided, write the word from the box needed to complete each sentence. Then put the **letter** of that word in the column at the left. Use each word once.

a. **acute**	b. **anonymous**	c. **apprehensive**	d. **arrogant**	e. **bestow**
f. **donor**	g. **phobia**	h. **prominent**	i. **prudent**	j. **recipient**

_____ 1. Some airlines offer classes to help people overcome their _____s about air travel.

_____ 2. Because the dentist had said the root canal would hurt "only a little," Doug wasn't prepared for the _____ pain that followed.

_____ 3. It isn't _____ for a worker to insult the boss when quitting a job. The worker might need the boss later for a reference.

_____ 4. The generous parents of the young man killed on the highway _____(e)d his organs on transplant banks.

_____ 5. The "No Smoking" sign was placed in a(n) _____ spot near the restaurant's door so that customers would be sure to see it before entering.

_____ 6. As the _____ of an athletic scholarship, Brad has to keep up a B average or leave the team.

_____ 7. The caller told police about a robbery going on at Fifth and Walnut, but she wouldn't give her name. For her own protection, she wanted her tip to remain _____.

_____ 8. Knowing he was wealthier than his classmates, the new boy was at first _____, but his attitude changed when he realized he was one of the worst students in the class.

_____ 9. The landscapers were _____ about planting the bushes when the homeowner wasn't there, since he had strong opinions about the way his yard should look.

_____ 10. Peggy volunteered to be a blood _____ during the Red Cross drive, but a nurse said she weighed too little to give blood.

SCORE: (Number correct) _____ × 10 = _____ %

Mastery Test: *Chapter 8 (Our Headstrong Baby)*

In the space provided, write the word from the box needed to complete each sentence. Then put the **letter** of that word in the column at the left. Use each word once.

a. **accessible** ✓	b. **awe**	c. **cite**	d. **compatible**	e. **exempt**
f. **prevail** ✓	g. **propel**	h. **rational**	i. **retort**	j. **retrieve**

_____ 1. I hate to say that Hank is a liar, but I could _____ many things he's told me that weren't true.

_____ 2. The wheels that used to _____ Joshua's toy train are jammed with sand, so now it just sits there going "toot toot."

_____ 3. The friendly way that Muffy and Ralph play together proves that a cat and dog can be

_____ .

_____ 4. The sixth-graders looked up with _____ at the visiting professional baseball player.

_____ 5. Because the prisoner had a weak heart, he was _____ from the hard physical labor required of the others.

_____ 6. When my little nephew visited, I needed to move my supply of candy from a(n) _____ cupboard to one out of his reach.

_____ 7. The paper boy threw the newspaper onto the Smiths' front porch and then went to _____ it when he remembered that the Smiths were out of town.

_____ 8. When Lydia and Jeff discuss money, they always start out calm and _____ and end up yelling and unreasonable.

_____ 9. If their best player is back in form tonight, the basketball team is sure to _____ over their opponents.

_____ 10. When the rude customer tried to cut into the line, saying, "I don't like to be kept waiting," the clerk gave this _____: "Then I won't make you wait to hear just what I think of you."

SCORE: (Number correct) _____ × 10 = _____ %

Name: _____

Mastery Test: *Chapter 9 (A Narrow Escape)*

In the space provided, write the word from the box needed to complete each sentence. Then put the **letter** of that word in the column at the left. Use each word once.

a. **elapse**	b. **evasive**	c. **fluent**	d. **futile**	e. **harass**
f. **infer**	g. **lethal**	h. **obsession**	i. **ordeal**	j. **persistent**

_____ 1. Grady's efforts to start his damaged car were _____, so he had to call a tow truck.

_____ 2. The striking workers outside the factory _____(e)d people who crossed the picket line by yelling at them and calling them names.

_____ 3. At first, the college counselor refused to let Chris retake the English entrance exam. But Chris was _____ in asking and was finally allowed to retake the test.

_____ 4. When Yolanda discovered that Ben had been in prison for ten years, she understood why he had been so _____ about his past.

_h_ 5. Being either extremely thin or very overweight indicates that food may be a(n) _____.

_____ 6. Tara is not speaking to her mother, so I _____ that they have had a fight.

_____ 7. People who were abused as children often suffer an emotional _____ that goes on long after the physical pain is over.

_g_ 8. Dogs love chocolate, but the sweet stuff can be _____ for them. More than one family has seen its pet die after it ate chocolate candy.

_____ 9. In order to control his temper, Ira let some time _____ before scolding his daughter about the broken lamp.

_____ 10. You can learn a foreign language from books and records. But to become truly _____ in the language, you must also converse with native speakers.

SCORE: (Number correct) _____ × 10 = _____ %

Name: _____

Mastery Test: *Chapter 10 (The Power of Advertising)*

In the space provided, write the word from the box needed to complete each sentence. Then put the **letter** of that word in the column at the left. Use each word once.

a. **convey**	b. **delusion**	c. **devise**	d. **savor**	e. **stimulate**
f. **subtle**	g. **unique**	h. **universal**	i. **versatile**	j. **vivid**

_____ 1. We must _____ a way to keep Tia away from the house until we finish setting up her surprise party.

_____ 2. Although Georgia dyed her hair, the color change was so _____ that few people noticed it.

_____ 3. Because my brother's Volkswagen is _____, I would know it anywhere. It's painted in day-glo colors and has a bumper sticker that says, "Yo! I'm here!"

_____ 4. As her Alzheimer's disease worsened, my grandmother held the _____ that people on TV could see her.

_____ 5. Naomi's photo of hot-air balloons is _____—red, orange, and purple balloons were sailing through a bright blue sky.

_____ 6. A talented actor can _____ emotions through gestures and postures, as well as through words.

_____ 7. When we go to the movies, Sam fills his shirt pocket with M&Ms. Eating them one at a time, he_____s them until the picture's end.

_____ 8. "We're looking for someone really _____ for this position," said the interviewer, "someone who can write well, speak well in public, and demonstrate our new hang glider."

_____ 9. The fruit cup served before the main course was supposed to _____ my appetite. Instead, it satisfied my hunger.

_____ 10. Knowing that no movie can have _____ appeal, producers must decide what type of person they hope to reach.

SCORE: (Number correct) _____ × 10 = _____ %

Mastery Test: *Chapter 11 (Waiter)*

In the space provided, write the word from the box needed to complete each sentence. Then put the **letter** of that word in the column at the left. Use each word once.

a. **defer**	b. **endeavor**	c. **equate**	d. **impose**	e. **indignant**
f. **inevitable**	g. **malicious**	h. **option**	i. **passive**	j. **patron**

_____ 1. Donna wrote a letter of complaint to the publisher of a textbook. She was _____ that the book always referred to doctors as "he" and nurses as "she."

_____ 2. Some people believe any spanking of a child is wrong. They _____ it with child abuse.

_____ 3. If Vince continues to talk on his cell phone while he's driving, it's _____ that he'll cause an accident.

_____ 4. We've become loyal _____ s of the Lebanese restaurant because we enjoy its delicious Middle Eastern food.

_____ 5. Devan's dog is the most _____ animal I've ever seen. A mouse actually ran over its paw, and it didn't even bother to raise its head.

_____ 6. I know you don't like Barry, but please _____ to be polite to him when he's here as a guest.

_____ 7. When you order a pizza here, you have the choice of usual toppings, like mushrooms and pepperoni, as well as unusual _____ s such as avocado, broccoli, or pineapple.

_____ 8. My brother often _____ s on my mother's generosity by asking her for money.

_____ 9. The children playing baseball broke a window by accident—it wasn't a(n) _____ act.

_____ 10. "When it comes to decorating our apartment," Jasmin said, "I _____ to my husband's judgment. He has better taste than I do."

SCORE: (Number correct) _____ × 10 = _____ %

Mastery Test: *Chapter 12 (Adjusting to a New Culture)*

In the space provided, write the word from the box needed to complete each sentence. Then put the **letter** of that word in the column at the left. Use each word once.

a. **adapt**	b. **dismay**	c. **exile**	d. **gesture**	e. **recede**
f. **reciprocate**	g. **refute**	h. **retain**	i. **revert**	j. **ritual**

_____ 1. The _____ of shaking one's head back and forth does not mean "no" in all cultures.

_____ 2. The neatness of Bill's house _____s his claim that he is lazy and sloppy.

_____ 3. Grandma sold most of her belongings when she moved to a retirement apartment, but she _____(e)d what had been Grandpa's favorite chair.

_____ 4. After Alice Weston died, her dog would at first only lie quietly in his new owner's home. But after a few weeks, he _____(e)d to the situation and became livelier.

_____ 5. The Bensons have had us over so often that we really should _____, but I don't know how we'll fit their large family into our small dining room.

_____ 6. The long line outside the box office so _____(e)d Bryan that he didn't even attempt to buy a ticket.

_____ 7. After he lost his throne, the Shah of Iran spent the rest of his life in _____, never returning to his native country.

_____ 8. The pickpocket grabbed a wallet and then _____(e)d into the crowd before the victim even knew anything was wrong.

_____ 9. Mr. Byron is so fearful of germs that several times a day he goes through a(n) _____ of wiping his hands with alcohol and then rinsing them.

_____ 10. Many teenagers speak politely in the presence of adults but _____ to rough slang when talking among themselves.

SCORE: (Number correct) _____ × 10 = _____ %

Mastery Test: *Chapter 13 (A Dream About Wealth)*

In the space provided, write the word from the box needed to complete each sentence. Then put the **letter** of that word in the column at the left. Use each word once.

a. **elaborate**	b. **emerge**	c. **exotic**	d. **frugal**	e. **impulsive**
f. **indifferent**	g. **indulgent**	h. **liberal**	i. **mediocre**	j. **notable**

_____ 1. The Gilmans are _____ supporters of their local public TV station; they make a large donation every year.

_____ 2. The crowd scene in the painting was so _____ that even the buttons on people's coats were carefully painted in.

_____ 3. Aunt Mary shows how _____ she is when she carefully opens a gift so that the wrapping can be re-used.

_____ 4. Maggie is _____, but she often regrets doing whatever she feels like, such as sliding down a muddy slide in her best pants.

_____ 5. When the rock star _____(e)d from his car, screaming fans rushed forward to get his autograph.

_____ 6. Before Ronald Reagan was President, he was _____ as a film star and TV actor.

_____ 7. Kevin gets a haircut only to prevent hair from falling into his eyes. He's _____ about how stylish or well-groomed he looks.

_____ 8. Phyllis loves to browse through shops with Indian brass work, African wood carvings, and other _____ arts and crafts.

_____ 9. Eddy's _____ parents spoil him. They buy him lots of candy and toys and let his worst behavior go without even a scolding.

_____ 10. The clothes at that shop are _____. They aren't as shabby as those in some of the cheapest stores, but they aren't as well-made as clothing in the best department stores.

SCORE: (Number correct) _____ × 10 = _____ %

Name: _____

Mastery Test: *Chapter 14 (Children and Drugs)*

In the space provided, write the word from the box needed to complete each sentence. Then put the **letter** of that word in the column at the left. Use each word once.

a. **affirm**	b. **alleged**	c. **allude**	d. **coerce**	e. **elite**
f. **essence**	g. **immunity**	h. **impair**	i. **query**	j. **sadistic**

_____ 1. The Loch Ness Monster is _____ to live in a lake in Scotland, but there's no proof that the dinosaur-like creature even exists.

_____ 2. Aging tends to _____ people's vision. They can't see as well as they used to.

_____ 3. "The only part of Mr. Hart's story that I can _____," the boss said, "is that he's my employee. I can't say if the other parts of his story are true because I see him only at the office."

_____ 4. The teacher promised _____ from punishment to whoever had broken the classroom window—if that person confessed immediately.

_____ 5. Paul _____(e)d to his adoption when he said, "Not surprisingly, I don't look like either of my parents."

_____ 6. Russell had several questions, but he was too shy to _____ the famous speaker.

_____ 7. The _____ of Santa Claus is loving generosity.

_____ 8. Some consider Columbian to be the _____ coffee—the best in aroma and flavor.

_____ 9. When I was younger, my parents _____(e)d me into drinking eggnog every day. Not surprisingly, I still hate the taste of the stuff.

_____ 10. Before being fired, the _____ teacher enjoyed embarrassing any student who displeased him in the slightest.

SCORE: (Number correct) _____ × 10 = _____ %

Name: _____

Mastery Test: *Chapter 15 (Party House)*

In the space provided, write the word from the box needed to complete each sentence. Then put the **letter** of that word in the column at the left. Use each word once.

a. **plausible**	b. **provoke**	c. **recur**	d. **reprimand**	e. **revoke**
f. **ridicule**	g. **shrewd**	h. **skeptical**	i. **stereotype**	j. **tactic**

_____ 1. It _____s me if someone tries to step in line in front of me. I feel like shoving the person away.

_____ 2. Singer Dolly Parton laughs at the _____ of the "dumb blonde." "I know I'm not dumb," she says. "And I'm not really blonde, either."

_____ 3. "Have some of this delicious wheat-and-bean-sprouts cake," I said to Tom, whose _____ look showed he doubted it was wise to accept the offer.

_____ 4. Since Chet was wearing a neck brace, the teacher found his excuse for missing the test—an auto accident—to be entirely _____.

_____ 5. When Derrick was a teen, his parents' most effective weapon against him was the threat that they would _____ his driving privileges.

_____ 6. In children's stories, the fox is often presented as a _____ individual who outsmarts all his enemies.

_____ 7. The political cartoon _____(e)d the senator, but he found the mockery so clever that he couldn't help laughing.

_____ 8. I have a frightening dream that _____s two or three times a year. I dream I'm in an elevator that gets stuck between floors, and I have no way to let anyone know where I am.

_____ 9. My brother and I agreed on our _____ before asking to go to the fair. He would tell Mom that Dad said we could go, and I would tell Dad that Mom said we could go.

_____ 10. People were angry when the police officer who had beaten an innocent bystander received only a _____. Community members felt he should have received a greater punishment.

SCORE: (Number correct) _____ × 10 = _____ %

Name: _____

Mastery Test: *Chapter 16 (Procrastinator)*

In the space provided, write the word from the box needed to complete each sentence. Then put the **letter** of that word in the column at the left. Use each word once.

a. **consequence**	b. **destiny**	c. **detain**	d. **diminish**	e. **procrastinate**
f. **simultaneous**	g. **strategy**	h. **tedious**	i. **transaction**	j. **vital**

_____ 1. "If it is _____ that you marry Roger, it will happen no matter what else happens," Aunt Blanche told my sister. "No one can escape fate."

_____ 2. To celebrate the city's 200th birthday, there were several _____ parties in city parks and streets. They were all scheduled to take place from 8 p.m. to midnight.

_____ 3. When you buy something major, keep the receipt for a while. Then if you return the purchase, you'll have proof the _____ took place.

_____ 4. "I need this delivered across town as quickly as possible," Will's boss told him. "Don't let anything _____ you."

_____ 5. Flo's _____ for weight loss includes a three-mile walk every morning and absolutely no snacking at night.

_____ 6. If the ivory trade is not stopped, the world's population of elephants will _____ to such a low number that they could disappear from the wild.

_____ 7. When you're involved in a _____ task like window-washing, it helps to have someone to talk to—unless, of course, the person is as boring as the window-washing.

_____ 8. Martin insulted several guests at Bea's party. As a _____, Bea won't ever invite him over again.

_____ 9. The restaurant failed because the owners overlooked one _____ fact: There were already too many seafood restaurants in the area.

_____ 10. When the brakes on Betsy's car began to make a strange sound, she took the car to a mechanic immediately. "I don't _____ when my safety is involved," she said.

SCORE: (Number correct) _____ × 10 = _____ %

Mastery Test: *Chapter 17 (A Change in View)*

In the space provided, write the word from the box needed to complete each sentence. Then put the **letter** of that word in the column at the left. Use each word once.

a. **discriminate**	b. **dismal**	c. **dispense**	d. **profound**	e. **severity**
f. **site**	g. **subside**	h. **summon**	i. **theoretical**	j. **vocation**

_____ 1. The relief workers _____(e)d bags of rice to the hungry refugees waiting in line.

_____ 2. It's no use talking to Paul until his anger _____s and he becomes more reasonable.

_____ 3. Discussions about possible life on planets around other suns are _____ since no one has ever visited there.

_____ 4. When Amy's uncle found her playing with his woodworking tools, he scolded her with such _____ that she started to cry.

_____ 5. Randy feared a long lecture when he was _____(e)d to the principal's office.

_____ 6. That rock band plays only on weekends. And you'd never guess the full-time _____ of its lead singer—he's a lawyer.

_____ 7. The _____ of the music festival had to be changed because local residents didn't want it nearby.

_____ 8. The movie was so _____—with its sad story, cheerless characters, and gray skies—that afterwards we all felt low.

_____ 9. Because he's color blind, Tom cannot _____ between blue and purple.

_____ 10. After watching a man threaten to jump off a ledge, Maggie felt _____ relief when he was persuaded to climb back inside the building.

SCORE: (Number correct) _____ × 10 = _____ %

Mastery Test: *Chapter 18 (Family Differences)*

In the space provided, write the word from the box needed to complete each sentence. Then put the **letter** of that word in the column at the left. Use each word once.

a. **data**	b. **inept**	c. **innate**	d. **intervene**	e. **lament**
f. **morbid**	g. **obstinate**	h. **parallel**	i. **perceptive**	j. **sedate**

_____ 1. Do most people have a(n)_____ fear of spiders, or do they gain the fear after birth, through experience?

_____ 2. The town council spent months studying _____ on the town recreation center before approving its construction.

_____ 3. Some newspapers appeal to people's curiosity about horrible events by publishing every _____ detail of accidents and crimes.

_____ 4. Rather than take a risk and _____ in the fight between two armed men, Ralph called the police to come and end the fight.

_____ 5. The children shrieked as they splashed and dived, while I, remaining _____, swam calmly around the pool.

_____ 6. Dad was such a(n) _____ handyman that when he tried to do home repairs, he usually made the problem worse.

_____ 7. Train tracks are _____ and thus never meet, but when you look down the tracks at a distance, they appear to move closer and closer together.

_____ 8. Diane, who _____s whenever she sees a dead animal on the road, keeps her own cats inside to protect them.

_____ 9. The boss thinks he's _____ enough to know when there are problems at work, but the truth is that he's not aware of half of what goes on in the office.

_____ 10. Sometimes it can be good to be _____. The author of the now-famous Dr. Seuss books stubbornly kept trying to get his first one published even though it was rejected 23 times.

SCORE: (Number correct) _____ × 10 = _____ %	

Mastery Test: *Chapter 19 (Chicken Pox)*

In the space provided, write the word from the box needed to complete each sentence. Then put the **letter** of that word in the column at the left. Use each word once.

a. **confirm**	b. **deceptive**	c. **defy**	d. **restrain**	e. **seclusion**
f. **submit**	g. **susceptible**	h. **transmit**	i. **valid**	j. **vigorous**

_____ 1. The little girl, very frightened of Santa Claus, was so determined to run out of the mall that her parents could hardly _____ her.

_____ 2. Martin recently went into _____ for an entire weekend. He needed to be alone in order to figure out his taxes.

_____ 3. It's good Larry called to _____ our reservations because the motel had no record of our request for a room.

_____ 4. Junk mail can be so _____. Often mail advertisements are designed to seem like announcements of wonderful prizes.

_____ 5. Crystal loses one job after another because she won't _____ to anyone's orders. She argues with her supervisors constantly.

_____ 6. It's no wonder Brad is out of shape. The most _____ exercise he gets is walking a block to the ice cream parlor.

_____ 7. Because Carlos is so _____ to poison ivy, he wears long pants and long sleeves if he thinks he might get anywhere near the pesky plant.

_____ 8. Since Mary's parents didn't approve of musicians, Mary had to _____ them if she wanted to go out with Buddy.

_____ 9. If one child in a day-care center gets measles, he or she is likely to _____ the catching illness to other children.

_____ 10. Joan has a _____ reason for not trusting Paul: she's heard him lie many times.

SCORE: (Number correct) _____ × 10 = _____ %

Mastery Test: *Chapter 20 (Walking)*

In the space provided, write the word from the box needed to complete each sentence. Then put the **letter** of that word in the column at the left. Use each word once.

a. **accelerate**	b. **adverse**	c. **advocate**	d. **audible**	e. **coherent**
f. **comparable**	g. **competent**	h. **consecutive**	i. **conspicuous**	j. **deteriorate**

_____ 1. Polly's family became frightened when she had a(n) _____ reaction to penicillin.

_____ 2. One lawyer's presentation was a model of logic and order, but the other's was far from _____.

_____ 3. Year after year, my grandfather's eyesight _____s. Every time he goes to the eye doctor, he needs stronger lenses.

_____ 4. The drugstore's own brand of lotion and shampoo seems _____ to name brands in quality. There doesn't seem to be any difference.

_____ 5. My mother opposed my sister's marrying Jim, but my father was a strong _____ of their marriage.

_____ 6. The teenagers thought that if they whispered, they would not be heard by others in the movie theater. However, their conversation was _____ to many who sat nearby.

_____ 7. Since both candidates for the job were equally _____, the employer chose the one with the more pleasant personality.

_____ 8. The test was designed to be taken in three _____ parts: first, some multiple-choice questions; next, a matching exercise; and finally, an essay question.

_____ 9. Not only is the cheetah the fastest mammal in the world; it takes this wild cat only two seconds to _____ from a standing start to a speed of 45 miles an hour.

_____ 10. To tease his wife, Vic pretended not to see the "Happy Birthday" sign strung along the living room wall, even though the sign was so big it was too _____ to miss.

SCORE: (Number correct) _____ × 10 = _____ %

Answers to the Mastery Tests:
BUILDING VOCABULARY SKILLS, SHORT VERSION

Chapter 1 (Taking Exams)

1. d
2. e
3. c
4. g
5. b
6. h
7. a
8. i
9. j
10. f

Chapter 2 (Nate the Woodsman)

1. j
2. a
3. e
4. g
5. i
6. b
7. f
8. h
9. c
10. d

Chapter 3 (Who's on Trial?)

1. c
2. a
3. f
4. i
5. g
6. e
7. b
8. j
9. h
10. d

Chapter 4 (Night Nurse)

1. g
2. a
3. f
4. h
5. i
6. c
7. e
8. j
9. b
10. d

Chapter 5 (Relating to Parents)

1. j
2. c
3. b
4. e
5. d
6. h
7. f
8. a
9. g
10. i

Chapter 6 (Job Choices)

1. b
2. h
3. f
4. d
5. c
6. e
7. j
8. i
9. g
10. a

Chapter 7 (Museum Pet)

1. g
2. a
3. i
4. e
5. h
6. j
7. b
8. d
9. c
10. f

Chapter 8 (Our Headstrong Baby)

1. c
2. g
3. d
4. b
5. e
6. a
7. j
8. h
9. f
10. i

Chapter 9 (A Narrow Escape)

1. d
2. e
3. j
4. b
5. h
6. f
7. i
8. g
9. a
10. c

Chapter 10 (The Power of Advertising)

1. c
2. f
3. g
4. b
5. j
6. a
7. d
8. i
9. e
10. h

Chapter 11 (Waiter)

1. e
2. c
3. f
4. j
5. i
6. b
7. h
8. d
9. g
10. a

Chapter 12 (Adjusting to a New Culture)

1. d
2. g
3. h
4. a
5. f
6. b
7. c
8. e
9. j
10. i

Chapter 13 (A Dream About Wealth)

1. h	6. j
2. a	7. f
3. d	8. c
4. e	9. g
5. b	10. i

Chapter 14 (Children and Drugs)

1. b	6. i
2. h	7. f
3. a	8. e
4. g	9. d
5. c	10. j

Chapter 15 (Party House)

1. b	6. g
2. i	7. f
3. h	8. c
4. a	9. j
5. e	10. d

Chapter 16 (Procrastinator)

1. b	6. d
2. f	7. h
3. i	8. a
4. c	9. j
5. g	10. e

Chapter 17 (A Change in View)

1. c	6. j
2. g	7. f
3. i	8. b
4. e	9. a
5. h	10. d

Chapter 18 (Family Differences)

1. c	6. b
2. a	7. h
3. f	8. e
4. d	9. i
5. j	10. g

Chapter 19 (Chicken Pox)

1. d	6. j
2. e	7. g
3. a	8. c
4. b	9. h
5. f	10. i

Chapter 20 (Walking)

1. b	6. d
2. e	7. g
3. j	8. h
4. f	9. a
5. c	10. i

Mastery Test: *Unit One*

PART A
Complete each sentence in a way that clearly shows you understand the meaning of the **boldfaced** word. Take a minute to plan your answer before you write.

Example: If you receive a wedding invitation, it is **appropriate** _____*to respond by the date requested*_____.

1. One common **transition** that people make in life is _____
_____.

2. Two things that can **illuminate** a room are _____
_____.

3. One way I **compel** myself to study is by _____
_____.

4. The driver **averted** a crash by _____
_____.

5. A sign of high **morale** on a team is _____
_____.

6. The judge was so **lenient** that _____
_____.

7. Being a **novice** as a waiter, Artic _____
_____.

8. Although the restaurant was attractive, its success was **undermined** by _____
_____."

9. I decided to take **drastic** action to improve my social life, so I _____
_____.

10. When Stephanie served roast goose and a delicious peanut-butter pie for Thanksgiving dinner, her
conservative brother said, " _____
_____."

(Continues on next page)

PART B

Use each of the following ten words in sentences of your own. Make it clear that you know the meaning of the word you use. Feel free to use the past tense or plural form of a word.

| a. **alternative** | b. **candid** | c. **deter** | d. **erratic** | e. **idealistic** |
| f. **illusion** | g. **legitimate** | h. **menace** | i. **superficial** | j. **sustain** |

11. _____

_____

12. _____

_____

13. _____

_____

14. _____

_____

15. _____

_____

16. _____

_____

17. _____

_____

18. _____

_____

19. _____

_____

20. _____

_____

SCORE: (Number correct) _____ × 5 = _____ %

Mastery Test: *Unit Two*

PART A
Complete each sentence in a way that clearly shows you understand the meaning of the **boldfaced** word. Take a minute to plan your answer before you write.

Example: I wanted to **verify** the program's starting time, so I _____*checked the listings in TV Guide.*_____.

1. Two ways a boat can be **propelled** are by _____

   _____."

2. People who write letters to advice columns like to be **anonymous** because _____

   _____.

3. My sister is so **versatile** that _____

   _____.

4. Fran decided to **supplement** her income by _____

   _____.

5. Wild teenagers on the street **harassed** passing cars by_____

   _____."

6. A man who believes he and his date are **compatible** might say at the end of the evening," _____

   _____."

7. Pauline is so **arrogant** that when Greg told her she looked pretty, she replied, " _____

   _____."

8. While waiting for my turn for a haircut, I felt **apprehensive** because _____

   _____.

9. My friend Ted is very **prudent** about his money. For instance, _____

   _____.

10. When Joanne asked her husband why he hadn't washed the dinner dishes, his **retort** was, " _____

   _____."

(Continues on next page)

PART B

Use each of the following ten words in sentences of your own. Make it clear that you know the meaning of the word you use. Feel free to use the past tense or plural form of a word.

a. **compensate**	b. **delusion**	c. **derive**	d. **elapse**	e. **infer**
f. **ordeal**	g. **persistent**	h. **prominent**	i. **retrieve**	j. **savor**

11. _____

_____

12. _____

_____

13. _____

_____

14. _____

_____

15. _____

_____

16. _____

_____

17. _____

_____

18. _____

_____

19. _____

_____

20. _____

_____

SCORE: (Number correct) _____ × 5 = _____ %

Mastery Test: *Unit Three*

PART A
Complete each sentence in a way that clearly shows you understand the meaning of the **boldfaced** word. Take a minute to plan your answer before you write.

Example: A **mediocre** essay is likely to _____ *receive a grade of C* _____ .

1. Lonnie needs to get from New York to Florida. One of his **options** is to _____

_____ .

2. A cab driver might respond to a **liberal** tip by _____

_____ .

3. When the heater broke, we **adapted** to the sudden drop in temperature by _____

_____ .

4. One **tactic** for dieting is _____

_____ .

5. After Gina invited Daniel out for coffee, he **reciprocated** by _____

_____ .

6. An animal-lover would become **indignant** if _____

_____ .

7. A **shrewd** shopper will probably spend a lot of time _____

_____ .

8. When I was little, my mother always used to give me this **reprimand**: " _____

_____ ."

9. One **exotic** place I'd like to visit some day is _____

_____ .

10. A **skeptical** response to "I love you" is " _____

_____ ."

(Continues on next page)

PART B

Use each of the following ten words in sentences of your own. Make it clear that you know the meaning of the word you use. Feel free to use the past tense or plural form of a word.

a. **coerce**	b. **emerge**	c. **equate**	d. **gesture**	e. **indifferent**
f. **passive**	g. **recur**	h. **ritual**	i. **sadistic**	j. **stereotype**

11. _____

_____

12. _____

_____

13. _____

_____

14. _____

_____

15. _____

_____

16. _____

_____

17. _____

_____

18. _____

_____

19. _____

_____

20. _____

_____

SCORE: (Number correct) _____ × 5 = _____ %

Mastery Test: *Unit Four*

PART A
Complete each sentence in a way that clearly shows you understand the meaning of the **boldfaced** word. Take a minute to plan your answer before you write.

Example: A child might **defy** a parent by _____ *refusing to mow the lawn* _____.

1. A camper might experience such **adverse** conditions as _____

   _____.

2. One **valid** reason for missing class is _____

   _____.

3. Drivers usually **accelerate** their cars when _____

   _____.

4. Ramon felt **dismal** because _____

   _____.

5. One activity I find especially **tedious** is _____

   _____.

6. I sometimes **procrastinate** when _____

   _____.

7. Our teacher **confirmed** the rumor that the test was being postponed when she _____

   _____.

8. Babies have an **innate** ability to _____

   _____.

9. If you were to **submit** to someone's demand for a loan, you would _____

   _____.

10. To stay healthy, it is **vital** that I _____

    _____.

(Continues on next page)

PART B

Use each of the following ten words in sentences of your own. Make it clear that you know the meaning of the word you use. Feel free to use the past tense or plural form of a word.

a. **audible**	b. **comparable**	c. **consequence**	d. **deteriorate**	e. **intervene**
f. **perceptive**	g. **profound**	h. **severity**	i. **subside**	j. **vocation**

11. _____

_____

12. _____

_____

13. _____

_____

14. _____

_____

15. _____

_____

16. _____

_____

17. _____

_____

18. _____

_____

19. _____

_____

20. _____

_____

SCORE: (Number correct) _____ × 5 = _____ %

NAME: _____

SECTION: _____ DATE: _____

Pretest

SCORE: _____

This test contains 100 items. In the space provided, write the letter of the choice that is closest in meaning to the **boldfaced** word.

Important: Keep in mind that this test is for diagnostic purposes only. **If you do not know a word, leave the space blank rather than guess at it.**

_____ 1. **animosity**   a) approval   b) ill will   c) fear   d) shyness

_____ 2. **encounter**   a) meeting   b) total   c) departure   d) attack

_____ 3. **adamant**   a) realistic   b) stubborn   c) weak   d) flexible

_____ 4. **eccentric**   a) odd   b) common   c) active   d) calm

_____ 5. **malign**   a) depend on   b) speak evil of   c) boast   d) praise

_____ 6. **tangible**   a) more than normal   b) touchable   c) hidden   d) orderly

_____ 7. **acclaim**   a) false name   b) great approval   c) disagreement   d) sadness

_____ 8. **escalate**   a) remove   b) lessen   c) include   d) intensify

_____ 9. **elicit**   a) draw forth   b) approve   c) praise   d) disprove

_____ 10. **obsolete**   a) current   b) difficult to believe   c) out-of-date   d) not sold

_____ 11. **allusion**   a) indirect reference   b) physical weakness   c) improvement   d) short story

_____ 12. **altruistic**   a) honest   b) lying   c) proud   d) unselfish

_____ 13. **euphemism**   a) false appearance   b) degree   c) substitute for offensive term   d) title

_____ 14. **arbitrary**   a) wordy   b) based on impulse   c) demanding   d) believable

_____ 15. **assail**   a) attack   b) travel   c) defend   d) confuse

_____ 16. **fluctuate**   a) stand still   b) vary irregularly   c) float   d) sink

_____ 17. **calamity**   a) disaster   b) storm   c) conference   d) breeze

_____ 18. **persevere**   a) treat harshly   b) mark   c) continue   d) delay

_____ 19. **comprehensive**   a) accidental   b) including much   c) delicate   d) small

_____ 20. **venture**   a) turn aside   b) urge   c) risk   d) misrepresent

_____ 21. **enhance**   a) reject   b) get   c) improve   d) free

_____ 22. **attribute**   a) admiration   b) program   c) disease   d) quality

_____ 23. **discern**   a) see clearly   b) devise   c) rule out   d) consider

_____ 24. **exemplify**   a) construct   b) represent   c) plan   d) test

_____ 25. **attest**   a) bear witness   b) examine   c) tear up   d) dislike

(Continues on next page)

____	26. **concurrent**	**a)** apart	**b)** happening together	**c)** north	**d)** off-and-on
____	27. **constitute**	**a)** make up	**b)** eliminate	**c)** separate	**d)** remove
____	28. **predominant**	**a)** smallest	**b)** most noticeable	**c)** having a tendency	**d)** hidden
____	29. **nominal**	**a)** open to harm	**b)** large	**c)** important	**d)** slight
____	30. **confiscate**	**a)** deny	**b)** make difficult	**c)** desire	**d)** seize with authority
____	31. **suffice**	**a)** think up	**b)** be enough	**c)** prevent	**d)** pay back
____	32. **degenerate**	**a)** give up	**b)** improve	**c)** stay the same	**d)** worsen
____	33. **implausible**	**a)** possible	**b)** hard to believe	**c)** imaginary	**d)** historical
____	34. **sinister**	**a)** frightened	**b)** lively	**c)** generous	**d)** evil
____	35. **intricate**	**a)** easy	**b)** complex	**c)** workable	**d)** touching
____	36. **qualm**	**a)** pleasure	**b)** dead end	**c)** feeling of doubt	**d)** place of safety
____	37. **garble**	**a)** refuse	**b)** mix up	**c)** claim	**d)** speak clearly
____	38. **immaculate**	**a)** roomy	**b)** clean	**c)** empty	**d)** complete
____	39. **retaliate**	**a)** repair	**b)** repeat	**c)** renew	**d)** pay back
____	40. **blatant**	**a)** sudden	**b)** immediate	**c)** quiet	**d)** obvious
____	41. **intermittent**	**a)** hesitant	**b)** nervous	**c)** off-and-on	**d)** constant
____	42. **digress**	**a)** stray	**b)** improve	**c)** resist	**d)** repeat
____	43. **incentive**	**a)** fear	**b)** pride	**c)** concern	**d)** encouragement
____	44. **succumb**	**a)** approach	**b)** repeat	**c)** give in	**d)** cut short
____	45. **devastate**	**a)** spread out	**b)** begin again	**c)** reassure	**d)** upset greatly
____	46. **speculate**	**a)** search	**b)** think about	**c)** inspect	**d)** state to be so
____	47. **infamous**	**a)** not known	**b)** small	**c)** having a bad reputation	**d)** related
____	48. **benefactor**	**a)** landlord	**b)** one who gives aid	**c)** optimist	**d)** kindness
____	49. **intrinsic**	**a)** belonging by its very nature	**b)** on the surface	**c)** not noticeable	**d)** careful
____	50. **alleviate**	**a)** make anxious	**b)** depart	**c)** infect	**d)** relieve

(Continues on next page)

_____	51. **mandatory**	**a)** masculine	**b)** sexist	**c)** required	**d)** threatening
_____	52. **lucrative**	**a)** silly	**b)** profitable	**c)** causing disease	**d)** attractive
_____	53. **aspire**	**a)** dislike	**b)** strongly desire	**c)** impress	**d)** deliver
_____	54. **benevolent**	**a)** kind	**b)** wealthy	**c)** nasty	**d)** poor
_____	55. **dissent**	**a)** approval	**b)** defeat	**c)** winning	**d)** disagreement
_____	56. **proponent**	**a)** foe	**b)** supporter	**c)** examiner	**d)** one part of the whole
_____	57. **quest**	**a)** search	**b)** request	**c)** place	**d)** memory
_____	58. **conversely**	**a)** rudely	**b)** uncooperative	**c)** in an opposite manner	**d)** unfriendly
_____	59. **prevalent**	**a)** famous	**b)** widespread	**c)** escapable	**d)** plain
_____	60. **traumatic**	**a)** causing painful emotions	**b)** reversed	**c)** delicate	**d)** harmless
_____	61. **flippant**	**a)** cold	**b)** formal	**c)** disrespectful	**d)** nervous
_____	62. **perception**	**a)** meeting	**b)** party	**c)** dead end	**d)** impression
_____	63. **prone**	**a)** disliked	**b)** tending	**c)** active	**d)** rested
_____	64. **rationale**	**a)** research paper	**b)** debate	**c)** logical basis	**d)** mood
_____	65. **impasse**	**a)** exit	**b)** central point	**c)** gate	**d)** dead end
_____	66. **divulge**	**a)** reveal	**b)** embarrass	**c)** hide	**d)** remove
_____	67. **nullify**	**a)** harm	**b)** allow	**c)** turn aside	**d)** cancel
_____	68. **elation**	**a)** trade	**b)** comparison	**c)** joy	**d)** majority opinion
_____	69. **ominous**	**a)** happy	**b)** threatening	**c)** depressed	**d)** friendly
_____	70. **averse**	**a)** attracted	**b)** fearful	**c)** warm	**d)** opposed
_____	71. **transcend**	**a)** send	**b)** travel	**c)** show off	**d)** rise above
_____	72. **deplete**	**a)** encourage	**b)** use up	**c)** delay	**d)** add to
_____	73. **complacent**	**a)** workable	**b)** easy	**c)** self-satisfied	**d)** healthy
_____	74. **empathy**	**a)** fear	**b)** encouragement	**c)** ability to share someone's feelings **d)** avoidance	
_____	75. **waive**	**a)** sleep	**b)** show off	**c)** give up	**d)** fly

(Continues on next page)

_____ 76. **gape**   a) stare   b) repair   c) beat   d) hide from

_____ 77. **punitive**   a) inexpensive   b) punishing   c) ridiculously inadequate   d) possible

_____ 78. **condone**   a) forgive   b) represent   c) arrest   d) appoint

_____ 79. **precedent**   a) gift   b) example   c) fee   d) later event

_____ 80. **contemplate**   a) think seriously about   b) create   c) add to   d) reveal

_____ 81. **detrimental**   a) dirty   b) nutritious   c) harmful   d) helpful

_____ 82. **ironic**   a) deeply felt   b) meaning opposite of what is said   c) simple   d) great

_____ 83. **vindictive**   a) not easily understood   b) gentle   c) vengeful   d) temporary

_____ 84. **saturate**   a) break apart   b) put down   c) fully soak   d) describe

_____ 85. **deficient**   a) forgotten   b) lacking   c) complete   d) well-known

_____ 86. **fallible**   a) capable of error   b) complete   c) incomplete   d) simple

_____ 87. **exhaustive**   a) respected   b) nervous   c) complete   d) tired

_____ 88. **habitat**   a) headache   b) natural environment   c) importance   d) usual behavior

_____ 89. **vile**   a) offensive   b) secretive   c) nice   d) tricky

_____ 90. **pragmatic**   a) ordinary   b) slow   c) wise   d) practical

_____ 91. **pacify**   a) betray   b) calm   c) retreat   d) remove

_____ 92. **esteem**   a) age   b) doubt   c) respect   d) length of life

_____ 93. **transient**   a) stubborn   b) temporary   c) permanent   d) easy-going

_____ 94. **avid**   a) bored   b) disliked   c) enthusiastic   d) plentiful

_____ 95. **nurture**   a) harden   b) thank   c) nourish   d) starve

_____ 96. **augment**   a) change   b) cause to become   c) increase   d) describe

_____ 97. **explicit**   a) everyday   b) distant   c) permanent   d) stated exactly

_____ 98. **magnitude**   a) importance   b) attraction   c) respect   d) example

_____ 99. **ambivalent**   a) everyday   b) having mixed feelings   c) temporary   d) able to be done

_____ 100. **dispel**   a) assist   b) anger   c) describe   d) cause to vanish

---

STOP. This is the end of the test. If there is time remaining, you may go back and recheck your answers. When the time is up, hand in both your answer sheet and this test booklet to your instructor.

NAME: _____

SECTION: _____ DATE: _____

SCORE: _____

Posttest

> This test contains 100 items. In the space provided, write the letter of the choice that is closest in meaning to the **boldfaced** word.

_____ 1. **enhance**   **a)** free   **b)** get   **c)** improve   **d)** reject

_____ 2. **encounter**   **a)** departure   **b)** total   **c)** meeting   **d)** attack

_____ 3. **obsolete**   **a)** current   **b)** out-of date   **c)** difficult to believe   **d)** not sold

_____ 4. **eccentric**   **a)** active   **b)** common   **c)** calm   **d)** odd

_____ 5. **escalate**   **a)** remove   **b)** include   **c)** lessen   **d)** intensify

_____ 6. **euphemism**   **a)** degree   **b)** false appearance   **c)** substitute for offensive term   **d)** title

_____ 7. **exemplify**   **a)** test   **b)** construct   **c)** represent   **d)** plan

_____ 8. **adamant**   **a)** flexible   **b)** stubborn   **c)** weak   **d)** realistic

_____ 9. **comprehensive**   **a)** delicate   **b)** including much   **c)** accidental   **d)** small

_____ 10. **animosity**   **a)** fear   **b)** shyness   **c)** approval   **d)** ill will

_____ 11. **discern**   **a)** rule out   **b)** devise   **c)** see clearly   **d)** consider

_____ 12. **allusion**   **a)** indirect reference   **b)** physical weakness   **c)** improvement   **d)** short story

_____ 13. **altruistic**   **a)** unselfish   **b)** honest   **c)** lying   **d)** proud

_____ 14. **malign**   **a)** praise   **b)** boast   **c)** speak evil of   **d)** depend on

_____ 15. **arbitrary**   **a)** based on impulse   **b)** wordy   **c)** believable   **d)** demanding

_____ 16. **assail**   **a)** defend   **b)** travel   **c)** attack   **d)** confuse

_____ 17. **fluctuate**   **a)** sink   **b)** vary irregularly   **c)** float   **d)** stand still

_____ 18. **elicit**   **a)** praise   **b)** disprove   **c)** draw forth   **d)** approve

_____ 19. **persevere**   **a)** mark   **b)** treat harshly   **c)** continue   **d)** delay

_____ 20. **venture**   **a)** misrepresent   **b)** turn aside   **c)** urge   **d)** risk

_____ 21. **attest**   **a)** examine   **b)** bear witness   **c)** tear up   **d)** dislike

_____ 22. **acclaim**   **a)** disagreement   **b)** great approval   **c)** false name   **d)** sadness

_____ 23. **calamity**   **a)** conference   **b)** breeze   **c)** disaster   **d)** storm

_____ 24. **attribute**   **a)** admiration   **b)** quality   **c)** disease   **d)** program

_____ 25. **tangible**   **a)** more than normal   **b)** touchable   **c)** hidden   **d)** orderly

(Continues on next page)

_____ 26. **retaliate**   a) repair   b) pay back   c) renew   d) repeat

_____ 27. **qualm**   a) pleasure   b) place of safety   c) feeling of doubt   d) dead end

_____ 28. **intrinsic**   a) belonging by its very nature   b) not noticeable   c) on the surface
d) careful

_____ 29. **confiscate**   a) make difficult   b) deny   c) seize with authority   d) desire

_____ 30. **immaculate**   a) roomy   b) clean   c) empty   d) complete

_____ 31. **degenerate**   a) give up   b) improve   c) stay the same   d) worsen

_____ 32. **implausible**   a) possible   b) hard to believe   c) imaginary   d) historical

_____ 33. **devastate**   a) reassure   b) upset greatly   c) spread out   d) begin again

_____ 34. **sinister**   a) frightened   b) generous   c) lively   d) evil

_____ 35. **nominal**   a) slight   b) large   c) important   d) open to harm

_____ 36. **speculate**   a) inspect   b) think about   c) search   d) state to be so

_____ 37. **succumb**   a) cut short   b) approach   c) give in   d) repeat

_____ 38. **garble**   a) claim   b) mix up   c) refuse   d) speak clearly

_____ 39. **constitute**   a) make up   b) remove   c) eliminate   d) separate

_____ 40. **blatant**   a) quiet   b) sudden   c) immediate   d) obvious

_____ 41. **intricate**   a) complex   b) easy   c) workable   d) touching

_____ 42. **predominant**   a) hidden   b) having a tendency   c) most noticeable   d) smallest

_____ 43. **incentive**   a) fear   b) concern   c) pride   d) encouragement

_____ 44. **infamous**   a) having a bad reputation   b) not known   c) small   d) related

_____ 45. **concurrent**   a) apart   b) north   c) happening together   d) off-and-on

_____ 46. **benefactor**   a) landlord   b) one who gives aid   c) optimist   d) kindness

_____ 47. **intermittent**   a) hesitant   b) nervous   c) off-and-on   d) constant

_____ 48. **suffice**   a) think up   b) prevent   c) be enough   d) pay back

_____ 49. **alleviate**   a) infect   b) relieve   c) make anxious   d) depart

_____ 50. **digress**   a) resist   b) improve   c) stray   d) repeat

(Continues on next page)

_____ 51. **averse**   a) opposed   b) fearful   c) warm   d) attracted

_____ 52. **conversely**   a) unfriendly   b) rudely   c) uncooperative   d) in an opposite manner

_____ 53. **aspire**   a) dislike   b) strongly desire   c) impress   d) deliver

_____ 54. **elation**   a) comparison   b) trade   c) joy   d) majority opinion

_____ 55. **quest**   a) place   b) memory   c) search   d) request

_____ 56. **mandatory**   a) sexist   b) threatening   c) required   d) masculine

_____ 57. **ominous**   a) happy   b) depressed   c) threatening   d) friendly

_____ 58. **traumatic**   a) harmless   b) reversed   c) delicate   d) causing painful emotions

_____ 59. **lucrative**   a) causing disease   b) profitable   c) silly   d) attractive

_____ 60. **impasse**   a) gate   b) exit   c) central point   d) dead end

_____ 61. **transcend**   a) send   b) travel   c) show off   d) rise above

_____ 62. **complacent**   a) workable   b) self-satisfied   c) healthy   d) easy

_____ 63. **divulge**   a) remove   b) reveal   c) hide   d) embarrass

_____ 64. **benevolent**   a) poor   b) kind   c) wealthy   d) nasty

_____ 65. **rationale**   a) mood   b) debate   c) logical basis   d) research paper

_____ 66. **proponent**   a) supporter   b) examiner   c) foe   d) one part of the whole

_____ 67. **nullify**   a) cancel   b) turn aside   c) allow   d) harm

_____ 68. **flippant**   a) cold   b) disrespectful   c) formal   d) nervous

_____ 69. **prone**   a) active   b) tending   c) disliked   d) rested

_____ 70. **empathy**   a) fear   b) encouragement   c) ability to share someone's feelings
d) avoidance

_____ 71. **waive**   a) fly   b) sleep   c) show off   d) give up

_____ 72. **prevalent**   a) plain   b) widespread   c) escapable   d) famous

_____ 73. **dissent**   a) disagreement   b) winning   c) defeat   d) approval

_____ 74. **perception**   a) impression   b) meeting   c) dead end   d) party

_____ 75. **deplete**   a) add to   b) delay   c) use up   d) encourage

(Continues on next page)

_____ 76. **vindictive**   a) not easily understood   b) gentle   c) vengeful   d) temporary

_____ 77. **precedent**   a) gift   b) fee   c) example   d) later event

_____ 78. **vile**   a) tricky   b) nice   c) secretive   d) offensive

_____ 79. **ironic**   a) simple   b) meaning opposite of what is said   c) deeply felt   d) great

_____ 80. **saturate**   a) fully soak   b) put down   c) break apart   d) describe

_____ 81. **pacify**   a) betray   b) remove   c) retreat   d) calm

_____ 82. **detrimental**   a) harmful   b) nutritious   c) dirty   d) helpful

_____ 83. **explicit**   a) everyday   b) permanent   c) distant   d) stated exactly

_____ 84. **exhaustive**   a) complete   b) nervous   c) respected   d) tired

_____ 85. **ambivalent**   a) everyday   b) temporary   c) having mixed feelings   d) able to be done

_____ 86. **dispel**   a) cause to vanish   b) anger   c) describe   d) assist

_____ 87. **pragmatic**   a) practical   b) slow   c) wise   d) ordinary

_____ 88. **esteem**   a) respect   b) doubt   c) age   d) length of life

_____ 89. **contemplate**   a) think seriously about   b) create   c) add to   d) reveal

_____ 90. **transient**   a) permanent   b) easy-going   c) stubborn   d) temporary

_____ 91. **augment**   a) cause to become   b) change   c) describe   d) increase

_____ 92. **fallible**   a) incomplete   b) complete   c) capable of error   d) simple

_____ 93. **punitive**   a) punishing   b) inexpensive   c) ridiculously inadequate   d) possible

_____ 94. **avid**   a) enthusiastic   b) disliked   c) bored   d) plentiful

_____ 95. **habitat**   a) headache   b) natural environment   c) importance   d) usual behavior

_____ 96. **nurture**   a) harden   b) thank   c) nourish   d) starve

_____ 97. **deficient**   a) forgotten   b) well-known   c) complete   d) lacking

_____ 98. **gape**   a) hide from   b) beat   c) stare   d) repair

_____ 99. **magnitude**   a) importance   b) attraction   c) respect   d) example

_____ 100. **condone**   a) arrest   b) represent   c) forgive   d) appoint

---

STOP. This is the end of the test. If there is time remaining, you may go back and recheck your answers. When the time is up, hand in both your answer sheet and this test booklet to your instructor.

Unit One: *Pretest*

In the space provided, write the letter of the choice that is closest in meaning to the **boldfaced** word.

_____ 1. **animosity**   a) approval   b) ill will   c) fear   d) shyness

_____ 2. **encounter**   a) meeting   b) total   c) departure   d) attack

_____ 3. **absolve**   a) make guilty   b) reject   c) clear from guilt   d) approve

_____ 4. **adamant**   a) realistic   b) stubborn   c) weak   d) flexible

_____ 5. **eccentric**   a) odd   b) common   c) active   d) calm

_____ 6. **amoral**   a) honest   b) poor   c) without principles   d) generous

_____ 7. **malign**   a) depend on   b) speak evil of   c) boast   d) praise

_____ 8. **antagonist**   a) friend   b) relative   c) boss   d) opponent

_____ 9. **tangible**   a) more than normal   b) touchable   c) hidden   d) orderly

_____ 10. **acclaim**   a) false name   b) great approval   c) disagreement   d) sadness

_____ 11. **escalate**   a) remove   b) lessen   c) include   d) intensify

_____ 12. **elicit**   a) draw forth   b) approve   c) praise   d) disprove

_____ 13. **exploit**   a) save   b) throw away   c) use selfishly   d) sell overseas

_____ 14. **obsolete**   a) current   b) difficult to believe   c) out-of-date   d) not sold

_____ 15. **engross**   a) destroy   b) impress   c) disgust   d) hold the attention of

_____ 16. **terminate**   a) stop   b) continue   c) begin   d) approach

_____ 17. **banal**   a) humid   b) commonplace   c) secret   d) true

_____ 18. **appease**   a) make calm   b) tell the truth   c) attack   d) approve

_____ 19. **allusion**   a) indirect reference   b) physical weakness   c) improvement   d) short story

_____ 20. **altruistic**   a) honest   b) lying   c) proud   d) unselfish

_____ 21. **mercenary**   a) clean   b) mean   c) calm   d) greedy

_____ 22. **euphemism**   a) false appearance   b) degree   c) substitute for offensive term   d) title

_____ 23. **arbitrary**   a) wordy   b) based on impulse   c) demanding   d) believable

_____ 24. **assail**   a) attack   b) travel   c) defend   d) confuse

_____ 25. **fluctuate**   a) stand still   b) vary irregularly   c) float   d) sink

(Continues on next page)

_____ 26. **rehabilitate**   a) restore to normal life   b) relax   c) plan in meetings   d) interpret

_____ 27. **calamity**   a) disaster   b) storm   c) conference   d) breeze

_____ 28. **persevere**   a) treat harshly   b) mark   c) continue   d) delay

_____ 29. **comprehensive**   a) accidental   b) including much   c) delicate   d) small

_____ 30. **venture**   a) turn aside   b) urge   c) risk   d) misrepresent

_____ 31. **ponder**   a) think deeply about   b) allow   c) reduce   d) flatten

_____ 32. **turmoil**   a) workplace   b) quiet setting   c) fire   d) uproar

_____ 33. **enhance**   a) reject   b) get   c) improve   d) free

_____ 34. **mobile**   a) firm in opinion   b) able to move   c) stationary   d) restricted

_____ 35. **orient**   a) determine the location of   b) lose   c) represent   d) consist of

_____ 36. **attribute**   a) admiration   b) program   c) disease   d) quality

_____ 37. **discern**   a) see clearly   b) devise   c) rule out   d) consider

_____ 38. **exemplify**   a) construct   b) represent   c) plan   d) test

_____ 39. **nocturnal**   a) supposed   b) not logical   c) complex   d) active at night

_____ 40. **attest**   a) bear witness   b) examine   c) tear up   d) dislike

_____ 41. **amiable**   a) stingy   b) rude   c) proud   d) good-natured

_____ 42. **epitome**   a) perfect example   b) large hole   c) horrible sight   d) tallest point

_____ 43. **adjacent**   a) above   b) under   c) next to   d) within

_____ 44. **methodical**   a) religious   b) systematic   c) careless   d) immoral

_____ 45. **syndrome**   a) attitude   b) thought   c) something required   d) group of symptoms

_____ 46. **taint**   a) surprise   b) dishonor   c) annoy   d) boast

_____ 47. **flagrant**   a) sweet-smelling   b) outrageous   c) hidden   d) slight

_____ 48. **conventional**   a) large   b) at a conference   c) outstanding   d) ordinary

_____ 49. **enigma**   a) rash   b) puzzle   c) tool   d) cleanser

_____ 50. **dispatch**   a) recall   b) remove   c) send   d) plant

SCORE: (Number correct) _____ × 2 = _____ %

Unit One: *Posttest*

In the space provided, write the letter of the choice that is closest in meaning to the **boldfaced** word.

____ 1. **enhance**　　　**a)** free　　**b)** get　　**c)** improve　　**d)** reject

____ 2. **encounter**　　**a)** total　　**b)** attack　　**c)** departure　　**d)** meeting

____ 3. **mercenary**　　**a)** calm　　**b)** greedy　　**c)** clean　　**d)** mean

____ 4. **obsolete**　　　**a)** current　　**b)** out-of date　　**c)** difficult to believe　　**d)** not sold

____ 5. **eccentric**　　　**a)** active　　**b)** common　　**c)** calm　　**d)** odd

____ 6. **mobile**　　　**a)** firm in opinion　　**b)** able to move　　**c)** stationary　　**d)** restricted

____ 7. **nocturnal**　　**a)** complex　　**b)** active at night　　**c)** supposed　　**d)** not logical

____ 8. **appease**　　　**a)** attack　　**b)** tell the truth　　**c)** make calm　　**d)** approve

____ 9. **turmoil**　　　**a)** fire　　**b)** uproar　　**c)** workplace　　**d)** quiet setting

____ 10. **antagonist**　　**a)** boss　　**b)** relative　　**c)** friend　　**d)** opponent

____ 11. **escalate**　　　**a)** remove　　**b)** include　　**c)** lessen　　**d)** intensify

____ 12. **cuphemism**　　**a)** degree　　**b)** false appearance　　**c)** substitute for offensive term　　**d)** title

____ 13. **engross**　　　**a)** destroy　　**b)** impress　　**c)** disgust　　**d)** hold the attention of

____ 14. **excmplify**　　**a)** test　　**b)** construct　　**c)** represent　　**d)** plan

____ 15. **adamant**　　　**a)** flexible　　**b)** stubborn　　**c)** weak　　**d)** realistic

____ 16. **terminate**　　**a)** begin　　**b)** stop　　**c)** continue　　**d)** approach

____ 17. **comprehensive**　　**a)** delicate　　**b)** including much　　**c)** accidental　　**d)** small

____ 18. **animosity**　　**a)** fear　　**b)** shyness　　**c)** approval　　**d)** ill will

____ 19. **banal**　　　**a)** commonplace　　**b)** humid　　**c)** secret　　**d)** true

____ 20. **discern**　　　**a)** rule out　　**b)** devise　　**c)** see clearly　　**d)** consider

____ 21. **allusion**　　　**a)** indirect reference　　**b)** physical weakness　　**c)** improvement　　**d)** short story

____ 22. **altruistic**　　**a)** unselfish　　**b)** honest　　**c)** lying　　**d)** proud

____ 23. **malign**　　　**a)** praise　　**b)** boast　　**c)** speak evil of　　**d)** depend on

____ 24. **orient**　　　**a)** lose　　**b)** determine the location of　　**c)** consist of　　**d)** represent

____ 25. **arbitrary**　　**a)** based on impulse　　**b)** wordy　　**c)** believable　　**d)** demanding

(Continues on next page)

_____ 26. **absolve**   **a)** make guilty   **b)** reject   **c)** clear from guilt   **d)** approve

_____ 27. **assail**   **a)** defend   **b)** travel   **c)** attack   **d)** confuse

_____ 28. **fluctuate**   **a)** sink   **b)** vary irregularly   **c)** float   **d)** stand still

_____ 29. **elicit**   **a)** praise   **b)** disprove   **c)** draw forth   **d)** approve

_____ 30. **exploit**   **a)** use selfishly   **b)** throw away   **c)** save   **d)** sell overseas

_____ 31. **amoral**   **a)** honest   **b)** poor   **c)** without principles   **d)** generous

_____ 32. **persevere**   **a)** mark   **b)** treat harshly   **c)** continue   **d)** delay

_____ 33. **venture**   **a)** misrepresent   **b)** turn aside   **c)** urge   **d)** risk

_____ 34. **attest**   **a)** examine   **b)** bear witness   **c)** tear up   **d)** dislike

_____ 35. **acclaim**   **a)** disagreement   **b)** great approval   **c)** false name   **d)** sadness

_____ 36. **ponder**   **a)** think deeply about   **b)** reduce   **c)** allow   **d)** flatten

_____ 37. **calamity**   **a)** conference   **b)** breeze   **c)** disaster   **d)** storm

_____ 38. **attribute**   **a)** admiration   **b)** quality   **c)** disease   **d)** program

_____ 39. **rehabilitate**   **a)** restore to normal life   **b)** relax   **c)** plan in meetings   **d)** interpret

_____ 40. **tangible**   **a)** more than normal   **b)** touchable   **c)** hidden   **d)** orderly

_____ 41. **flagrant**   **a)** slight   **b)** hidden   **c)** outrageous   **d)** sweet-smelling

_____ 42. **amiable**   **a)** good-natured   **b)** stingy   **c)** proud   **d)** rude

_____ 43. **adjacent**   **a)** under   **b)** above   **c)** next to   **d)** within

_____ 44. **taint**   **a)** dishonor   **b)** boast   **c)** annoy   **d)** surprise

_____ 45. **dispatch**   **a)** recall   **b)** remove   **c)** send   **d)** plant

_____ 46. **methodical**   **a)** careless   **b)** systematic   **c)** immoral   **d)** religious

_____ 47. **epitome**   **a)** horrible sight   **b)** large hole   **c)** tallest point   **d)** perfect example

_____ 48. **conventional**   **a)** large   **b)** outstanding   **c)** at a conference   **d)** ordinary

_____ 49. **enigma**   **a)** tool   **b)** puzzle   **c)** cleanser   **d)** rash

_____ 50. **syndrome**   **a)** something required   **b)** thought   **c)** attitude   **d)** group of symptoms

SCORE: (Number correct) _____ × 2 = _____ %

Unit Two: *Pretest*

In the space provided, write the letter of the choice that is closest in meaning to the **boldfaced** word.

_____ 1. **concurrent**   a) apart   b) happening together   c) north   d) off-and-on

_____ 2. **constitute**   a) make up   b) eliminate   c) separate   d) remove

_____ 3. **predominant**   a) smallest   b) most noticeable   c) having a tendency   d) hidden

_____ 4. **decipher**   a) interpret   b) study   c) improve   d) pay back

_____ 5. **default**   a) jump   b) do automatically   c) fail to do something required   d) seize

_____ 6. **nominal**   a) open to harm   b) large   c) important   d) slight

_____ 7. **prerequisite**   a) requirement beforehand   b) test   c) close inspection   d) extra credit

_____ 8. **confiscate**   a) deny   b) make difficult   c) desire   d) seize with authority

_____ 9. **sanctuary**   a) opinion   b) hardship   c) place of safety   d) something complicated

_____ 10. **suffice**   a) think up   b) be enough   c) prevent   d) pay back

_____ 11. **degenerate**   a) give up   b) improve   c) stay the same   d) worsen

_____ 12. **vulnerable**   a) kind   b) intelligent   c) wicked   d) sensitive

_____ 13. **implausible**   a) possible   b) hard to believe   c) imaginary   d) historical

_____ 14. **sinister**   a) frightened   b) lively   c) generous   d) evil

_____ 15. **incoherent**   a) not logical   b) well-spoken   c) quiet   d) unable to read

_____ 16. **intricate**   a) easy   b) complex   c) workable   d) touching

_____ 17. **qualm**   a) pleasure   b) dead end   c) feeling of doubt   d) place of safety

_____ 18. **blight**   a) something that damages   b) natural environment   c) example   d) storm

_____ 19. **garble**   a) refuse   b) mix up   c) claim   d) speak clearly

_____ 20. **immaculate**   a) roomy   b) clean   c) empty   d) complete

_____ 21. **retaliate**   a) repair   b) repeat   c) renew   d) pay back

_____ 22. **gloat**   a) express spiteful pleasure   b) give up   c) eat   d) deny

_____ 23. **plagiarism**   a) support   b) contribution   c) stealing someone's writings   d) removal

_____ 24. **blatant**   a) sudden   b) immediate   c) quiet   d) obvious

_____ 25. **incorporate**   a) anger   b) separate   c) combine   d) calm

(Continues on next page)

_____ 26. **intermittent**   **a)** hesitant   **b)** nervous   **c)** off-and-on   **d)** constant

_____ 27. **digress**   **a)** stray   **b)** improve   **c)** resist   **d)** repeat

_____ 28. **incentive**   **a)** fear   **b)** pride   **c)** concern   **d)** encouragement

_____ 29. **succumb**   **a)** approach   **b)** repeat   **c)** give in   **d)** cut short

_____ 30. **curtail**   **a)** urge   **b)** join   **c)** cut short   **d)** relieve

_____ 31. **indispensable**   **a)** necessary   **b)** not important   **c)** saved up   **d)** wasted

_____ 32. **devastate**   **a)** spread out   **b)** begin again   **c)** reassure   **d)** upset greatly

_____ 33. **speculate**   **a)** search   **b)** think about   **c)** inspect   **d)** state to be so

_____ 34. **infamous**   **a)** not known   **b)** small   **c)** having a bad reputation   **d)** related

_____ 35. **benefactor**   **a)** landlord   **b)** one who gives aid   **c)** optimist   **d)** kindness

_____ 36. **covert**   **a)** distant   **b)** hidden   **c)** changed   **d)** adjusted

_____ 37. **virile**   **a)** healthy   **b)** manly   **c)** wrinkled   **d)** required

_____ 38. **intrinsic**   **a)** belonging by its very nature   **b)** on the surface   **c)** not noticeable   **d)** careful

_____ 39. **alleviate**   **a)** make anxious   **b)** depart   **c)** infect   **d)** relieve

_____ 40. **revulsion**   **a)** confession   **b)** great disgust   **c)** attraction   **d)** compassion

_____ 41. **hypothetical**   **a)** moral   **b)** factual   **c)** avoidable   **d)** supposed

_____ 42. **recession**   **a)** parade   **b)** amusement   **c)** giving in   **d)** business decline

_____ 43. **intercede**   **a)** ask for a favor   **b)** remove   **c)** isolate   **d)** come between to help solve

_____ 44. **scrutiny**   **a)** knowledge   **b)** lack of interest   **c)** close inspection   **d)** ignorance

_____ 45. **contrive**   **a)** allow   **b)** inspect   **c)** think up   **d)** prepare

_____ 46. **gaunt**   **a)** tired   **b)** complex   **c)** well   **d)** bony

_____ 47. **rigor**   **a)** ease   **b)** hardship   **c)** slowness   **d)** meanness

_____ 48. **squander**   **a)** waste   **b)** lose   **c)** insult   **d)** strongly desire

_____ 49. **cynic**   **a)** pessimist   **b)** serious person   **c)** single person   **d)** clown

_____ 50. **demise**   **a)** trick   **b)** death   **c)** disguise   **d)** departure

SCORE: (Number correct) _____ × 2 = _____ %

Unit Two: *Posttest*

In the space provided, write the letter of the choice that is closest in meaning to the **boldfaced** word.

_____ 1. **decipher** **a)** interpret **b)** study **c)** improve **d)** pay back

_____ 2. **retaliate** **a)** repair **b)** pay back **c)** renew **d)** repeat

_____ 3. **qualm** **a)** pleasure **b)** place of safety **c)** feeling of doubt **d)** dead end

_____ 4. **curtail** **a)** relieve **b)** join **c)** urge **d)** cut short

_____ 5. **default** **a)** jump **b)** seize **c)** fail to do something required **d)** do automatically

_____ 6. **plagiarism** **a)** removal **b)** stealing someone's writings **c)** contribution **d)** support

_____ 7. **intrinsic** **a)** belonging by its very nature **b)** not noticeable **c)** on the surface **d)** careful

_____ 8. **gloat** **a)** eat **b)** give up **c)** express spiteful pleasure **d)** deny

_____ 9. **prerequisite** **a)** close inspection **b)** test **c)** requirement beforehand **d)** extra credit

_____ 10. **confiscate** **a)** make difficult **b)** deny **c)** seize with authority **d)** desire

_____ 11. **immaculate** **a)** roomy **b)** clean **c)** empty **d)** complete

_____ 12. **degenerate** **a)** give up **b)** improve **c)** stay the same **d)** worsen

_____ 13. **vulnerable** **a)** wicked **b)** sensitive **c)** kind **d)** intelligent

_____ 14. **indispensable** **a)** necessary **b)** not important **c)** saved up **d)** wasted

_____ 15. **implausible** **a)** possible **b)** hard to believe **c)** imaginary **d)** historical

_____ 16. **devastate** **a)** reassure **b)** upset greatly **c)** spread out **d)** begin again

_____ 17. **sinister** **a)** frightened **b)** generous **c)** lively **d)** evil

_____ 18. **sanctuary** **a)** hardship **b)** opinion **c)** something complicated **d)** place of safety

_____ 19. **nominal** **a)** slight **b)** large **c)** important **d)** open to harm

_____ 20. **speculate** **a)** inspect **b)** think about **c)** search **d)** state to be so

_____ 21. **blight** **a)** storm **b)** natural environment **c)** something that damages **d)** example

_____ 22. **succumb** **a)** cut short **b)** approach **c)** give in **d)** repeat

_____ 23. **garble** **a)** claim **b)** mix up **c)** refuse **d)** speak clearly

_____ 24. **constitute** **a)** make up **b)** remove **c)** eliminate **d)** separate

_____ 25. **virile** **a)** healthy **b)** wrinkled **c)** manly **d)** required

(Continues on next page)

_____ 26. **blatant**   a) quiet   b) sudden   c) immediate   d) obvious

_____ 27. **revulsion**   a) great disgust   b) confession   c) attraction   d) compassion

_____ 28. **incorporate**   a) calm   b) separate   c) combine   d) anger

_____ 29. **intricate**   a) complex   b) easy   c) workable   d) touching

_____ 30. **predominant**   a) hidden   b) having a tendency   c) most noticeable   d) smallest

_____ 31. **incentive**   a) fear   b) concern   c) pride   d) encouragement

_____ 32. **infamous**   a) having a bad reputation   b) not known   c) small   d) related

_____ 33. **concurrent**   a) apart   b) north   c) happening together   d) off-and-on

_____ 34. **benefactor**   a) landlord   b) one who gives aid   c) optimist   d) kindness

_____ 35. **intermittent**   a) hesitant   b) nervous   c) off-and-on   d) constant

_____ 36. **incoherent**   a) unable to read   b) well-spoken   c) not logical   d) quiet

_____ 37. **covert**   a) changed   b) adjusted   c) distant   d) hidden

_____ 38. **suffice**   a) think up   b) prevent   c) be enough   d) pay back

_____ 39. **alleviate**   a) infect   b) relieve   c) make anxious   d) depart

_____ 40. **digress**   a) resist   b) improve   c) stray   d) repeat

_____ 41. **intercede**   a) remove   b) come between to help solve   c) isolate   d) strike

_____ 42. **demise**   a) disguise   b) death   c) departure   d) trick

_____ 43. **rigor**   a) meanness   b) ease   c) slowness   d) hardship

_____ 44. **contrive**   a) inspect   b) prepare   c) allow   d) think up

_____ 45. **squander**   a) insult   b) lose   c) strongly desire   d) waste

_____ 46. **cynic**   a) serious person   b) clown   c) single person   d) pessimist

_____ 47. **hypothetical**   a) factual   b) avoidable   c) moral   d) supposed

_____ 48. **gaunt**   a) complex   b) bony   c) well   d) tired

_____ 49. **recession**   a) parade   b) business decline   c) giving in   d) amusement

_____ 50. **scrutiny**   a) lack of interest   b) ignorance   c) close inspection   d) knowledge

Name: _____

Unit Three: *Pretest*

In the space provided, write the letter of the choice that is closest in meaning to the **boldfaced** word.

_____ 1. **deficit**　　　　**a)** surplus　　**b)** remainder　　**c)** part of the whole　　**d)** shortage

_____ 2. **mandatory**　　　**a)** masculine　　**b)** sexist　　**c)** required　　**d)** threatening

_____ 3. **abstain**　　　　**a)** do without　　**b)** disagree　　**c)** prepare　　**d)** approve of

_____ 4. **lucrative**　　　**a)** silly　　**b)** profitable　　**c)** causing disease　　**d)** attractive

_____ 5. **agnostic**　　　**a)** one who is unsure there's a God　　**b)** saint　　**c)** believer　　**d)** genius

_____ 6. **aspire**　　　　**a)** dislike　　**b)** strongly desire　　**c)** impress　　**d)** deliver

_____ 7. **benevolent**　　**a)** kind　　**b)** wealthy　　**c)** nasty　　**d)** poor

_____ 8. **dissent**　　　　**a)** approval　　**b)** defeat　　**c)** winning　　**d)** disagreement

_____ 9. **proponent**　　　**a)** foe　　**b)** supporter　　**c)** examiner　　**d)** one part of the whole

_____ 10. **charisma**　　　**a)** friendship　　**b)** kindness　　**c)** obedience　　**d)** charm

_____ 11. **quest**　　　　**a)** search　　**b)** request　　**c)** place　　**d)** memory

_____ 12. **conversely**　　**a)** rudely　　**b)** uncooperative　　**c)** in an opposite manner　　**d)** unfriendly

_____ 13. **contemporary**　**a)** modern　　**b)** odd　　**c)** old-fashioned　　**d)** futuristic

_____ 14. **extrovert**　　　**a)** shy person　　**b)** magnetism　　**c)** main point　　**d)** outgoing person

_____ 15. **prevalent**　　　**a)** famous　　**b)** widespread　　**c)** escapable　　**d)** plain

_____ 16. **traumatic**　　　**a)** causing painful emotions　　**b)** reversed　　**c)** delicate　　**d)** harmless

_____ 17. **rapport**　　　　**a)** support　　**b)** close relationship　　**c)** view　　**d)** report

_____ 18. **flippant**　　　**a)** cold　　**b)** formal　　**c)** disrespectful　　**d)** nervous

_____ 19. **perception**　　　**a)** meeting　　**b)** party　　**c)** dead end　　**d)** impression

_____ 20. **congenial**　　　**a)** pleasant　　**b)** intelligent　　**c)** mixed-up　　**d)** lacking

_____ 21. **prone**　　　　**a)** disliked　　**b)** tending　　**c)** active　　**d)** rested

_____ 22. **rationale**　　　**a)** research paper　　**b)** debate　　**c)** logical basis　　**d)** mood

_____ 23. **impasse**　　　**a)** exit　　**b)** central point　　**c)** gate　　**d)** dead end

_____ 24. **prompt**　　　　**a)** urge　　**b)** avoid　　**c)** waste　　**d)** lie

_____ 25. **divulge**　　　**a)** reveal　　**b)** embarrass　　**c)** hide　　**d)** remove

(Continues on next page)

____	26. **endow**	a) name	b) tease	c) give a quality to	d) cancel
____	27. **expulsion**	a) promotion	b) dismissal	c) award	d) attack
____	28. **detract**	a) provide	b) compete	c) lessen	d) compliment
____	29. **nullify**	a) harm	b) allow	c) turn aside	d) cancel
____	30. **elation**	a) trade	b) comparison	c) joy	d) majority opinion
____	31. **ominous**	a) happy	b) threatening	c) depressed	d) friendly
____	32. **averse**	a) attracted	b) fearful	c) warm	d) opposed
____	33. **transcend**	a) send	b) travel	c) show off	d) rise above
____	34. **deplete**	a) encourage	b) use up	c) delay	d) add to
____	35. **complacent**	a) workable	b) easy	c) self-satisfied	d) healthy
____	36. **niche**	a) memory	b) wild outburst	c) main idea	d) one's place
____	37. **diligent**	a) careful in work	b) odd	c) obvious	d) gentle
____	38. **empathy**	a) fear	b) encouragement	c) ability to share someone's feelings	d) avoidance
____	39. **consensus**	a) majority opinion	b) counting	c) study	d) approval
____	40. **waive**	a) sleep	b) show off	c) give up	d) fly
____	41. **affiliate**	a) impress	b) approve	c) reject	d) join
____	42. **diversion**	a) awareness	b) practice	c) amusement	d) fate
____	43. **contend**	a) join	b) claim	c) arouse	d) allow
____	44. **poignant**	a) annoying	b) beautiful	c) careless	d) touching
____	45. **reprisal**	a) getting even	b) defeat	c) question	d) search
____	46. **relentless**	a) angry	b) persistent	c) cruel	d) kind
____	47. **mortify**	a) humiliate	b) praise	c) entertain	d) remember
____	48. **disdain**	a) discouragement	b) pain	c) scorn	d) approval
____	49. **menial**	a) important	b) unkind	c) lowly	d) odd
____	50. **commemorate**	a) forget	b) imitate	c) add new members	d) honor the memory of

SCORE: (Number correct) _____ × 2 = _____ %

Unit Three: *Posttest*

In the space provided, write the letter of the choice that is closest in meaning to the **boldfaced** word.

_____ 1. **agnostic**   a) believer   b) saint   c) one who is unsure there's a God   d) genius

_____ 2. **averse**   a) opposed   b) fearful   c) warm   d) attracted

_____ 3. **conversely**   a) unfriendly   b) rudely   c) uncooperative   d) in an opposite manner

_____ 4. **aspire**   a) dislike   b) strongly desire   c) impress   d) deliver

_____ 5. **charisma**   a) charm   b) kindness   c) obedience   d) friendship

_____ 6. **elation**   a) comparison   b) trade   c) joy   d) majority opinion

_____ 7. **quest**   a) place   b) memory   c) search   d) request

_____ 8. **contemporary**   a) modern   b) old-fashioned   c) futuristic   d) odd

_____ 9. **mandatory**   a) sexist   b) threatening   c) required   d) masculine

_____ 10. **niche**   a) memory   b) wild outburst   c) main idea   d) one's place

_____ 11. **ominous**   a) happy   b) depressed   c) threatening   d) friendly

_____ 12. **traumatic**   a) harmless   b) reversed   c) delicate   d) causing painful emotions

_____ 13. **rapport**   a) support   b) view   c) close relationship   d) report

_____ 14. **congenial**   a) lacking   b) pleasant   c) intelligent   d) mixed-up

_____ 15. **lucrative**   a) causing disease   b) profitable   c) silly   d) attractive

_____ 16. **impasse**   a) gate   b) exit   c) central point   d) dead end

_____ 17. **transcend**   a) send   b) travel   c) show off   d) rise above

_____ 18. **prompt**   a) avoid   b) urge   c) lie   d) waste

_____ 19. **complacent**   a) workable   b) self-satisfied   c) healthy   d) easy

_____ 20. **abstain**   a) prepare   b) disagree   c) do without   d) approve of

_____ 21. **consensus**   a) majority opinion   b) counting   c) study   d) approval

_____ 22. **divulge**   a) remove   b) reveal   c) hide   d) embarrass

_____ 23. **extrovert**   a) shy person   b) magnetism   c) main point   d) outgoing person

_____ 24. **endow**   a) cancel   b) name   c) tease   d) give a quality to

_____ 25. **deficit**   a) shortage   b) remainder   c) part of the whole   d) surplus

(Continues on next page)

_____ 26. **diligent**   a) obvious   b) odd   c) careful in work   d) gentle

_____ 27. **perception**   a) impression   b) meeting   c) dead end   d) party

_____ 28. **expulsion**   a) promotion   b) dismissal   c) award   d) attack

_____ 29. **benevolent**   a) poor   b) kind   c) wealthy   d) nasty

_____ 30. **rationale**   a) mood   b) debate   c) logical basis   d) research paper

_____ 31. **proponent**   a) supporter   b) examiner   c) foe   d) one part of the whole

_____ 32. **nullify**   a) cancel   b) turn aside   c) allow   d) harm

_____ 33. **flippant**   a) cold   b) disrespectful   c) formal   d) nervous

_____ 34. **prone**   a) active   b) tending   c) disliked   d) rested

_____ 35. **empathy**   a) fear   b) encouragement   c) ability to share someone's feelings   d) avoidance

_____ 36. **waive**   a) fly   b) sleep   c) show off   d) give up

_____ 37. **prevalent**   a) plain   b) widespread   c) escapable   d) famous

_____ 38. **dissent**   a) disagreement   b) winning   c) defeat   d) approval

_____ 39. **detract**   a) provide   b) compete   c) lessen   d) compliment

_____ 40. **deplete**   a) add to   b) delay   c) use up   d) encourage

_____ 41. **mortify**   a) humiliate   b) remember   c) entertain   d) praise

_____ 42. **affiliate**   a) approve   b) reject   c) impress   d) join

_____ 43. **poignant**   a) touching   b) annoying   c) careless   d) beautiful

_____ 44. **disdain**   a) pain   b) approval   c) scorn   d) discouragement

_____ 45. **commemorate**   a) imitate   b) honor the memory of   c) add new members   d) forget

_____ 46. **menial**   a) unkind   b) lowly   c) important   d) odd

_____ 47. **relentless**   a) kind   b) persistent   c) cruel   d) angry

_____ 48. **contend**   a) arouse   b) allow   c) claim   d) join

_____ 49. **reprisal**   a) defeat   b) search   c) question   d) getting even

_____ 50. **diversion**   a) practice   b) fate   c) amusement   d) awareness

---

SCORE: (Number correct) _____ × 2 = _____ %

Unit Four: *Pretest*

In the space provided, write the letter of the choice that is closest in meaning to the **boldfaced** word.

_____ 1. **feign** a) offend b) avoid c) overlook d) pretend

_____ 2. **gape** a) stare b) repair c) beat d) hide from

_____ 3. **punitive** a) inexpensive b) punishing c) ridiculously inadequate d) possible

_____ 4. **condone** a) forgive b) represent c) arrest d) appoint

_____ 5. **pathetic** a) rich b) puzzling c) wonderful d) pitifully lacking

_____ 6. **precedent** a) gift b) example c) fee d) later event

_____ 7. **contemplate** a) think seriously about b) create c) add to d) reveal

_____ 8. **furtive** a) loud b) quiet c) public d) secretive

_____ 9. **detrimental** a) dirty b) nutritious c) harmful d) helpful

_____ 10. **ironic** a) deeply felt b) meaning opposite of what is said c) simple d) great

_____ 11. **implicit** a) lacking b) attached c) above d) unstated but understood

_____ 12. **vindictive** a) not easily understood b) gentle c) vengeful d) temporary

_____ 13. **saturate** a) break apart b) put down c) fully soak d) describe

_____ 14. **inhibition** a) attack b) delay c) holding back d) exhibit

_____ 15. **deficient** a) forgotten b) lacking c) complete d) well-known

_____ 16. **rupture** a) burst b) fill c) damage d) overlook

_____ 17. **constrict** a) control b) prove c) make smaller d) regard

_____ 18. **fallible** a) capable of error b) complete c) incomplete d) simple

_____ 19. **exhaustive** a) respected b) nervous c) complete d) tired

_____ 20. **formulate** a) allow b) move c) purchase d) develop

_____ 21. **habitat** a) headache b) natural environment c) importance d) usual behavior

_____ 22. **vile** a) offensive b) secretive c) nice d) tricky

_____ 23. **reconcile** a) refine b) redo c) accept d) increase

_____ 24. **pragmatic** a) ordinary b) slow c) wise d) practical

_____ 25. **pacify** a) betray b) calm c) retreat d) remove

(Continues on next page)

_____ 26. **esteem**   a) age   b) doubt   c) respect   d) length of life

_____ 27. **transient**   a) stubborn   b) temporary   c) permanent   d) easy-going

_____ 28. **legacy**   a) size   b) anything serving as an example for a later case   c) inheritance   d) length of life

_____ 29. **muted**   a) softened   b) strangled   c) bright   d) puzzling

_____ 30. **avid**   a) bored   b) disliked   c) enthusiastic   d) plentiful

_____ 31. **dwindle**   a) strip   b) shrink   c) weave   d) cut

_____ 32. **nurture**   a) harden   b) thank   c) nourish   d) starve

_____ 33. **aloof**   a) cool   b) friendly   c) not clearly expressed   d) ordinary

_____ 34. **augment**   a) change   b) cause to become   c) increase   d) describe

_____ 35. **explicit**   a) everyday   b) distant   c) permanent   d) stated exactly

_____ 36. **longevity**   a) size   b) holding back   c) length of life   d) health

_____ 37. **magnitude**   a) importance   b) attraction   c) respect   d) example

_____ 38. **ambivalent**   a) everyday   b) having mixed feelings   c) temporary   d) able to be done

_____ 39. **dispel**   a) assist   b) anger   c) describe   d) cause to vanish

_____ 40. **render**   a) win out   b) reveal   c) cause to vanish   d) cause to become

_____ 41. **feasible**   a) unbelievable   b) possible   c) amazing   d) wild

_____ 42. **fiscal**   a) secretive   b) about government   c) financial   d) personal

_____ 43. **cryptic**   a) harmful   b) cruel   c) puzzling   d) loud

_____ 44. **depict**   a) describe   b) settle   c) accept   d) control

_____ 45. **genial**   a) practical   b) possible   c) inherited   d) pleasant

_____ 46. **pretentious**   a) pleasant   b) showy   c) required   d) practical

_____ 47. **evoke**   a) pull back   b) plant   c) vote   d) draw forth

_____ 48. **mundane**   a) odd   b) ordinary   c) softened   d) loud

_____ 49. **obscure**   a) enthusiastic   b) showy   c) hard to understand   d) bored

_____ 50. **mediate**   a) come between to settle   b) measure   c) explain in detail   d) change

---

SCORE: (Number correct) _____ × 2 = _____ %

Unit Four: *Posttest*

In the space provided, write the letter of the choice that is closest in meaning to the **boldfaced** word.

_____	1. **feign**	**a)** pretend	**b)** offend	**c)** overlook	**d)** avoid
_____	2. **vindictive**	**a)** not easily understood	**b)** gentle	**c)** vengeful	**d)** temporary
_____	3. **dwindle**	**a)** weave	**b)** cut	**c)** strip	**d)** shrink
_____	4. **inhibition**	**a)** attack	**b)** holding back	**c)** delay	**d)** exhibit
_____	5. **aloof**	**a)** friendly	**b)** cool	**c)** not clearly expressed	**d)** ordinary
_____	6. **precedent**	**a)** gift	**b)** fee	**c)** example	**d)** later event
_____	7. **vile**	**a)** tricky	**b)** nice	**c)** secretive	**d)** offensive
_____	8. **detrimental**	**a)** harmful	**b)** nutritious	**c)** dirty	**d)** helpful
_____	9. **ironic**	**a)** simple	**b)** meaning opposite of what is said	**c)** deeply felt	**d)** great
_____	10. **saturate**	**a)** fully soak	**b)** put down	**c)** break apart	**d)** describe
_____	11. **pacify**	**a)** betray	**b)** remove	**c)** retreat	**d)** calm
_____	12. **constrict**	**a)** control	**b)** regard	**c)** make smaller	**d)** prove
_____	13. **explicit**	**a)** everyday	**b)** permanent	**c)** distant	**d)** stated exactly
_____	14. **reconcile**	**a)** refine	**b)** accept	**c)** redo	**d)** increase
_____	15. **exhaustive**	**a)** complete	**b)** nervous	**c)** respected	**d)** tired
_____	16. **formulate**	**a)** move	**b)** allow	**c)** develop	**d)** purchase
_____	17. **ambivalent**	**a)** everyday	**b)** temporary	**c)** having mixed feelings	**d)** able to be done
_____	18. **dispel**	**a)** cause to vanish	**b)** anger	**c)** describe	**d)** assist
_____	19. **pathetic**	**a)** wonderful	**b)** pitifully lacking	**c)** rich	**d)** puzzling
_____	20. **render**	**a)** win out	**b)** cause to become	**c)** cause to vanish	**d)** reveal
_____	21. **pragmatic**	**a)** practical	**b)** slow	**c)** wise	**d)** ordinary
_____	22. **implicit**	**a)** unstated but understood	**b)** above	**c)** attached	**d)** lacking
_____	23. **furtive**	**a)** loud	**b)** secretive	**c)** public	**d)** quiet
_____	24. **augment**	**a)** cause to become	**b)** change	**c)** describe	**d)** increase
_____	25. **esteem**	**a)** respect	**b)** doubt	**c)** age	**d)** length of life

(Continues on next page)

_____ 26. **contemplate** a) think seriously about b) create c) add to d) reveal

_____ 27. **transient** a) permanent b) easy-going c) stubborn d) temporary

_____ 28. **fallible** a) incomplete b) complete c) capable of error d) simple

_____ 29. **longevity** a) health b) size c) length of life d) holding back

_____ 30. **legacy** a) size b) anything serving as an example for a later case c) inheritance d) length of life

_____ 31. **punitive** a) punishing b) inexpensive c) ridiculously inadequate d) possible

_____ 32. **muted** a) puzzling b) softened c) strangled d) bright

_____ 33. **avid** a) enthusiastic b) disliked c) bored d) plentiful

_____ 34. **habitat** a) headache b) natural environment c) importance d) usual behavior

_____ 35. **nurture** a) harden b) thank c) nourish d) starve

_____ 36. **deficient** a) forgotten b) well-known c) complete d) lacking

_____ 37. **gape** a) hide from b) beat c) stare d) repair

_____ 38. **rupture** a) overlook b) damage c) fill d) burst

_____ 39. **magnitude** a) importance b) attraction c) respect d) example

_____ 40. **condone** a) arrest b) represent c) forgive d) appoint

_____ 41. **depict** a) control b) settle c) accept d) describe

_____ 42. **pretentious** a) pleasant b) required c) showy d) practical

_____ 43. **evoke** a) pull back b) draw forth c) vote d) plant

_____ 44. **cryptic** a) puzzling b) cruel c) harmful d) loud

_____ 45. **mundane** a) odd b) softened c) ordinary d) loud

_____ 46. **fiscal** a) secretive b) personal c) financial d) about government

_____ 47. **obscure** a) hard to understand b) showy c) enthusiastic d) bored

_____ 48. **mediate** a) change b) measure c) explain in detail d) come between to settle

_____ 49. **feasible** a) unbelievable b) wild c) amazing d) possible

_____ 50. **genial** a) pleasant b) possible c) inherited d) practical

SCORE: (Number correct) _____ × 2 = _____ %

Pretest / Posttest

NAME: _____

SECTION: _____ DATE: _____

SCORE: _____

ANSWER SHEET

1. _____	26. _____	51. _____	76. _____
2. _____	27. _____	52. _____	77. _____
3. _____	28. _____	53. _____	78. _____
4. _____	29. _____	54. _____	79. _____
5. _____	30. _____	55. _____	80. _____
6. _____	31. _____	56. _____	81. _____
7. _____	32. _____	57. _____	82. _____
8. _____	33. _____	58. _____	83. _____
9. _____	34. _____	59. _____	84. _____
10. _____	35. _____	60. _____	85. _____
11. _____	36. _____	61. _____	86. _____
12. _____	37. _____	62. _____	87. _____
13. _____	38. _____	63. _____	88. _____
14. _____	39. _____	64. _____	89. _____
15. _____	40. _____	65. _____	90. _____
16. _____	41. _____	66. _____	91. _____
17. _____	42. _____	67. _____	92. _____
18. _____	43. _____	68. _____	93. _____
19. _____	44. _____	69. _____	94. _____
20. _____	45. _____	70. _____	95. _____
21. _____	46. _____	71. _____	96. _____
22. _____	47. _____	72. _____	97. _____
23. _____	48. _____	73. _____	98. _____
24. _____	49. _____	74. _____	99. _____
25. _____	50. _____	75. _____	100. _____

ANSWER KEY

1. b	26. b	51. c	76. a
2. a	27. a	52. b	77. b
3. b	28. b	53. b	78. a
4. a	29. d	54. a	79. b
5. b	30. d	55. d	80. a
6. b	31. b	56. b	81. c
7. b	32. d	57. a	82. b
8. d	33. b	58. c	83. c
9. a	34. d	59. b	84. c
10. c	35. b	60. a	85. b
11. a	36. c	61. c	86. a
12. d	37. b	62. d	87. c
13. c	38. b	63. b	88. b
14. b	39. d	64. c	89. a
15. a	40. d	65. d	90. d
16. b	41. c	66. a	91. b
17. a	42. a	67. d	92. c
18. c	43. d	68. c	93. b
19. b	44. c	69. b	94. c
20. c	45. d	70. d	95. c
21. c	46. b	71. d	96. c
22. d	47. c	72. b	97. d
23. a	48. b	73. c	98. a
24. b	49. a	74. c	99. b
25. a	50. d	75. c	100. d

ANSWER KEY

1. c	26. b	51. a	76. c
2. c	27. c	52. d	77. c
3. b	28. a	53. b	78. d
4. d	29. c	54. c	79. b
5. d	30. b	55. c	80. a
6. c	31. d	56. c	81. d
7. c	32. b	57. c	82. a
8. b	33. b	58. d	83. d
9. b	34. d	59. b	84. a
10. d	35. a	60. d	85. c
11. c	36. b	61. d	86. a
12. a	37. c	62. b	87. a
13. a	38. b	63. b	88. a
14. c	39. a	64. b	89. a
15. a	40. d	65. c	90. d
16. c	41. a	66. a	91. d
17. b	42. c	67. a	92. c
18. c	43. d	68. b	93. a
19. c	44. a	69. b	94. a
20. d	45. c	70. c	95. b
21. b	46. b	71. d	96. c
22. b	47. c	72. b	97. d
23. c	48. c	73. a	98. c
24. b	49. b	74. a	99. a
25. b	50. c	75. c	100. c

Answers to the Pretests and Posttests:

IMPROVING VOCABULARY SKILLS, SHORT VERSION

	Unit One			Unit Two			Unit Three			Unit Four	
	Pretest	*Posttest*		*Pretest*	*Posttest*		*Pretest*	*Posttest*		*Pretest*	*Posttest*
1.	b	1. c	1.	b	1. a	1.	d	1. c	1.	d	1. a
2.	a	2. d	2.	a	2. b	2.	c	2. a	2.	a	2. c
3.	c	3. b	3.	b	3. c	3.	a	3. d	3.	b	3. d
4.	b	4. b	4.	a	4. d	4.	b	4. b	4.	a	4. b
5.	a	5. d	5.	c	5. c	5.	a	5. a	5.	d	5. b
6.	c	6. b	6.	d	6. b	6.	b	6. c	6.	b	6. c
7.	b	7. b	7.	a	7. a	7.	a	7. c	7.	a	7. d
8.	d	8. c	8.	d	8. c	8.	d	8. a	8.	d	8. a
9.	b	9. b	9.	c	9. c	9.	b	9. c	9.	c	9. b
10.	b	10. d	10.	b	10. c	10.	d	10. d	10.	b	10. a
11.	d	11. d	11.	d	11. b	11.	a	11. c	11.	d	11. d
12.	a	12. c	12.	d	12. d	12.	c	12. d	12.	c	12. c
13.	c	13. d	13.	b	13. b	13.	a	13. c	13.	c	13. d
14.	c	14. c	14.	d	14. a	14.	d	14. b	14.	c	14. b
15.	d	15. b	15.	a	15. b	15.	b	15. b	15.	b	15. a
16.	a	16. b	16.	b	16. b	16.	a	16. d	16.	a	16. c
17.	b	17. b	17.	c	17. d	17.	b	17. d	17.	c	17. c
18.	a	18. d	18.	a	18. d	18.	c	18. b	18.	a	18. a
19.	a	19. a	19.	b	19. a	19.	d	19. b	19.	c	19. b
20.	d	20. c	20.	b	20. b	20.	a	20. c	20.	d	20. b
21.	d	21. a	21.	d	21. c	21.	b	21. a	21.	b	21. a
22.	c	22. a	22.	a	22. c	22.	c	22. b	22.	a	22. a
23.	b	23. c	23.	c	23. b	23.	d	23. d	23.	c	23. b
24.	a	24. b	24.	d	24. a	24.	a	24. d	24.	d	24. d
25.	b	25. a	25.	c	25. c	25.	a	25. a	25.	b	25. a
26.	a	26. c	26.	c	26. d	26.	c	26. c	26.	c	26. a
27.	a	27. c	27.	a	27. a	27.	b	27. a	27.	b	27. d
28.	c	28. b	28.	d	28. c	28.	c	28. b	28.	c	28. c
29.	b	29. c	29.	c	29. a	29.	d	29. b	29.	a	29. c
30.	c	30. a	30.	c	30. c	30.	c	30. c	30.	c	30. c
31.	a	31. c	31.	a	31. d	31.	b	31. a	31.	b	31. a
32.	d	32. c	32.	d	32. a	32.	d	32. a	32.	c	32. b
33.	c	33. d	33.	b	33. c	33.	d	33. b	33.	a	33. a
34.	b	34. b	34.	c	34. b	34.	b	34. b	34.	c	34. b
35.	a	35. b	35.	b	35. c	35.	c	35. c	35.	d	35. c
36.	d	36. a	36.	b	36. c	36.	d	36. d	36.	c	36. d
37.	a	37. c	37.	b	37. d	37.	a	37. b	37.	a	37. c
38.	b	38. b	38.	a	38. c	38.	c	38. a	38.	b	38. d
39.	d	39. a	39.	d	39. b	39.	a	39. c	39.	d	39. a
40.	a	40. b	40.	b	40. c	40.	c	40. c	40.	d	40. c
41.	d	41. c	41.	d	41. b	41.	d	41. a	41.	b	41. d
42.	a	42. a	42.	d	42. b	42.	c	42. d	42.	c	42. c
43.	c	43. c	43.	d	43. d	43.	b	43. a	43.	c	43. b
44.	b	44. a	44.	c	44. d	44.	d	44. c	44.	a	44. a
45.	d	45. c	45.	c	45. d	45.	a	45. b	45.	d	45. c
46.	b	46. b	46.	d	46. d	46.	b	46. b	46.	b	46. c
47.	b	47. d	47.	b	47. d	47.	a	47. b	47.	d	47. a
48.	d	48. d	48.	a	48. b	48.	c	48. c	48.	b	48. d
49.	b	49. b	49.	a	49. b	49.	c	49. d	49.	c	49. d
50.	c	50. d	50.	b	50. c	50.	d	50. c	50.	a	50. a

Chapter 1 (Joseph Palmer)

Ten Words in Context	Matching Words/Defs	Sentence Check 1	Sentence Check 2	Final Check
1. b 6. b	1. 2 6. 9	1. b 6. i	1–2. g, h	1. d 6. f
2. a 7. b	2. 4 7. 6	2. h 7. a	3–4. e, j	2. c 7. a
3. c 8. c	3. 7 8. 5	3. j 8. f	5–6. b, f	3. i 8. e
4. c 9. a	4. 1 9. 10	4. c 9. e	7–8. d, a	4. h 9. b
5. a 10. c	5. 8 10. 3	5. d 10. g	9–10. i, c	5. j 10. g

Chapter 2 (A Cruel Sport)

Ten Words in Context	Matching Words/Defs	Sentence Check 1	Sentence Check 2	Final Check
1. b 6. b	1. 3 6. 8	1. i 6. d	1–2. d, c	1. f 6. d
2. a 7. c	2. 10 7. 5	2. h 7. f	3–4. h, j	2. h 7. b
3. c 8. c	3. 7 8. 1	3. a 8. g	5–6. i, a	3. c 8. j
4. a 9. b	4. 2 9. 4	4. b 9. j	7–8. f, e	4. a 9. g
5. a 10. a	5. 9 10. 6	5. e 10. c	9–10. g, b	5. e 10. i

Chapter 3 (No Luck With Women)

Ten Words in Context	Matching Words/Defs	Sentence Check 1	Sentence Check 2	Final Check
1. b 6. b	1. 4 6. 3	1. h 6. j	1–2. b, h	1. e 6. c
2. a 7. b	2. 8 7. 6	2. a 7. c	3–4. e, c	2. f 7. d
3. c 8. c	3. 1 8. 10	3. b 8. i	5–6. d, g	3. h 8. i
4. c 9. a	4. 9 9. 5	4. e 9. d	7–8. i, j	4. a 9. b
5. a 10. b	5. 7 10. 2	5. g 10. f	9–10. f, a	5. j 10. g

Chapter 4 (Accident and Recovery)

Ten Words in Context	Matching Words/Defs	Sentence Check 1	Sentence Check 2	Final Check
1. b 6. c	1. 4 6. 9	1. a 6. f	1–2. j, a	1. d 6. h
2. a 7. c	2. 10 7. 1	2. g 7. h	3–4. h, f	2. a 7. j
3. c 8. b	3. 2 8. 5	3. d 8. i	5–6. c, d	3. e 8. g
4. a 9. b	4. 8 9. 7	4. b 9. e	7–8. g, b	4. i 9. f
5. b 10. a	5. 6 10. 3	5. c 10. j	9–10. e, i	5. b 10. c

Chapter 5 (Animal Senses)

Ten Words in Context	Matching Words/Defs	Sentence Check 1	Sentence Check 2	Final Check
1. a 6. b	1. 6 6. 3	1. e 6. i	1–2. e, c	1. d 6. b
2. c 7. a	2. 4 7. 5	2. a 7. c	3–4. h, j	2. j 7. i
3. a 8. c	3. 9 8. 8	3. d 8. j	5–6. b, g	3. f 8. g
4. b 9. c	4. 1 9. 2	4. g 9. h	7–8. d, f	4. e 9. h
5. a 10. a	5. 10 10. 7	5. f 10. h	9–10. a, i	5. c 10. a

Chapter 6 (Money Problems)

Ten Words in Context	Matching Words/Defs	Sentence Check 1	Sentence Check 2	Final Check
1. a 6. c	1. 3 6. 4	1. h 6. d	1–2. g, a	1. h 6. j
2. b 7. b	2. 5 7. 7	2. a 7. j	3–4. c, h	2. e 7. i
3. c 8. b	3. 8 8. 1	3. c 8. e	5–6. i, d	3. b 8. c
4. a 9. a	4. 9 9. 10	4. i 9. b	7–8. e, b	4. d 9. g
5. b 10. c	5. 2 10. 6	5. g 10. f	9–10. f, j	5. a 10. f

Chapter 7 (The New French Employee)

Ten Words in Context	Matching Words/Defs	Sentence Check 1	Sentence Check 2	Final Check
1. c 6. b	1. 5 6. 10	1. i 6. f	1–2. j, f	1. i 6. a
2. a 7. a	2. 9 7. 2	2. h 7. c	3–4. b, i	2. h 7. d
3. b 8. b	3. 1 8. 8	3. j 8. g	5–6. e, a	3. e 8. f
4. b 9. b	4. 6 9. 7	4. e 9. a	7–8. h, c	4. c 9. j
5. c 10. a	5. 4 10. 3	5. b 10. d	9–10. g, d	5. b 10. g

Chapter 8 (A Cruel Teacher)

Ten Words in Context	Matching Words/Defs	Sentence Check 1	Sentence Check 2	Final Check
1. a 6. b	1. 9 6. 3	1. g 6. d	1–2. g, a	1. e 6. g
2. c 7. b	2. 4 7. 10	2. b 7. j	3–4. j, i	2. a 7. h
3. a 8. b	3. 6 8. 1	3. f 8. e	5–6. e, c	3. d 8. i
4. c 9. a	4. 2 9. 7	4. a 9. i	7–8. h, d	4. f 9. j
5. a 10. b	5. 8 10. 5	5. c 10. h	9–10. b, f	5. c 10. b

Chapter 9 (Learning to Study)

Ten Words in Context	Matching Words/Defs	Sentence Check 1	Sentence Check 2	Final Check
1. b 6. b	1. 9 6. 2	1. g 6. h	1–2. i, h	1. h 6. a
2. c 7. a	2. 1 7. 10	2. b 7. i	3–4. a, e	2. i 7. f
3. b 8. c	3. 4 8. 6	3. e 8. a	5–6. g, j	3. b 8. j
4. a 9. b	4. 3 9. 5	4. f 9. c	7–8. b, c	4. d 9. g
5. b 10. a	5. 8 10. 7	5. d 10. j	9–10. d, f	5. c 10. c

Chapter 10 (The Mad Monk)

Ten Words in Context	Matching Words/Defs	Sentence Check 1	Sentence Check 2	Final Check
1. c 6. a	1. 3 6. 10	1. g 6. c	1–2. g, a	1. f 6. d
2. a 7. b	2. 4 7. 5	2. a 7. h	3–4. h, c	2. h 7. i
3. b 8. b	3. 7 8. 9	3. j 8. i	5–6. d, e	3. g 8. j
4. a 9. c	4. 6 9. 1	4. d 9. b	7–8. j, b	4. b 9. c
5. c 10. a	5. 2 10. 8	5. f 10. e	9–10. f, i	5. a 10. e

Chapter 11 (Conflict Over Holidays)

Ten Words in Context	Matching Words/Defs	Sentence Check 1	Sentence Check 2	Final Check
1. c 6. a	1. 4 6. 3	1. d 6. f	1–2. b, h	1. g 6. a
2. a 7. b	2. 9 7. 10	2. e 7. g	3–4. a, j	2. i 7. e
3. b 8. a	3. 6 8. 8	3. h 8. b	5–6. c, e	3. f 8. c
4. b 9. b	4. 1 9. 2	4. j 9. c	7–8. f, g	4. j 9. b
5. c 10. c	5. 5 10. 7	5. a 10. i	9–10. d, i	5. d 10. h

Chapter 12 (Dr. Martin Luther King, Jr.)

Ten Words in Context	Matching Words/Defs	Sentence Check 1	Sentence Check 2	Final Check
1. b 6. a	1. 4 6. 2	1. d 6. h	1–2. g, b	1. b 6. e
2. c 7. b	2. 1 7. 8	2. e 7. a	3–4. e, d	2. h 7. f
3. c 8. c	3. 9 8. 6	3. f 8. b	5–6. j, h	3. g 8. d
4. a 9. a	4. 7 9. 10	4. g 9. j	7–8. c, f	4. c 9. i
5. c 10. c	5. 3 10. 5	5. c 10. i	9–10. a, i	5. a 10. j

Chapter 13 (Relating to Parents)

Ten Words in Context	Matching Words/Defs	Sentence Check 1	Sentence Check 2	Final Check
1. c 6. a	1. 4 6. 1	1. f 6. c	1–2. a, g	1. j 6. i
2. a 7. b	2. 6 7. 5	2. a 7. i	3–4. h, e	2. h 7. a
3. a 8. b	3. 9 8. 10	3. b 8. d	5–6. f, b	3. c 8. g
4. b 9. c	4. 8 9. 3	4. e 9. j	7–8. d, c	4. b 9. f
5. c 10. b	5. 2 10. 7	5. g 10. h	9–10. i, j	5. d 10. e

Chapter 14 (The Nightmare of Gym)

Ten Words in Context	Matching Words/Defs	Sentence Check 1	Sentence Check 2	Final Check
1. a 6. a	1. 6 6. 1	1. b 6. f	1–2. a, i	1. f 6. c
2. c 7. b	2. 3 7. 8	2. j 7. g	3–4. f, b	2. g 7. a
3. b 8. a	3. 7 8. 2	3. a 8. c	5–6. d, g	3. b 8. e
4. c 9. c	4. 10 9. 5	4. e 9. d	7–8. h, c	4. h 9. d
5. c 10. b	5. 4 10. 9	5. i 10. h	9–10. j, e	5. j 10. i

Chapter 15 (A Model Teacher)

Ten Words in Context	Matching Words/Defs	Sentence Check 1	Sentence Check 2	Final Check
1. b 6. b	1. 7 6. 3	1. j 6. h	1–2. j, d	1. c 6. e
2. c 7. a	2. 6 7. 2	2. a 7. g	3–4. c, f	2. h 7. f
3. a 8. b	3. 9 8. 5	3. d 8. e	5–6. h, i	3. i 8. j
4. a 9. b	4. 1 9. 8	4. i 9. c	7–8. a, g	4. d 9. g
5. c 10. c	5. 10 10. 4	5. b 10. f	9–10. e, b	5. b 10. a

Chapter 16 (Shoplifter)

Ten Words in Context	Matching Words/Defs	Sentence Check 1	Sentence Check 2	Final Check
1. a 6. a	1. 3 6. 10	1. g 6. e	1–2. c, e	1. f 6. a
2. a 7. c	2. 6 7. 5	2. b 7. f	3–4. j, b	2. b 7. e
3. c 8. b	3. 7 8. 2	3. i 8. h	5–6. g, h	3. d 8. c
4. c 9. c	4. 9 9. 8	4. c 9. d	7–8. a, f	4. h 9. j
5. b 10. a	5. 1 10. 4	5. a 10. j	9–10. i, d	5. i 10. g

Chapter 17 (A Nutty Newspaper Office)

Ten Words in Context	Matching Words/Defs	Sentence Check 1	Sentence Check 2	Final Check
1. b 6. a	1. 6 6. 8	1. b 6. c	1–2. h, i	1. d 6. i
2. a 7. a	2. 1 7. 2	2. h 7. j	3–4. a, c	2. f 7. c
3. b 8. c	3. 5 8. 9	3. g 8. a	5–6. j, d	3. g 8. b
4. c 9. c	4. 10 9. 4	4. d 9. i	7–8. g, e	4. a 9. j
5. c 10. b	5. 3 10. 7	5. f 10. e	9–10. f, b	5. e 10. h

Chapter 18 (Roughing It)

Ten Words in Context	Matching Words/Defs	Sentence Check 1	Sentence Check 2	Final Check
1. c 6. c	1. 9 6. 2	1. j 6. b	1–2. i, c	1. j 6. g
2. b 7. a	2. 6 7. 5	2. e 7. h	3–4. d, f	2. h 7. b
3. c 8. b	3. 8 8. 10	3. i 8. f	5–6. g, j	3. c 8. d
4. a 9. a	4. 3 9. 4	4. a 9. g	7–8. b, a	4. a 9. e
5. c 10. c	5. 1 10. 7	5. d 10. c	9–10. e, h	5. f 10. i

Chapter 19 (Getting Scared)

Ten Words in Context	Matching Words/Defs	Sentence Check 1	Sentence Check 2	Final Check
1. b 6. b	1. 7 6. 2	1. i 6. j	1–2. c, j	1. a 6. g
2. c 7. a	2. 10 7. 6	2. d 7. c	3–4. a, b	2. i 7. c
3. b 8. c	3. 1 8. 3	3. b 8. a	5–6. g, i	3. j 8. d
4. a 9. c	4. 9 9. 8	4. g 9. e	7–8. h, e	4. f 9. b
5. c 10. b	5. 4 10. 5	5. h 10. f	9–10. f, d	5. h 10. e

Chapter 20 (My Sister's Date)

Ten Words in Context	Matching Words/Defs	Sentence Check 1	Sentence Check 2	Final Check
1. c 6. b	1. 4 6. 10	1. h 6. i	1–2. f, e	1. j 6. d
2. b 7. a	2. 7 7. 9	2. c 7. j	3–4. c, g	2. i 7. a
3. a 8. c	3. 8 8. 1	3. b 8. d	5–6. b, j	3. c 8. e
4. b 9. b	4. 5 9. 3	4. f 9. e	7–8. a, d	4. f 9. h
5. c 10. b	5. 2 10. 6	5. a 10. g	9–10. i, h	5. g 10. b

Mastery Test: *Chapter 1 (Joseph Palmer)*

In the space provided, write the word from the box needed to complete each sentence. Then put the **letter** of that word in the column at the left. Use each word once.

a. **absolve**	b. **adamant**	c. **amiable**	d. **amoral**	e. **animosity**
f. **antagonist**	g. **eccentric**	h. **encounter**	i. **epitome**	j. **malign**

_____ 1. Female students who took auto shop classes used to be considered _____. Now, however, it's not considered odd for women to learn to do car repairs.

_____ 2. The husband and wife were such bitter _____s at their divorce hearing that it was hard to believe they once loved each other.

_____ 3. Frank hates the thought that his teacher believes he cheated. He'll go to any lengths to _____ himself.

_____ 4. Elena intended to ask her father to lend her his car, but when she saw how grouchy he was, she decided to wait until he was in a more _____ mood.

_____ 5. The great baseball player and civil rights leader Jackie Robinson was the _____ of both physical and moral strength.

_____ 6. When Mrs. Haley visited the school she'd attended thirty years before, she unexpectedly had an _____ with one of her former teachers.

_____ 7. Bill is _____ about going to the park for a picnic, even though the weather report is predicting severe thunderstorms.

_____ 8. Although my emotionally disturbed neighbor makes rude comments to my visitors and scatters trash all over my steps, I don't feel any _____ toward her. I just feel sorry for her.

_____ 9. A newborn baby is _____. It's only as a child grows older that he or she develops a sense of "right" and "wrong."

_____ 10. People who say the female crocodile eats her young _____ her. She simply takes them into a protective pouch inside her mouth.

SCORE: (Number correct) _____ × 10 = _____ %	

Mastery Test: *Chapter 2 (A Cruel Sport)*

In the space provided, write the word from the box needed to complete each sentence. Then put the **letter** of that word in the column at the left. Use each word once.

a. **acclaim**	b. **adjacent**	c. **elicit**	d. **engross**	e. **escalate**
f. **exploit**	g. **methodical**	h. **obsolete**	i. **tangible**	j. **terminate**

_____ 1. The mystery story so _____(e)d Donna that she jumped in fright when I entered the room.

_____ 2. Dinah arranges the spices in her kitchen in a(n) _____ way: in alphabetical order.

_____ 3. The landlord would like to _____ the lease of the family in 4-A. Their loud parties and shouting disturb everyone in the building.

_____ 4. My woodworker friend lives _____ to his work. His workshop is next door to his house.

_____ 5. That supervisor knows how to _____ workers. She makes them work overtime without extra pay.

_____ 6. "Don't buy an old-fashioned electric typewriter," my brother advised me. "Computers will soon make typewriters _____."

_____ 7. Peter seems to think he deserves _____ just for showing up for school. His teachers, however, think that's the least he can do.

_____ 8. The protests of some small groups in Eastern Europe _____(e)d into full-scale rebellions against their governments.

_____ 9. Some people enjoy getting praised when they do a good job. I prefer a more _____ reward, like a raise in pay.

_____ 10. Flora is a bad-tempered child. Even the suggestion that she come to the dinner table is enough to _____ a tantrum.

SCORE: (Number correct) _____ × 10 = _____ %

Name: _____

Mastery Test: *Chapter 3 (No Luck with Women)*

In the space provided, write the word from the box needed to complete each sentence. Then put the **letter** of that word in the column at the left. Use each word once.

a. **allusion**	b. **altruistic**	c. **appease**	d. **arbitrary**	e. **assail**
f. **banal**	g. **euphemism**	h. **mercenary**	i. **syndrome**	j. **taint**

_____ 1. I expected the made-for-TV movie to be another _____ romance, but I was pleasantly surprised. It was both original and funny.

_____ 2. The little boy's slow speech and clumsy movements are all part of a(n) _____ caused by his lack of oxygen at birth.

_____ 3. A heckler in the audience _____(e)d the comedian with rude remarks until the bouncer forced the heckler to leave the club.

_____ 4. I'm afraid my sister is encouraging her children to be _____. Every time they do a chore or an errand, she gives them a dollar. Soon they won't do anything unless they get paid.

_____ 5. Being suspended for drug abuse _____s athletes' reputations.

_____ 6. So many people are afraid of dying that we use _____s to describe it, such as "passing away."

_____ 7. I admire Luis' _____ nature. He is truly more concerned for the welfare of those around him than he is for his own.

_____ 8. Apologizing for tearing Danny's shirt isn't enough. Nothing will _____ him until you buy him a new one.

_____ 9. Hoping to receive a cell phone for her birthday, Jeannie continually makes such _____s to it as "Mom, when I was at the mall today I saw a coat you would have loved! I wish I could have called you to tell you about it."

_____ 10. That judge's sentencing seems completely _____. Yesterday she sent a shoplifter to jail for three months, but today she gave a car thief probation and a suspended sentence.

SCORE: (Number correct) _____ × 10 = _____ %

Mastery Test: *Chapter 4 (Accident and Recovery)*

In the space provided, write the word from the box needed to complete each sentence. Then put the **letter** of that word in the column at the left. Use each word once.

a. **calamity**	b. **comprehensive**	c. **conventional**	d. **flagrant**	e. **fluctuate**
f. **persevere**	g. **ponder**	h. **rehabilitate**	i. **turmoil**	j. **venture**

_____ 1. The movie I saw last weekend really confused me. I have _____(e)d its meaning all week.

_____ 2. When a doctor sees a new patient, the doctor should ask for a _____ health history, beginning with childhood illnesses and ending with the patient's present physical condition.

_____ 3. After breaking his leg in a motorcycle accident, Lenny had to attend physical therapy classes to _____ himself so he could walk normally again.

_____ 4. The birthday party ended in complete _____, as the children ran around the room screaming, breaking balloons, and grabbing presents.

_____ 5. I'm not sure my answer is correct, but I'm feeling brave, so I'll _____ a guess.

_____ 6. While Fran enjoys unusual foods, such as curries and pasta, her husband Nick prefers more _____ dinners, like steak and French fries.

_____ 7. It takes a long time for Julio to know people well enough to trust them. You'll have to _____ if you want to win his friendship.

_____ 8. The recent earthquake was a terrible_____, killing thousands of people and leveling entire towns.

_____ 9. I was shocked by the new student's _____ refusal to observe the dress code at our school.

_____ 10. My feelings about my job _____ according to what kind of day I've had at work. Some days my job is good; some days it's terrible.

SCORE: (Number correct) _____ × 10 = _____ %	

Name: _____

Mastery Test: *Chapter 5 (Animal Senses)*

In the space provided, write the word from the box needed to complete each sentence. Then put the **letter** of that word in the column at the left. Use each word once.

a. **attest**	b. **attribute**	c. **discern**	d. **dispatch**	e. **enhance**
f. **enigma**	g. **exemplify**	h. **mobile**	i. **nocturnal**	j. **orient**

_____ 1. Every year our neighbors _____ the appearance of their home. Last year they redecorated the living room; this year, they planted a flowering tree in their front yard.

_____ 2. One interesting _____ of my family is that everyone in it was born in July.

_____ 3. Sailors used to _____ themselves by looking at the positions of the stars. Now they use modern instruments to figure out their location and direction at sea.

_____ 4. For many people, Adolf Hitler and the Nazis _____ the human potential for evil.

_____ 5. We keep our TV in the bedroom, but since it's on wheels, it's _____. We roll it into the living room or kitchen whenever we want to.

_____ 6. The victim's neighbor _____(e)d to the fact that she had never returned from her shopping trip. Her newspapers and mail hadn't been picked up for a week.

_____ 7. My brother's career plans are a(n) _____ to my parents. They can't understand why he wants to move to a small town in Maine and make furniture instead of getting an office job and making money.

_____ 8. I can't _____ any difference between diet soft drinks and the nondiet ones. They taste exactly the same to me.

_____ 9. Cats are _____ animals. They sleep most of the day and are active most of the night.

_____ 10. As soon as the emergency call was received, police and paramedics were _____(e)d to the scene of the accident.

SCORE: (Number correct) _____ × 10 = _____ %	

Mastery Test: *Chapter 6 (Money Problems)*

In the space provided, write the word from the box needed to complete each sentence. Then put the **letter** of that word in the column at the left. Use each word once.

a. **concurrent**	b. **confiscate**	c. **constitute**	d. **decipher**	e. **default**
f. **hypothetical**	g. **nominal**	h. **predominant**	i. **prerequisite**	j. **recession**

_____ 1. Myra won her case in small-claims court when the man she was suing _____(e)d by not showing up.

_____ 2. Although the delicious punch is made of a mixture of fruit juices, the _____ flavor is strawberry.

_____ 3. After a water fight broke out in the fourth-grade classroom, the teacher _____(e)d all the squirt guns.

_____ 4. During the _____, when business was bad, more than half the workers in the plastics factory were laid off.

_____ 5. Since Velma couldn't _____ her teacher's handwriting, she had no idea how to go about revising her paper.

_____ 6. I just realized that my school vacation and my sister's wedding are _____. I'll be able to help her get everything ready for the wedding.

_____ 7. Two scoops of vanilla fudge ice cream, hot fudge sauce, marshmallow topping, and walnut pieces _____ my favorite dessert—a walnut-marshmallow-hot-fudge sundae.

_____ 8. Let me ask you a _____ question. If you were teaching this course, what questions would you put on the final exam?

_____ 9. Being at least 16 years old is the usual _____ for obtaining a driver's license.

_____ 10. Although the dog fight looked serious, our German shepherd escaped with only _____ injuries.

SCORE: (Number correct) _____ × 10 = _____ %

Mastery Test: *Chapter 7 (The New French Employee)*

In the space provided, write the word from the box needed to complete each sentence. Then put the **letter** of that word in the column at the left. Use each word once.

a. **degenerate**	b. **implausible**	c. **incoherent**	d. **intercede**	e. **intricate**
f. **sanctuary**	g. **scrutiny**	h. **sinister**	i. **suffice**	j. **vulnerable**

_____ 1. Because the novel's plot was so _____, Alfonso was beginning to get confused. Then he had the bright idea of writing down the names of the many characters and their relationships to one another.

_____ 2. My close friendship with Ellen began to _____ after my school work began taking up most of my time. I then had no spare time in which to see her or have our usual long phone conversations.

_____ 3. Since his divorce, my older brother has felt extremely _____. He's afraid to get involved with anyone and run the risk of getting hurt again.

_____ 4. After the robbery, I gave the apartment a careful inspection to see what had been taken. My _____ extended even to the linen closet, where I counted the towels and sheets.

_____ 5. Thomas Jefferson once wrote, "He governs best who governs least." In other words, he thought government should _____ as little as possible into people's lives.

_____ 6. When Pat learned she had won the lottery, she became _____ with joy. She kept babbling: "You've got to be . . . Oh my . . . If this isn't . . ."

_____ 7. The Women's _____ in town is a shelter for women who are being abused at home.

_____ 8. "Who drew on the wall with crayon?" asked the angry mother. The little boy's _____ answer was, "A man came through the window and did it."

_____ 9. The food in the refrigerator will have to _____ for the rest of the week. There's no grocery money until the next family paycheck.

_____ 10. Everyone was shocked to learn that Mr. Johnson had murdered his wife. His cheerful, friendly manner gave no hint of his _____ past.

SCORE: (Number correct) _____ × 10 = _____ %

Mastery Test: *Chapter 8 (A Cruel Teacher)*

In the space provided, write the word from the box needed to complete each sentence. Then put the **letter** of that word in the column at the left. Use each word once.

a. **blatant**	b. **blight**	c. **contrive**	d. **garble**	e. **gaunt**
f. **gloat**	g. **immaculate**	h. **plagiarism**	i. **qualm**	j. **retaliate**

_____ 1. When the boss announced that everyone would have to work an hour overtime, the staff _____(e)d by taking a two-hour lunch.

_____ 2. Even though I knew I was doing the right thing, I felt a _____ of conscience as I told Mr. Lane that it was my friend who'd stolen his car.

_____ 3. To the family's amazement, the teenager's room was _____. The bed was made, the records were put away, and there wasn't a single piece of clothing on the floor.

_____ 4. It's hard not to _____ about Sharon being fired when she's been so unpleasant to all her coworkers.

_____ 5. That dogwood tree must be suffering from some _____. It didn't flower this year, and half the branches have no leaves.

_____ 6. Those ten-dollar bills are _____ forgeries. Even a ten-year-old could tell that they're fakes.

_____ 7. My uncle's stroke has _____(e)d his speech. Now it's almost impossible to understand what he's saying.

_____ 8. A writer accused a comedian of _____. He said that the comedian had taken the writer's script and turned it into a movie without paying the writer or giving him credit.

_____ 9. After losing forty pounds, Alice thought her figure was perfect. Actually, though, she looked unpleasantly _____ —as if she'd not quite recovered from a long illness.

_____ 10. Joanne has _____(e)d a clever way of making throw pillows. She sews two fancy washcloths together back to back and then stuffs them with foam rubber.

SCORE: (Number correct) _____ × 10 = _____ %

Name: _____

Mastery Test: *Chapter 9 (Learning to Study)*

In the space provided, write the word from the box needed to complete each sentence. Then put the **letter** of that word in the column at the left. Use each word once.

a. **curtail**	b. **devastate**	c. **digress**	d. **incentive**	e. **incorporate**
f. **indispensable**	g. **intermittent**	h. **rigor**	i. **squander**	j. **succumb**

____ 1. My fantasy apartment _____s several very desirable features: a huge living room for parties, an all-electronic kitchen, a whirlpool, and a balcony overlooking the ocean.

____ 2. The _____s of camping are too much for Elaine. She likes to sleep on a sturdy mattress in a safe, warm room, not in a flimsy tent with biting insects.

____ 3. My grandmother refused to _____ even one bit of food. Today's leftovers always became tomorrow's soup or hash.

____ 4. Are you going to stick to your diet, or are you going to _____ to temptation and have a piece of chocolate fudge cake?

____ 5. I don't understand how people got along without VCR's. I find my VCR _____; without it, I'd never get to see my favorite shows at the few times I have to watch them.

____ 6. A bad case of flu forced Gerald to _____ his vacation. He came home after only three days and spent the rest of the week lying in bed.

____ 7. When employers offer their workers _____s, such as vacations or a share in the profits, the employees usually work harder.

____ 8. Rico was _____(e)d to learn that he hadn't gotten the promotion. He had already planned how he would spend the extra money.

____ 9. My e-mails to my friend Steve are _____. Sometimes I write once a month, other times once a year.

____ 10. The candidate for the state senate must not know much about taxes. Every time she's asked about this topic, she _____(e)s and talks about other matters, like the homeless or public transportation.

SCORE: (Number correct) _____ × 10 = _____ %

Mastery Test: *Chapter 10 (The Mad Monk)*

In the space provided, write the word from the box needed to complete each sentence. Then put the **letter** of that word in the column at the left. Use each word once.

a. **alleviate**	b. **benefactor**	c. **covert**	d. **cynic**	e. **demise**
f. **infamous**	g. **intrinsic**	h. **revulsion**	i. **speculate**	j. **virile**

_____ 1. Everyone was shocked to learn of the sudden _____ of Jim Henson, creator of the Muppets. He died of pneumonia at the age of only 53.

_____ 2. My family photo album has little _____ value, but to me, it is worth more than any amount of money.

_____ 3. Nicotine gum can _____ the withdrawal symptoms of quitting smoking.

_____ 4. Someone once helped my uncle pay for college. Now that he can afford it, he's become a _____ to struggling students.

_____ 5. Brenda took a(n) _____ look at her watch, hoping her hosts didn't notice her glance and think she was anxious to leave.

_____ 6. Benjamin Franklin must have been a _____. He showed a lack of faith in human nature when he wrote, "Three may keep a secret if two of them are dead."

_____ 7. In her lecture, the history teacher _____(e)d about why countries go to war. She came up with three reasons: to get territory, to gain natural resources such as oil, and to have power over others.

_____ 8. In the past, men who cried or showed their emotions weren't considered _____. Today, though, it's acceptable for "real men" to be sensitive.

_____ 9. My husband was filled with such _____ during the horror movie that he had to leave the theater. He couldn't bear to watch the scientist turn into a giant fly.

_____ 10. Nearly every American has heard of John Wilkes Booth. He is _____ for murdering President Abraham Lincoln.

SCORE: (Number correct) _____ × 10 = _____ %

Mastery Test: *Chapter 11 (Conflict Over Holidays)*

In the space provided, write the word from the box needed to complete each sentence. Then put the **letter** of that word in the column at the left. Use each word once.

a. **abstain**	b. **affiliate**	c. **agnostic**	d. **aspire**	e. **benevolent**
f. **deficit**	g. **dissent**	h. **diversion**	i. **lucrative**	j. **mandatory**

_____ 1. The famous American lawyer, Clarence Darrow, said it was impossible to know if God exists. "I do not consider it an insult, but a compliment, to be called an _____. I do not pretend to know where many ignorant men are sure."

_____ 2. Laura loves salty foods, but she has to _____ from them. Her blood pressure is high and salt makes it higher.

_____ 3. Organizations such as the Boy Scouts and Girl Scouts reward their members for performing _____ actions like volunteering at a hospital or a shelter for the homeless.

_____ 4. The Taylors were considering a divorce around Christmas time, so there was a noticeable _____ of good cheer in their house.

_____ 5. To get a construction job, workers usually have to _____ with the union. Few bosses are willing to risk hiring non-union employees.

_____ 6. The Johnsons were sorry to lose their favorite babysitter, but they understood that she needed a more _____ job in order to earn money for college.

_____ 7. That teacher won't put up with any _____ in her classroom. The only opinions she likes to listen to are her own.

_____ 8. Many Little League players _____ to become major league ballplayers. That's why they take the game so seriously.

_____ 9. At this school, a course in writing is _____. Even art students must take it.

_____ 10. JoJo the Clown visits Children's Hospital every Saturday to provide a(n) _____ for children who are bedridden or about to undergo operations.

SCORE: (Number correct) _____ × 10 = _____ %

Mastery Test: *Chapter 12 (Dr. Martin Luther King, Jr.)*

In the space provided, write the word from the box needed to complete each sentence. Then put the **letter** of that word in the column at the left. Use each word once.

a. **charisma**	b. **contemporary**	c. **contend**	d. **conversely**	e. **extrovert**
f. **poignant**	g. **prevalent**	h. **proponent**	i. **quest**	j. **traumatic**

_____ 1. My little sister doesn't enjoy old classic movies like *The Wizard of Oz* or *Gone with the Wind.* She'd rather see something more _____, with actors who are still alive.

_____ 2. My friend Bob is so outgoing that he can joke and make friends easily. I wish I were as much of a(n) _____ as he is.

_____ 3. Holly's most _____ childhood experience was getting lost in a department store. She's never forgotten how frightened and upset she was before her parents found her.

_____ 4. Many people on Spring Street object to the plan to build a shopping center there. They _____ that it will create too much traffic and noise.

_____ 5. Squirrels are _____ in our neighborhood. We see them everywhere.

_____ 6. Gold was discovered in California in January, 1848. The following year, 80,000 people traveled there in a(n) _____ for the precious metal.

_____ 7. My mother raised my brother and me after getting her college degree. _____, my aunt raised a family before getting her degree.

_____ 8. Some sports stars have so much _____ that their fans will wait outside the stadium for hours just to get a look at them.

_____ 9. Donna and Greg's wedding ceremony was full of touching details. An especially _____ moment came when the bride and groom gave a rose to each other's parents.

_____ 10. Our doctor is a(n) _____ of home care. She sends patients home from the hospital as soon as possible, believing they'll recover more quickly in familiar surroundings.

SCORE: (Number correct) _____ × 10 = _____ %

Mastery Test: *Chapter 13 (Relating to Parents)*

In the space provided, write the word from the box needed to complete each sentence. Then put the **letter** of that word in the column at the left. Use each word once.

a. **congenial**	b. **flippant**	c. **impasse**	d. **perception**	e. **prompt**
f. **prone**	g. **rapport**	h. **rationale**	i. **relentless**	j. **reprisal**

_____ 1. We were at a frustrating _____. Our old car needed major repairs in order to keep running, but it wasn't really worth saving. However, a new car would simply cost too much.

_____ 2. The rain has been _____. It has poured down every day for the past week.

_____ 3. Reba's _____ of big cities is that they're exciting, interesting places. Her husband, however, sees them only as noisy, dirty places to avoid.

_____ 4. Why am I more _____ to upset stomachs on the days I have tests? I wish I didn't get so tense then.

_____ 5. In the days when parents arranged their children's marriages, it could take a long time for the newlyweds to develop a _____.

_____ 6. When the fourth-grade teacher asked her class, " Who discovered America?" my little brother gave the _____ answer, "Not me, Teacher!"

_____ 7. The boss's _____ for not letting us leave the building during our lunch hour is "It gives you the chance to get to know each other better." We don't think that's a good enough reason for keeping us cooped up.

_____ 8. The sing-along at Sally's party was so much fun that it _____(e)d my father to get out his dusty old guitar when we got home.

_____ 9. Henry is such a _____ fellow that all the other waiters at the restaurant like him, even though he does get more tips than any of them.

_____ 10. The Thompsons, our next-door neighbors, didn't invite us to their Fourth of July barbecue. In _____, we didn't invite them to our Labor Day picnic.

SCORE: (Number correct) _____ × 10 = _____ %

Mastery Test: *Chapter 14 (The Nightmare of Gym)*

In the space provided, write the word from the box needed to complete each sentence. Then put the **letter** of that word in the column at the left. Use each word once.

a. **averse**	b. **detract**	c. **disdain**	d. **divulge**	e. **elation**
f. **endow**	g. **expulsion**	h. **mortified**	i. **nullified**	j. **ominous**

_____ 1. My parents couldn't give me much materially, but they did _____ me with a healthy self-confidence.

_____ 2. Patti's _____ at being elected class president was lessened by the knowledge that her best friend had lost the election for class secretary.

_____ 3. Some superstitious people are _____ to anything with the number thirteen on it.

_____ 4. The still air and strangely green sky were signs of a(n) _____ change in the weather.

_____ 5. Elise felt _____ when she jumped on the trampoline and her shorts fell off, but everyone else laughed.

_____ 6. A year in college has made Gina feel superior. She now looks with _____ upon old friends who haven't gone beyond high school.

_____ 7. Officials _____(e)d the results of the race when they learned that the winning horse had been given an illegal drug.

_____ 8. Rudy's noisy and insulting behavior resulted in his _____ from the restaurant.

_____ 9. The continual crying of a baby in the auditorium _____(e)d from our enjoyment of the movie.

_____ 10. Because the Academy Awards program is so long, I fall asleep long before the names of the top winners are _____(e)d.

SCORE: (Number correct) _____ × 10 = _____ %

Mastery Test: *Chapter 15 (A Model Teacher)*

In the space provided, write the word from the box needed to complete each sentence. Then put the **letter** of that word in the column at the left. Use each word once.

a. **commemorate**	b. **complacent**	c. **consensus**	d. **deplete**	e. **diligent**
f. **empathy**	g. **menial**	h. **niche**	i. **transcend**	j. **waive**

_____ 1. Although we have only one house guest, his huge appetite quickly _____s our supplies of certain foods. I've had to make three trips to the supermarket this week.

_____ 2. To be a good therapist, one must have _____ for others.

_____ 3. Tony never became _____ about his store's success. He continued to work as hard as he did the first day it was opened.

_____ 4. To _____ my aunt and uncle's wedding anniversary, I made a donation to one of their favorite charities.

_____ 5. Amy isn't skilled at dealing with people, but she has found a(n) _____ as a computer repair specialist, working mainly with machines, not humans.

_____ 6. There was rarely a(n) _____ in our large family on where to eat. Three always wanted Mexican food, and the others usually preferred Italian or Chinese.

_____ 7. With special training, Philip was able to _____ his learning disability and become a successful accountant.

_____ 8. Ben cheerfully accepted a job as a dishwasher at a summer resort. He didn't mind the _____ work as long as he could enjoy the beautiful resort in his free time.

_____ 9. Once the librarian gets to know you, she _____s the requirement that you show your student identification every time you wish to take out a book.

_____ 10. Herb is not at the top of the honor roll month after month because he's so brilliant, but because he's very _____ about his school work.

SCORE: (Number correct) _____ × 10 = _____ %

Mastery Test: *Chapter 16 (Shoplifter)*

In the space provided, write the word from the box needed to complete each sentence. Then put the **letter** of that word in the column at the left. Use each word once.

a. **condone**	b. **contemplate**	c. **feasible**	d. **feign**	e. **fiscal**
f. **furtive**	g. **gape**	h. **pathetic**	i. **precedent**	j. **punitive**

_____   1. Although Dr. Simpson often seems rude, we _____ his bad manners because of the many kind things he's done for our family over the years.

_____   2. The _____ rules at some banks allowed them to lend huge amounts of money. When the economy turned bad and the loans weren't repaid, those banks failed.

_____   3. Many young people _____ joining the Army because of the free career training it could provide them.

_____   4. Should prisons only be _____? Or should they also teach prisoners useful skills?

_____   5. We _____(e)d in astonishment at the huge hole in the ground left by the earthquake.

_____   6. Alex's attempts to repair his car were so _____ that he made the situation even worse.

_____   7. Lawyers rely heavily on legal _____. When a question arises, they look for past cases in which similar questions were dealt with.

_____   8. Little Emily tried to act as if she wasn't thinking about her Christmas presents, but she kept taking _____ glances at the beautifully wrapped packages under the tree.

_____   9. I wonder if it will someday be _____ for an average person to take a vacation somewhere in space.

_____   10. When I open one of Grandma's birthday presents, I usually have to _____ delighted surprise. She often gives me something that's either ugly or useless.

SCORE: (Number correct) _____ × 10 = _____ %

Mastery Test: *Chapter 17 (A Nutty Newspaper Office)*

In the space provided, write the word from the box needed to complete each sentence. Then put the **letter** of that word in the column at the left. Use each word once.

a. **cryptic**	b. **deficient**	c. **depict**	d. **detrimental**	e. **implicit**
f. **inhibition**	g. **ironic**	h. **rupture**	i. **saturate**	j. **vindictive**

_____ 1. The _____ note my girlfriend left on my door said only, "A bridge over troubled waters."

_____ 2. Throughout the hilarious movie, my visiting cousin didn't laugh once or even crack a smile. He seemed completely _____ in a sense of humor.

_____ 3. Most plants need as much sunshine as possible. But for shade-loving plants, direct sunlight is actually _____ to their well-being.

_____ 4. The expensive two-week, eight-hour-a day language course _____s students' minds with the new language.

_____ 5. "Wouldn't you be more comfortable on the couch?" was a(n) _____ request for the 300-pound guest not to sit on Jane's fragile antique chair.

_____ 6. Celia felt as if she'd kept all her anger at her roommate trapped in a box inside her. Suddenly, the box _____(e)d, and angry words came spilling out of her mouth.

_____ 7. Although Bill Cosby was in the same elevator with me, my _____ against bothering people kept me from asking for his autograph.

_____ 8. "It's a(n) _____ fact of life," said Aunt Lucy, "that we are often attracted to our mates by the very qualities that later drive us crazy."

_____ 9. Bertha had _____(e)d her father as such a monster that when I finally met him, I was surprised to find him soft-spoken and pleasant.

_____ 10. Mona was angry because her brother had refused to lend her a favorite CD. Feeling _____, Mona went through her brother's room and removed everything she had ever given him.

SCORE: (Number correct) _____ × 10 = _____ %

Mastery Test: *Chapter 18 (Roughing It)*

In the space provided, write the word from the box needed to complete each sentence. Then put the **letter** of that word in the column at the left. Use each word once.

a. **constrict**	b. **exhaustive**	c. **fallible**	d. **formulate**	e. **genial**
f. **habitat**	g. **pragmatic**	h. **pretentious**	i. **reconcile**	j. **vile**

_____ 1. The octopus is very good at squeezing into small spaces. It can _____ its flexible legs and body enough to slip into what seems an impossibly small area.

_____ 2. My fifth-grade teacher's _____ manner disguised a truly unpleasant personality.

_____ 3. Instead of denying it when she makes a mistake, our English teacher simply says, "Like everyone else, I'm _____."

_____ 4. Jan doesn't often mention the fact that she has two doctoral degrees because she doesn't want to be _____.

_____ 5. I don't really like my biology lab partner, but he asked me out so suddenly that I didn't have time to _____ an excuse. Instead I just stammered, "Uh, well, I guess so."

_____ 6. Although several specialists ran a(n) _____ series of tiring tests and exams, they could discover no cause for Eric's terrible headaches.

_____ 7. My twelve-year-old sister enjoyed creating a natural _____ inside a large aquarium for her hermit crab.

_____ 8. It's more _____ to buy clothing that can be mixed and matched into various outfits than to buy clothes that can be worn in only one outfit.

_____ 9. When Sara decided to stay home with the baby, she and Andy _____(e)d themselves to living on considerably less money for a while.

_____ 10. Why do millions of people enjoy seeing movies about such _____ subjects as chain-saw murders?

SCORE: (Number correct) _____ × 10 = _____ %

Name: _____

Mastery Test: *Chapter 19 (Getting Scared)*

In the space provided, write the word from the box needed to complete each sentence. Then put the **letter** of that word in the column at the left. Use each word once.

a. **avid**	b. **dwindle**	c. **esteem**	d. **evoke**	e. **legacy**
f. **mediate**	g. **muted**	h. **nurture**	i. **pacify**	j. **transient**

_____ 1. If we aren't careful, our _____ to our children and grandchildren may be an environment damaged beyond saving.

_____ 2. The children were annoyed to return from lunch and find that their formerly huge snowman had _____ under the midday sun to only a stump.

_____ 3. "I don't know what to say!" gasped the woman when she met her favorite actor. "I'm your most _____(e)d fan. I've seen each of your movies at least three times."

_____ 4. The smell of lilac cologne always _____s memories in me of my grandmother.

_____ 5. Kay looks more attractive now that she's traded in her harsh, bright make-up for more _____ colors.

_____ 6. It was hard for Toni to see the restaurant she had _____(e)d from a tiny take-out stand to a thriving pizzeria disappear in a blaze of fire.

_____ 7. Al was about to offer to _____ the dispute between his two angry neighbors, but when he noticed one of them had a knife, he decided instead to call the police.

_____ 8. My _____ for my rich uncle grew when I learned how much work he did for charities and how much money he gave them.

_____ 9. When my brother is really angry, nothing I say can _____ him. I just listen until he's had his say, and then he quickly calms down again.

_____ 10. My joy at seeing an A at the top of the returned math paper was _____, passing quickly when I realized the teacher had mistakenly given me someone else's paper.

SCORE: (Number correct) _____ × 10 = _____ %

Name: _____

Mastery Test: *Chapter 20 (My Sister's Date)*

In the space provided, write the word from the box needed to complete each sentence. Then put the **letter** of that word in the column at the left. Use each word once.

a. **aloof**	b. **ambivalent**	c. **augment**	d. **dispel**	e. **explicit**
f. **longevity**	g. **magnitude**	h. **mundane**	i. **obscure**	j. **render**

_____ 1. I've tried to _____ superstitions from my mind, but I still find myself walking around ladders, not under them.

_____ 2. I don't know how Tom could have made such a mess of painting the garage. He was given _____ instructions as to how it was to be done.

_____ 3. Perry decided to _____ his muscles by lifting weights every other day.

_____ 4. Cats are usually thought of as more _____ than dogs, keeping their distance from everyone but a chosen few.

_____ 5. Doug is _____ about the job offer he's received. The job itself sounds great, but accepting it would mean moving far from his family and friends.

_____ 6. Many scientists believe our sun will die someday, but since that event wouldn't happen for millions of years, it seems of little _____ today.

_____ 7. People often marry expecting never-ending romance and excitement. However, marriages are full of _____ details like bill-paying and finding baby sitters.

_____ 8. After staying awake all night, Duane wrote what he thought was a brilliant letter to his girlfriend. But this morning he found it so _____ that even he couldn't understand it all.

_____ 9. A new coat of off-white paint _____(e)d the old kitchen much brighter and more attractive.

_____ 10. Just when you are determined to stop all unhealthy habits, you read about some lively 100-year-old who says his or her _____ stems from daily doses of whiskey and cigars.

SCORE: (Number correct) _____ × 10 = _____ %

Answers to the Mastery Tests:
IMPROVING VOCABULARY SKILLS, SHORT VERSION

Chapter 1 (Joseph Palmer)

1.	g	6.	h
2.	f	7.	b
3.	a	8.	e
4.	c	9.	d
5.	i	10.	j

Chapter 2 (A Cruel Sport)

1.	d	6.	h
2.	g	7.	a
3.	j	8.	e
4.	b	9.	i
5.	f	10.	c

Chapter 3 (No Luck with Women)

1.	f	6.	g
2.	i	7.	b
3.	e	8.	c
4.	h	9.	a
5.	j	10.	d

Chapter 4 (Accident and Recovery)

1.	g	6.	c
2.	b	7.	f
3.	h	8.	a
4.	i	9.	d
5.	j	10.	e

Chapter 5 (Animal Senses)

1.	e	6.	a
2.	b	7.	f
3.	j	8.	c
4.	g	9.	i
5.	h	10.	d

Chapter 6 (Money Problems)

1.	e	6.	a
2.	h	7.	c
3.	b	8.	f
4.	j	9.	i
5.	d	10.	g

Chapter 7 (The New French Employee)

1.	e	6.	c
2.	a	7.	f
3.	j	8.	b
4.	g	9.	i
5.	d	10.	h

Chapter 8 (A Cruel Teacher)

1.	j	6.	a
2.	i	7.	d
3.	g	8.	h
4.	f	9.	e
5.	b	10.	c

Chapter 9 (Learning to Study)

1.	e	6.	a
2.	h	7.	d
3.	i	8.	b
4.	j	9.	g
5.	f	10.	c

Chapter 10 (The Mad Monk)

1.	e	6.	d
2.	g	7.	i
3.	a	8.	j
4.	b	9.	h
5.	c	10.	f

Chapter 11 (Conflict Over Holidays)

1.	c	6.	i
2.	a	7.	g
3.	e	8.	d
4.	f	9.	j
5.	b	10.	h

Chapter 12 (Dr. Martin Luther King, Jr.)

1.	b	6.	i
2.	e	7.	d
3.	j	8.	a
4.	c	9.	f
5.	g	10.	h

Chapter 13 (Relating to Parents)

1. c		6. b	
2. i		7. h	
3. d		8. e	
4. f		9. a	
5. g		10. j	

Chapter 14 (The Nightmare of Gym)

1. f		6. c	
2. e		7. i	
3. a		8. g	
4. j		9. b	
5. h		10. d	

Chapter 15 (A Model Teacher)

1. d		6. c	
2. f		7. i	
3. b		8. g	
4. a		9. j	
5. h		10. e	

Chapter 16 (Shoplifter)

1. a		6. h	
2. e		7. i	
3. b		8. f	
4. j		9. c	
5. g		10. d	

Chapter 17 (A Nutty Newspaper Office)

1. a		6. h	
2. b		7. f	
3. d		8. g	
4. i		9. c	
5. e		10. j	

Chapter 18 (Roughing It)

1. a		6. b	
2. e		7. f	
3. c		8. g	
4. h		9. i	
5. d		10. j	

Chapter 19 (Getting Scared)

1. e		6. h	
2. b		7. f	
3. a		8. c	
4. d		9. i	
5. g		10. j	

Chapter 20 (My Sister's Date)

1. d		6. g	
2. e		7. h	
3. c		8. i	
4. a		9. j	
5. b		10. f	

Name: _____

Mastery Test: *Unit One*

PART A
Complete each sentence in a way that clearly shows you understand the meaning of the **boldfaced** word. Take a minute to plan your answer before you write.

Example: Being **nocturnal** animals, raccoons _____ *raid our garbage cans only at night* _____.

1. The news program reported a **calamity** in which _____
   _____.

2. Typewriters are now almost **obsolete** because _____
   _____.

3. Three personal **attributes** that I possess are _____
   _____.

4. One **tangible** symbol of affection is _____
   _____.

5. When I'm alone, I often **ponder** _____
   _____.

6. The **eccentric** teacher has a habit of _____
   _____.

7. One advantage of a **mobile** library might be _____
   _____.

8. The most **altruistic** thing I ever saw anyone do was to _____
   _____.

9. The actor received this **acclaim** for his performance: " _____
   _____."

10. I plan to **persevere** in _____
    _____.

(Continues on next page)

PART B

Use each of the following ten words in sentences of your own. Make it clear that you know the meaning of the word you use. Feel free to use the past tense or plural form of a word.

a. **absolve**	b. **animosity**	c. **antagonist**	d. **appease**	e. **banal**
f. **encounter**	g. **engross**	h. **euphemism**	i. **mercenary**	j. **turmoil**

11. _____

_____

12. _____

_____

13. _____

_____

14. _____

_____

15. _____

_____

16. _____

_____

17. _____

_____

18. _____

_____

19. _____

_____

20. _____

_____

SCORE: (Number correct) _____ × 5 = _____ %

Mastery Test: *Unit Two*

PART A
Complete each sentence in a way that clearly shows you understand the meaning of the **boldfaced** word. Take a minute to plan your answer before you write.

Example: As an **incentive** to work better, the company   *gives bonuses to workers who show special effort* .

1. One of the most **infamous** people I've heard of is _____

_____.

2. One sight that makes me feel **revulsion** is _____

_____.

3. The reason the plan was **covert** was that _____

_____.

4. When Carolyn saw her essay grade, she **gloated**, saying, " _____

_____."

5. During the math class, the teacher **digressed** by _____

_____.

6. My apartment is so **immaculate** that _____

_____.

7. A good friend of mine was once **devastated** by _____

_____.

8. The novel's main character is a **sinister** doctor who _____

_____.

9. When our neighbor cut lilacs off our bush for her home, we **retaliated** by _____

_____.

10. One **prerequisite** for getting married ought to be _____

_____.

(Continues on next page)

PART B

Use each of the following ten words in sentences of your own. Make it clear that you know the meaning of the word you use. Feel free to use the past tense or plural form of a word.

a. **blight**	b. **curtail**	c. **decipher**	d. **implausible**	e. **predominant**
f. **qualm**	g. **sanctuary**	h. **speculate**	i. **virile**	j. **vulnerable**

11. _____

_____

12. _____

_____

13. _____

_____

14. _____

_____

15. _____

_____

16. _____

_____

17. _____

_____

18. _____

_____

19. _____

_____

20. _____

_____

SCORE: (Number correct) _____ × 5 = _____ %

Mastery Test: *Unit Three*

PART A
Complete each sentence in a way that clearly shows you understand the meaning of the **boldfaced** word. Take a minute to plan your answer before you write.

Example: I **abstain** from _____ *staying up late and watching TV the night before a test* _____ .

1. Luis showed his **elation** at the news by _____

_____ .

2. I **aspire** to _____

_____ .

3. Jon, who is a **proponent** of daily exercise, advised me, " _____

_____ _____ ."

4. At our school, it is **mandatory** to _____

_____ .

5. At parties, Shawna, who is an **extrovert** , likes to _____

_____ .

6. I find it **detracts** from a restaurant meal when _____

_____ .

7. Lamont is **averse** to city life because _____

_____ .

8. Our father told us how **traumatic** it was for him to _____

_____ .

9. My **rationale** for going to college is _____

_____ .

10. When asked by the restaurant owner to pay his bill, the young man's **flippant** reply was " _____

_____ ."

(Continues on next page)

PART B

Use each of the following ten words in sentences of your own. Make it clear that you know the meaning of the word you use. Feel free to use the past tense or plural form of a word.

| a. **consensus** | b. **deplete** | c. **dissent** | d. **empathy** | e. **niche** |
| f. **perception** | g. **prone** | h. **quest** | i. **rapport** | j. **waive** |

11. _____

_____

12. _____

_____

13. _____

_____

14. _____

_____

15. _____

_____

16. _____

_____

17. _____

_____

18. _____

_____

19. _____

_____

20. _____

_____

SCORE: (Number correct) _____ × 5 = _____ %

Mastery Test: *Unit Four*

PART A

Complete each sentence in a way that clearly shows you understand the meaning of the **boldfaced** word. Take a minute to plan your answer before you write.

Example: To increase your **longevity**, *exercise frequently and avoid tobacco, alcohol, and high-fat foods* .

1. **Pragmatic** Ramona spends her money on such things as _____
_____ .

2. One thing the nursery-school teacher did to **nurture** each child each day was _____
_____ .

3. The critic summed up how **pathetic** the actor's performance was with this comment: "_____
_____ ."

4. The car accident **rendered** Philip _____
_____ .

5. The **magnitude** of Carol's musical talent became clear to us when _____
_____ .

6. A student **deficient** in study skills might _____
_____ .

7. We learned how **fallible** the house builder was when _____
_____ .

8. I have had to **reconcile** myself to the fact that _____
_____ .

9. When he wasn't invited to the wedding, the bride's **vindictive** cousin _____
_____ .

10. I'm such an **avid** fan of _____ that I'll _____
_____ .

(Continues on next page)

PART B

Use each of the following ten words in sentences of your own. Make it clear that you know the meaning of the word you use. Feel free to use the past tense or plural form of a word.

a. **condone**	b. **contemplate**	c. **esteem**	d. **feign**	e. **furtive**
f. **gape**	g. **habitat**	h. **inhibition**	i. **pacify**	j. **vile**

11. _____

_____

12. _____

_____

13. _____

_____

14. _____

_____

15. _____

_____

16. _____

_____

17. _____

_____

18. _____

_____

19. _____

_____

20. _____

_____

SCORE: (Number correct) _____ × 5 = _____ %

126

NAME: _____

SECTION: _____ DATE: _____

Pretest

SCORE: _____

> This test contains 100 items. In the space provided, write the letter of the choice that is closest in meaning to the **boldfaced** word.
>
> *Important:* Keep in mind that this test is for diagnostic purposes only. **If you do not know a word, leave the space blank rather than guess at it.**

____ 1. **scrupulous**   a) sociable   b) careless   c) clean   d) conscientious

____ 2. **vicarious**   a) experienced indirectly   b) lively   c) inactive   d) occasional

____ 3. **facetious**   a) ill-mannered   b) joking   c) careless   d) depressed

____ 4. **discretion**   a) independence   b) gladness   c) slyness   d) tact

____ 5. **gregarious**   a) wordy   b) depressed   c) sociable   d) religious

____ 6. **despondent**   a) depressed   b) tired   c) encouraged   d) well-behaved

____ 7. **rudimentary**   a) rude   b) planned   c) partial   d) elementary

____ 8. **retrospect**   a) expecting   b) repetition   c) removal   d) looking back

____ 9. **instigate**   a) stir to action   b) investigate   c) prepare   d) suppress

____ 10. **venerate**   a) protect   b) create   c) make unfriendly   d) respect

____ 11. **subsidize**   a) support financially   b) lift up   c) fall over   d) calculate

____ 12. **dissident**   a) political supporter   b) visitor   c) candidate   d) one who disagrees

____ 13. **juxtapose**   a) replace   b) place side by side   c) remove   d) imagine

____ 14. **embellish**   a) remove   b) keep   c) decorate   d) hide

____ 15. **inadvertent**   a) unintentional   b) not for sale   c) distant   d) near

____ 16. **relinquish**   a) enjoy   b) gather   c) criticize   d) give up

____ 17. **impetuous**   a) lazy   b) calm   c) teasing   d) impulsive

____ 18. **euphoric**   a) undecided   b) depressed   c) lonely   d) overjoyed

____ 19. **infallible**   a) incapable of error   b) accident-prone   c) human   d) wild

____ 20. **regress**   a) make progress   b) restrict   c) return to previous behavior   d) adjust

____ 21. **fortuitous**   a) lucky   b) sad   c) having never happened before   d) brave

____ 22. **sham**   a) type   b) imitation   c) disturbance   d) belief

____ 23. **predisposed**   a) against   b) reluctant to speak   c) undecided   d) tending beforehand

____ 24. **propensity**   a) relation   b) job   c) tendency   d) hobby

____ 25. **reprehensible**   a) blameworthy   b) well-filled   c) affordable   d) admirable

(Continues on next page)

____ 26. **attrition**   **a)** becoming fewer   **b)** connection   **c)** multiplying   **d)** imitation

____ 27. **reticent**   **a)** forgiving   **b)** sad   **c)** reluctant to speak   **d)** contrary to reason

____ 28. **circumvent**   **a)** avoid   **b)** fail to notice   **c)** distribute   **d)** socialize

____ 29. **inundate**   **a)** delay   **b)** flood   **c)** swallow   **d)** approve

____ 30. **oblivious**   **a)** courageous   **b)** unaware   **c)** quiet   **d)** reliable

____ 31. **inquisitive**   **a)** cheerful   **b)** nervous   **c)** curious   **d)** in pain

____ 32. **relegate**   **a)** bring back into use   **b)** assign to a lesser place   **c)** blend   **d)** raise

____ 33. **bolster**   **a)** support   **b)** protect   **c)** protest   **d)** hide

____ 34. **terse**   **a)** nervous   **b)** sad   **c)** brief   **d)** cool

____ 35. **sedentary**   **a)** sitting   **b)** excessive   **c)** harmless   **d)** repeated

____ 36. **superfluous**   **a)** extra   **b)** unclear   **c)** useful   **d)** ahead

____ 37. **exonerate**   **a)** encourage   **b)** condemn   **c)** hide   **d)** free from blame

____ 38. **contingency**   **a)** contest   **b)** disapproval   **c)** theory   **d)** possibility

____ 39. **clandestine**   **a)** well-lit   **b)** secret   **c)** noble   **d)** harmless

____ 40. **liability**   **a)** drawback   **b)** hatred   **c)** favor   **d)** indirect remark

____ 41. **austere**   **a)** wealthy   **b)** plain   **c)** complex   **d)** far

____ 42. **perfunctory**   **a)** unenthusiastic   **b)** troubled   **c)** on time   **d)** well-prepared

____ 43. **provocative**   **a)** careful   **b)** able to improve   **c)** inconsistent   **d)** arousing interest

____ 44. **esoteric**   **a)** public   **b)** uniform   **c)** well-written   **d)** understood by few

____ 45. **metamorphosis**   **a)** journey   **b)** change   **c)** secret plot   **d)** fantasy

____ 46. **verbose**   **a)** wordy   **b)** active   **c)** noisy   **d)** forceful

____ 47. **connoisseur**   **a)** one who likes to suffer   **b)** egotist   **c)** expert   **d)** painter

____ 48. **contrite**   **a)** indecent   **b)** sorry   **c)** lacking confidence   **d)** careful

____ 49. **plight**   **a)** difficult situation   **b)** minor weakness   **c)** environment   **d)** travel

____ 50. **distraught**   **a)** educated   **b)** too noticeable   **c)** troubled   **d)** rehearsed

(Continues on next page)

_____ 51. **encompass**   **a)** include   **b)** draw   **c)** separate   **d)** purchase

_____ 52. **stringent**   **a)** dry   **b)** strict   **c)** loose   **d)** long

_____ 53. **eradicate**   **a)** wipe out   **b)** scold   **c)** restore   **d)** hold onto

_____ 54. **sordid**   **a)** slow   **b)** unprepared   **c)** morally low   **d)** injured

_____ 55. **presumptuous**   **a)** indecent   **b)** lacking standards of selection   **c)** nervous   **d)** too bold

_____ 56. **meticulous**   **a)** broken-down   **b)** curious   **c)** careful and exact   **d)** irregular

_____ 57. **magnanimous**   **a)** nameless   **b)** proud   **c)** generous in forgiving   **d)** lacking standards

_____ 58. **exhort**   **a)** strongly urge   **b)** travel   **c)** escape   **d)** hint

_____ 59. **innocuous**   **a)** delightful   **b)** harmless   **c)** dangerous   **d)** disappointing

_____ 60. **masochist**   **a)** one who likes to suffer   **b)** egotist   **c)** fan
d) one who expects the worst

_____ 61. **deplore**   **a)** command   **b)** disapprove of   **c)** encourage   **d)** prevent

_____ 62. **atrophy**   **a)** weaken   **b)** reward   **c)** expand   **d)** strengthen

_____ 63. **unprecedented**   **a)** overly noticeable   **b)** without authority   **c)** unexpected
d) having never happened before

_____ 64. **mitigate**   **a)** make worse   **b)** make less severe   **c)** remove   **d)** hide

_____ 65. **exacerbate**   **a)** make worse   **b)** remove   **c)** bring closer   **d)** strengthen

_____ 66. **exorbitant**   **a)** absorbent   **b)** excessive   **c)** quarrelsome   **d)** well-timed

_____ 67. **facilitate**   **a)** approve   **b)** serve   **c)** make easier   **d)** clear from blame

_____ 68. **synchronize**   **a)** spread throughout   **b)** separate   **c)** reduce   **d)** cause to occur together

_____ 69. **extricate**   **a)** run away   **b)** confuse   **c)** free from difficulty   **d)** complicate

_____ 70. **exhilaration**   **a)** freedom   **b)** thirst   **c)** wisdom   **d)** gladness

_____ 71. **proficient**   **a)** proud   **b)** wise   **c)** skilled   **d)** well-known

_____ 72. **annihilate**   **a)** guide   **b)** misunderstand   **c)** carry out   **d)** destroy

_____ 73. **criterion**   **a)** philosophy   **b)** standard for judgment   **c)** political theory
d) state of mind

_____ 74. **vindicate**   **a)** clear from blame   **b)** ridicule   **c)** escape   **d)** formally question

_____ 75. **subversive**   **a)** being a servant   **b)** acting to overthrow   **c)** willing
d) planning to build

(Continues on next page)

_____ 76. **forestall**   a) prevent   b) predict   c) rent   d) hurry

_____ 77. **retribution**   a) donation   b) looking back   c) evil   d) punishment

_____ 78. **insinuate**   a) demand   b) state   c) deny   d) hint

_____ 79. **disparity**   a) sadness   b) inequality   c) blemish   d) similarity

_____ 80. **opportune**   a) generous   b) more important   c) well-timed   d) belittling

_____ 81. **fastidious**   a) not planned   b) attentive to details   c) quick   d) inferior

_____ 82. **heinous**   a) evil   b) mischievous   c) stubborn   d) depressed

_____ 83. **implement**   a) encourage   b) carry out   c) insult   d) prevent

_____ 84. **complement**   a) praise   b) sin   c) make fun of   d) add what is needed

_____ 85. **impromptu**   a) forceful   b) unplanned   c) delayed   d) on time

_____ 86. **transgress**   a) follow   b) round out   c) travel   d) sin

_____ 87. **extenuating**   a) excusing   b) inferior   c) forceful   d) overly noticeable

_____ 88. **vehement**   a) forceful   b) wicked   c) rude   d) calm

_____ 89. **auspicious**   a) threatening   b) lazy   c) favorable   d) not trusting

_____ 90. **rebuke**   a) compromise   b) fix   c) scold   d) admire

_____ 91. **macabre**   a) frightful   b) depressed   c) cheerful   d) common

_____ 92. **fabricate**   a) misinterpret   b) put away   c) clothe   d) invent

_____ 93. **turbulent**   a) ambitious   b) wildly disturbed   c) mixed   d) fast

_____ 94. **impending**   a) about to happen   b) illegal   c) historical   d) usual

_____ 95. **paramount**   a) dramatic   b) disturbed   c) unknown   d) chief

_____ 96. **emulate**   a) be tardy   b) misunderstand   c) imitate   d) prepare

_____ 97. **antithesis**   a) disorder   b) theory   c) effect   d) opposite

_____ 98. **incapacitate**   a) disable   b) allow   c) increase   d) fight

_____ 99. **abrasive**   a) rough   b) friendly   c) mild   d) foolish

_____ 100. **prognosis**   a) hope   b) memory   c) opposite   d) prediction

---

STOP. This is the end of the test. If there is time remaining, you may go back and recheck your answers. When the time is up, hand in both your answer sheet and this test booklet to your instructor.

Posttest

This test contains 100 items. In the space provided, write the letter of the choice that is closest in meaning to the **boldfaced** word.

_____ 1. **juxtapose**   a) place side by side   b) replace   c) remove   d) imagine

_____ 2. **embellish**   a) remove   b) decorate   c) keep   d) hide

_____ 3. **facetious**   a) joking   b) ill-mannered   c) careless   d) depressed

_____ 4. **infallible**   a) wild   b) accident-prone   c) incapable of error   d) human

_____ 5. **discretion**   a) independence   b) tact   c) slyness   d) gladness

_____ 6. **inadvertent**   a) near   b) not for sale   c) distant   d) unintentional

_____ 7. **gregarious**   a) religious   b) sociable   c) depressed   d) wordy

_____ 8. **rudimentary**   a) rude   b) planned   c) partial   d) elementary

_____ 9. **retrospect**   a) repetition   b) looking back   c) removal   d) expecting

_____ 10. **regress**   a) restrict   b) make progress   c) adjust   d) return to previous behavior

_____ 11. **instigate**   a) stir to action   b) suppress   c) prepare   d) investigate

_____ 12. **venerate**   a) protect   b) respect   c) make unfriendly   d) create

_____ 13. **propensity**   a) hobby   b) relation   c) job   d) tendency

_____ 14. **subsidize**   a) fall over   b) lift up   c) support financially   d) calculate

_____ 15. **dissident**   a) political supporter   b) candidate   c) visitor   d) one who disagrees

_____ 16. **despondent**   a) tired   b) depressed   c) encouraged   d) well-behaved

_____ 17. **relinquish**   a) give up   b) criticize   c) gather   d) enjoy

_____ 18. **scrupulous**   a) clean   b) careless   c) sociable   d) conscientious

_____ 19. **sham**   a) type   b) imitation   c) disturbance   d) belief

_____ 20. **impetuous**   a) impulsive   b) lazy   c) teasing   d) calm

_____ 21. **fortuitous**   a) having never happened before   b) brave   c) lucky   d) sad

_____ 22. **predisposed**   a) against   b) reluctant to speak   c) tending beforehand   d) undecided

_____ 23. **reprehensible**   a) affordable   b) well-filled   c) blameworthy   d) admirable

_____ 24. **vicarious**   a) occasional   b) experienced indirectly   c) lively   d) inactive

_____ 25. **euphoric**   a) undecided   b) depressed   c) lonely   d) overjoyed

(Continues on next page)

_____ 26. **contrite** a) careful b) lacking confidence c) sorry d) indecent

_____ 27. **attrition** a) becoming fewer b) imitation c) multiplying d) connection

_____ 28. **terse** a) nervous b) sad c) brief d) cool

_____ 29. **esoteric** a) public b) uniform c) well-written d) understood by few

_____ 30. **clandestine** a) secret b) well-lit c) noble d) harmless

_____ 31. **inquisitive** a) cheerful b) curious c) nervous d) in pain

_____ 32. **contingency** a) contest b) disapproval c) theory d) possibility

_____ 33. **relegate** a) blend b) assign to a lesser place c) bring back into use d) raise

_____ 34. **verbose** a) noisy b) active c) wordy d) forceful

_____ 35. **exonerate** a) encourage b) hide c) condemn d) free from blame

_____ 36. **connoisseur** a) one who likes to suffer b) egotist c) expert d) painter

_____ 37. **liability** a) hatred b) drawback c) indirect remark d) favor

_____ 38. **circumvent** a) distribute b) socialize c) avoid d) fail to notice

_____ 39. **bolster** a) hide b) protest c) protect d) support

_____ 40. **austere** a) far b) wealthy c) plain d) complex

_____ 41. **reticent** a) forgiving b) reluctant to speak c) sad d) contrary to reason

_____ 42. **distraught** a) troubled b) too noticeable c) educated d) rehearsed

_____ 43. **superfluous** a) useful b) unclear c) extra d) ahead

_____ 44. **provocative** a) careful b) arousing interest c) inconsistent d) able to improve

_____ 45. **metamorphosis** a) secret plot b) fantasy c) journey d) change

_____ 46. **sedentary** a) excessive b) sitting c) repeated d) harmless

_____ 47. **oblivious** a) courageous b) unaware c) quiet d) reliable

_____ 48. **plight** a) minor weakness b) difficult situation c) travel d) environment

_____ 49. **inundate** a) flood b) delay c) approve d) swallow

_____ 50. **perfunctory** a) unenthusiastic b) on time c) troubled d) well-prepared

(Continues on next page)

_____ 51. **encompass** **a)** separate **b)** draw **c)** include **d)** purchase

_____ 52. **vindicate** **a)** ridicule **b)** escape **c)** clear from blame **d)** formally question

_____ 53. **meticulous** **a)** irregular **b)** broken-down **c)** curious **d)** careful and exact

_____ 54. **annihilate** **a)** destroy **b)** misunderstand **c)** carry out **d)** guide

_____ 55. **exacerbate** **a)** bring closer **b)** strengthen **c)** make worse **d)** remove

_____ 56. **magnanimous** **a)** nameless **b)** generous in forgiving **c)** proud **d)** lacking standards

_____ 57. **exhort** **a)** hint **b)** strongly urge **c)** travel **d)** escape

_____ 58. **stringent** **a)** long **b)** loose **c)** strict **d)** dry

_____ 59. **innocuous** **a)** delightful **b)** harmless **c)** dangerous **d)** disappointing

_____ 60. **facilitate** **a)** make easier **b)** serve **c)** approve **d)** clear from blame

_____ 61. **presumptuous** **a)** indecent **b)** lacking standards of selection **c)** nervous **d)** too bold

_____ 62. **unprecedented** **a)** overly noticeable **b)** without authority **c)** unexpected
d) having never happened before

_____ 63. **mitigate** **a)** make less severe **b)** make worse **c)** hide **d)** remove

_____ 64. **subversive** **a)** being a servant **b)** willing **c)** planning to build **d)** acting to overthrow

_____ 65. **atrophy** **a)** strengthen **b)** reward **c)** expand **d)** weaken

_____ 66. **sordid** **a)** slow **b)** morally low **c)** unprepared **d)** injured

_____ 67. **extricate** **a)** run away **b)** free from difficulty **c)** confuse **d)** complicate

_____ 68. **exhilaration** **a)** gladness **b)** freedom **c)** thirst **d)** wisdom

_____ 69. **masochist** **a)** one who expects the worst **b)** egotist **c)** fan
d) one who likes to suffer

_____ 70. **eradicate** **a)** wipe out **b)** scold **c)** restore **d)** hold onto

_____ 71. **proficient** **a)** wise **b)** proud **c)** well-known **d)** skilled

_____ 72. **exorbitant** **a)** excessive **b)** absorbent **c)** quarrelsome **d)** well-timed

_____ 73. **synchronize** **a)** cause to occur together **b)** separate **c)** reduce **d)** spread throughout

_____ 74. **deplore** **a)** command **b)** encourage **c)** disapprove of **d)** prevent

_____ 75. **criterion** **a)** philosophy **b)** political theory **c)** standard for judgment
d) state of mind

(Continues on next page)

____ 76. **forestall**   a) rent   b) predict   c) prevent   d) hurry

____ 77. **complement**   a) sin   b) praise   c) add what is needed   d) make fun of

____ 78. **prognosis**   a) memory   b) hope   c) prediction   d) opposite

____ 79. **vehement**   a) wicked   b) forceful   c) calm   d) rude

____ 80. **auspicious**   a) threatening   b) lazy   c) not trusting   d) favorable

____ 81. **disparity**   a) sadness   b) similarity   c) inequality   d) blemish

____ 82. **heinous**   a) depressed   b) evil   c) mischievous   d) stubborn

____ 83. **impromptu**   a) forceful   b) on time   c) delayed   d) unplanned

____ 84. **antithesis**   a) disorder   b) theory   c) opposite   d) effect

____ 85. **incapacitate**   a) allow   b) disable   c) increase   d) fight

____ 86. **implement**   a) carry out   b) encourage   c) insult   d) prevent

____ 87. **insinuate**   a) demand   b) state   c) deny   d) hint

____ 88. **rebuke**   a) compromise   b) scold   c) fix   d) admire

____ 89. **impending**   a) illegal   b) about to happen   c) historical   d) usual

____ 90. **abrasive**   a) foolish   b) rough   c) friendly   d) mild

____ 91. **fastidious**   a) not planned   b) attentive to details   c) quick   d) inferior

____ 92. **macabre**   a) depressed   b) frightful   c) common   d) cheerful

____ 93. **opportune**   a) well-timed   b) more important   c) generous   d) belittling

____ 94. **turbulent**   a) wildly disturbed   b) ambitious   c) mixed   d) fast

____ 95. **transgress**   a) round out   b) follow   c) sin   d) travel

____ 96. **extenuating**   a) overly noticeable   b) excusing   c) inferior   d) forceful

____ 97. **paramount**   a) disturbed   b) dramatic   c) chief   d) unknown

____ 98. **fabricate**   a) put away   b) misinterpret   c) invent   d) clothe

____ 99. **retribution**   a) looking back   b) donation   c) punishment   d) evil

____ 100. **emulate**   a) be tardy   b) imitate   c) misunderstand   d) prepare

---

STOP. This is the end of the test. If there is time remaining, you may go back and recheck your answers. When the time is up, hand in both your answer sheet and this test booklet to your instructor.

Unit One: *Pretest*

In the space provided, write the letter of the choice that is closest in meaning to the **boldfaced** word.

_____ 1. **dexterous**   a) young   b) accidental   c) skillful   d) skinny

_____ 2. **scrupulous**   a) sociable   b) careless   c) clean   d) conscientious

_____ 3. **vicarious**   a) experienced indirectly   b) lively   c) inactive   d) occasional

_____ 4. **sensory**   a) in the mind   b) sensible   c) of the senses   d) on the surface

_____ 5. **facetious**   a) ill-mannered   b) joking   c) careless   d) depressed

_____ 6. **discretion**   a) independence   b) gladness   c) slyness   d) tact

_____ 7. **ostentatious**   a) showy   b) lazy   c) courageous   d) playfully witty

_____ 8. **gregarious**   a) wordy   b) depressed   c) sociable   d) religious

_____ 9. **despondent**   a) depressed   b) tired   c) encouraged   d) well-behaved

_____ 10. **rudimentary**   a) rude   b) planned   c) partial   d) elementary

_____ 11. **collaborate**   a) respect   b) work hard   c) search   d) work together

_____ 12. **resilient**   a) able to recover quickly   b) strong   c) heavy   d) light

_____ 13. **retrospect**   a) expecting   b) repetition   c) removal   d) looking back

_____ 14. **instigate**   a) stir to action   b) investigate   c) prepare   d) suppress

_____ 15. **scoff**   a) impress   b) inquire   c) make fun of   d) show off

_____ 16. **venerate**   a) protect   b) create   c) make unfriendly   d) respect

_____ 17. **ambiguous**   a) under   b) not clear   c) widespread   d) too large

_____ 18. **subsidize**   a) support financially   b) lift up   c) fall over   d) calculate

_____ 19. **inane**   a) brilliant   b) measurable   c) causing pain   d) silly

_____ 20. **dissident**   a) political supporter   b) visitor   c) candidate   d) one who disagrees

_____ 21. **juxtapose**   a) replace   b) place side by side   c) remove   d) imagine

_____ 22. **fritter**   a) waste   b) prove   c) wander   d) collect

_____ 23. **embellish**   a) remove   b) keep   c) decorate   d) hide

_____ 24. **inadvertent**   a) unintentional   b) not for sale   c) distant   d) near

_____ 25. **relinquish**   a) enjoy   b) gather   c) criticize   d) give up

(Continues on next page)

_____ 26. **estrange** a) state again b) depart c) make unsympathetic d) enter

_____ 27. **impetuous** a) lazy b) calm c) teasing d) impulsive

_____ 28. **euphoric** a) undecided b) depressed c) lonely d) overjoyed

_____ 29. **zenith** a) cure-all b) peak c) drawback d) authority

_____ 30. **infallible** a) incapable of error b) accident-prone c) human d) wild

_____ 31. **regress** a) make progress b) restrict c) return to previous behavior d) adjust

_____ 32. **berate** a) urge b) criticize c) branch off d) lie

_____ 33. **fortuitous** a) lucky b) sad c) having never happened before d) brave

_____ 34. **impeccable** a) built-in b) unnecessary c) mischievous d) faultless

_____ 35. **sham** a) type b) imitation c) disturbance d) belief

_____ 36. **equivocate** a) be vague on purpose b) dedicate c) approve d) agree

_____ 37. **predisposed** a) against b) reluctant to speak c) undecided d) tending beforehand

_____ 38. **solicitous** a) trying to impress b) sitting c) showing concern d) negative

_____ 39. **propensity** a) relation b) job c) tendency d) hobby

_____ 40. **reprehensible** a) blameworthy b) well-filled c) affordable d) admirable

_____ 41. **detriment** a) outward behavior b) something damaging c) failure d) silence

_____ 42. **optimum** a) highest b) most favorable c) brightest d) heaviest

_____ 43. **squelch** a) make fun of b) stretch c) suppress d) approve

_____ 44. **zealot** a) dictator b) person devoted to a cause c) casual person d) leader

_____ 45. **sporadic** a) tiny b) particular c) occasional d) wasteful

_____ 46. **lethargy** a) strength b) highest point c) hunger d) lack of energy

_____ 47. **maudlin** a) kind b) sentimental c) useful d) clever

_____ 48. **ubiquitous** a) existing everywhere b) all-knowing c) all-powerful d) perfect

_____ 49. **liaison** a) reference b) plan c) go-between d) accusation

_____ 50. **solace** a) relaxation b) comfort c) sleep d) comedy

SCORE: (Number correct) _____ × 2 = _____ %

Unit One: *Posttest*

In the space provided, write the letter of the choice that is closest in meaning to the **boldfaced** word.

_____ 1. **inane**   **a)** silly   **b)** brilliant   **c)** measurable   **d)** causing pain

_____ 2. **juxtapose**   **a)** place side by side   **b)** replace   **c)** remove   **d)** imagine

_____ 3. **dexterous**   **a)** young   **b)** skillful   **c)** accidental   **d)** skinny

_____ 4. **ambiguous**   **a)** under   **b)** not clear   **c)** widespread   **d)** too large

_____ 5. **embellish**   **a)** remove   **b)** decorate   **c)** keep   **d)** hide

_____ 6. **facetious**   **a)** joking   **b)** ill-mannered   **c)** careless   **d)** depressed

_____ 7. **infallible**   **a)** wild   **b)** accident-prone   **c)** incapable of error   **d)** human

_____ 8. **zenith**   **a)** cure-all   **b)** drawback   **c)** peak   **d)** authority

_____ 9. **resilient**   **a)** able to recover quickly   **b)** light   **c)** heavy   **d)** strong

_____ 10. **discretion**   **a)** independence   **b)** tact   **c)** slyness   **d)** gladness

_____ 11. **inadvertent**   **a)** near   **b)** not for sale   **c)** distant   **d)** unintentional

_____ 12. **scoff**   **a)** show off   **b)** make fun of   **c)** inquire   **d)** impress

_____ 13. **gregarious**   **a)** religious   **b)** sociable   **c)** depressed   **d)** wordy

_____ 14. **solicitous**   **a)** trying to impress   **b)** showing concern   **c)** sitting   **d)** negative

_____ 15. **rudimentary**   **a)** rude   **b)** planned   **c)** partial   **d)** elementary

_____ 16. **collaborate**   **a)** search   **b)** work together   **c)** respect   **d)** work hard

_____ 17. **retrospect**   **a)** repetition   **b)** looking back   **c)** removal   **d)** expecting

_____ 18. **regress**   **a)** restrict   **b)** make progress   **c)** adjust   **d)** return to previous behavior

_____ 19. **instigate**   **a)** stir to action   **b)** suppress   **c)** prepare   **d)** investigate

_____ 20. **ostentatious**   **a)** showy   **b)** courageous   **c)** playfully witty   **d)** lazy

_____ 21. **berate**   **a)** lie   **b)** urge   **c)** branch off   **d)** criticize

_____ 22. **venerate**   **a)** protect   **b)** respect   **c)** make unfriendly   **d)** create

_____ 23. **propensity**   **a)** hobby   **b)** relation   **c)** job   **d)** tendency

_____ 24. **subsidize**   **a)** fall over   **b)** lift up   **c)** support financially   **d)** calculate

_____ 25. **dissident**   **a)** political supporter   **b)** candidate   **c)** visitor   **d)** one who disagrees

(Continues on next page)

_____ 26. **despondent**   a) tired   b) depressed   c) encouraged   d) well-behaved

_____ 27. **relinquish**   a) give up   b) criticize   c) gather   d) enjoy

_____ 28. **equivocate**   a) approve   b) dedicate   c) be vague on purpose   d) agree

_____ 29. **estrange**   a) enter   b) depart   c) make unsympathetic   d) state again

_____ 30. **scrupulous**   a) clean   b) careless   c) sociable   d) conscientious

_____ 31. **sham**   a) type   b) imitation   c) disturbance   d) belief

_____ 32. **impetuous**   a) impulsive   b) lazy   c) teasing   d) calm

_____ 33. **fortuitous**   a) having never happened before   b) brave   c) lucky   d) sad

_____ 34. **impeccable**   a) mischievous   b) unnecessary   c) built-in   d) faultless

_____ 35. **sensory**   a) in the mind   b) sensible   c) of the senses   d) on the surface

_____ 36. **predisposed**   a) against   b) reluctant to speak   c) tending beforehand   d) undecided

_____ 37. **fritter**   a) collect   b) wander   c) prove   d) waste

_____ 38. **reprehensible**   a) affordable   b) well-filled   c) blameworthy   d) admirable

_____ 39. **vicarious**   a) occasional   b) experienced indirectly   c) lively   d) inactive

_____ 40. **euphoric**   a) undecided   b) depressed   c) lonely   d) overjoyed

_____ 41. **sporadic**   a) tiny   b) particular   c) occasional   d) wasteful

_____ 42. **liaison**   a) accusation   b) plan   c) go-between   d) reference

_____ 43. **maudlin**   a) clever   b) sentimental   c) useful   d) kind

_____ 44. **squelch**   a) make fun of   b) stretch   c) suppress   d) approve

_____ 45. **lethargy**   a) highest point   b) strength   c) hunger   d) lack of energy

_____ 46. **ubiquitious**   a) existing everywhere   b) all-knowing   c) all-powerful   d) perfect

_____ 47. **solace**   a) sleep   b) comfort   c) relaxation   d) comedy

_____ 48. **zealot**   a) dictator   b) person devoted to a cause   c) casual person   d) leader

_____ 49. **detriment**   a) silence   b) something damaging   c) failure   d) outward behavior

_____ 50. **optimum**   a) heaviest   b) brightest   c) highest   d) most favorable

SCORE: (Number correct) _____ × 2 = _____ %

138

Name: _____

Unit Two: *Pretest*

In the space provided, write the letter of the choice that is closest in meaning to the **boldfaced** word.

_____ 1. **grievous**   a) funny   b) boring   c) impressive   d) causing pain

_____ 2. **attrition**   a) becoming fewer   b) connection   c) multiplying   d) imitation

_____ 3. **reticent**   a) forgiving   b) sad   c) reluctant to speak   d) contrary to reason

_____ 4. **robust**   a) extremely careful   b) vigorous   c) tall   d) loyal

_____ 5. **circumvent**   a) avoid   b) fail to notice   c) distribute   d) socialize

_____ 6. **sanction**   a) present   b) prepare   c) authorize   d) free from a difficulty

_____ 7. **inundate**   a) delay   b) flood   c) swallow   d) approve

_____ 8. **oblivious**   a) courageous   b) unaware   c) quiet   d) reliable

_____ 9. **inquisitive**   a) cheerful   b) nervous   c) curious   d) in pain

_____ 10. **depreciate**   a) set free   b) come forth   c) support   d) fall in value

_____ 11. **relegate**   a) bring back into use   b) assign to a lesser place   c) blend   d) raise

_____ 12. **bolster**   a) support   b) protect   c) protest   d) hide

_____ 13. **terse**   a) nervous   b) sad   c) brief   d) cool

_____ 14. **sedentary**   a) sitting   b) excessive   c) harmless   d) repeated

_____ 15. **indiscriminate**   a) self-centered   b) especially generous   c) painful   d) not choosing carefully

_____ 16. **nebulous**   a) contrary to reason   b) unclear   c) complete   d) calm

_____ 17. **prolific**   a) wise   b) overly cautious   c) fertile   d) holding firmly

_____ 18. **superfluous**   a) extra   b) unclear   c) useful   d) ahead

_____ 19. **exonerate**   a) encourage   b) condemn   c) hide   d) free from blame

_____ 20. **contingency**   a) contest   b) disapproval   c) theory   d) possibility

_____ 21. **reinstate**   a) make more severe   b) suggest   c) restore   d) visit

_____ 22. **egocentric**   a) unbalanced   b) circular   c) square   d) self-centered

_____ 23. **clandestine**   a) well-lit   b) secret   c) noble   d) harmless

_____ 24. **liability**   a) drawback   b) hatred   c) favor   d) indirect remark

_____ 25. **austere**   a) wealthy   b) plain   c) complex   d) far

(Continues on next page)

_____ 26. **notorious**   **a)** too bold   **b)** written   **c)** known widely but unfavorably
         d) lacking skill

_____ 27. **facsimile**   **a)** authority   **b)** copy   **c)** comparison   **d)** accusation

_____ 28. **perfunctory**   **a)** unenthusiastic   **b)** troubled   **c)** on time   **d)** well-prepared

_____ 29. **mesmerize**   **a)** wipe out   **b)** control   **c)** hypnotize   **d)** slow down

_____ 30. **provocative**   **a)** careful   **b)** able to improve   **c)** inconsistent   **d)** arousing interest

_____ 31. **esoteric**   **a)** public   **b)** uniform   **c)** well-written   **d)** understood by few

_____ 32. **metamorphosis**   **a)** journey   **b)** change   **c)** secret plot   **d)** fantasy

_____ 33. **verbose**   **a)** wordy   **b)** active   **c)** noisy   **d)** forceful

_____ 34. **connoisseur**   **a)** one who likes to suffer   **b)** egotist   **c)** expert   **d)** painter

_____ 35. **contrite**   **a)** indecent   **b)** sorry   **c)** lacking confidence   **d)** careful

_____ 36. **lucid**   **a)** clear   **b)** generous in forgiving   **c)** careful   **d)** bold

_____ 37. **conspiracy**   **a)** robbery   **b)** revenge   **c)** project   **d)** secret plot

_____ 38. **superficially**   **a)** strictly   **b)** carefully   **c)** totally   **d)** hastily

_____ 39. **plight**   **a)** difficult situation   **b)** minor weakness   **c)** environment   **d)** travel

_____ 40. **distraught**   **a)** educated   **b)** too noticeable   **c)** troubled   **d)** rehearsed

_____ 41. **cohesive**   **a)** slippery   **b)** risky   **c)** separating   **d)** sticking together

_____ 42. **vociferous**   **a)** vicious   **b)** talented   **c)** noisy   **d)** busy

_____ 43. **tenet**   **a)** principle   **b)** apartment dweller   **c)** disadvantage   **d)** peculiarity

_____ 44. **replete**   **a)** unclear   **b)** well-filled   **c)** finished   **d)** empty

_____ 45. **indigenous**   **a)** underground   **b)** native   **c)** following established rules   **d)** distant

_____ 46. **incongruous**   **a)** not noticeable   **b)** inborn   **c)** inconsistent   **d)** gathered together

_____ 47. **travesty**   **a)** mockery   **b)** copy   **c)** campaign   **d)** ill will

_____ 48. **grotesque**   **a)** harmless   **b)** unclear   **c)** dirty   **d)** distorted

_____ 49. **germane**   **a)** evil   **b)** chief   **c)** relevant   **d)** growing

_____ 50. **symmetrical**   **a)** extra   **b)** well-proportioned   **c)** uniform   **d)** colorful

SCORE: (Number correct) _____ × 2 = _____ %

Unit Two: *Posttest*

In the space provided, write the letter of the choice that is closest in meaning to the **boldfaced** word.

_____ 1. **nebulous**   a) contrary to reason   b) unclear   c) complete   d) calm

_____ 2. **egocentric**   a) self-centered   b) square   c) circular   d) unbalanced

_____ 3. **prolific**   a) holding firmly   b) fertile   c) overly cautious   d) wise

_____ 4. **grievous**   a) boring   b) impressive   c) funny   d) causing pain

_____ 5. **contrite**   a) careful   b) lacking confidence   c) sorry   d) indecent

_____ 6. **facsimile**   a) comparison   b) accusation   c) authority   d) copy

_____ 7. **attrition**   a) becoming fewer   b) imitation   c) multiplying   d) connection

_____ 8. **terse**   a) nervous   b) sad   c) brief   d) cool

_____ 9. **esoteric**   a) public   b) uniform   c) well-written   d) understood by few

_____ 10. **clandestine**   a) secret   b) well-lit   c) noble   d) harmless

_____ 11. **inquisitive**   a) cheerful   b) curious   c) nervous   d) in pain

_____ 12. **depreciate**   a) set free   b) come forth   c) fall in value   d) support

_____ 13. **contingency**   a) contest   b) disapproval   c) theory   d) possibility

_____ 14. **relegate**   a) blend   b) assign to a lesser place   c) bring back into use   d) raise

_____ 15. **verbose**   a) noisy   b) active   c) wordy   d) forceful

_____ 16. **indiscriminate**   a) painful   b) especially generous   c) self-centered   d) not choosing carefully

_____ 17. **exonerate**   a) encourage   b) hide   c) condemn   d) free from blame

_____ 18. **connoisseur**   a) one who likes to suffer   b) egotist   c) expert   d) painter

_____ 19. **reinstate**   a) restore   b) suggest   c) make more severe   d) visit

_____ 20. **superficially**   a) strictly   b) carefully   c) totally   d) hastily

_____ 21. **liability**   a) hatred   b) drawback   c) indirect remark   d) favor

_____ 22. **circumvent**   a) distribute   b) socialize   c) avoid   d) fail to notice

_____ 23. **bolster**   a) hide   b) protest   c) protect   d) support

_____ 24. **austere**   a) far   b) wealthy   c) plain   d) complex

_____ 25. **conspiracy**   a) secret plot   b) revenge   c) project   d) robbery

(Continues on next page)

_____ 26. **reticent**   **a)** forgiving   **b)** reluctant to speak   **c)** sad   **d)** contrary to reason

_____ 27. **distraught**   **a)** troubled   **b)** too noticeable   **c)** educated   **d)** rehearsed

_____ 28. **robust**   **a)** extremely careful   **b)** vigorous   **c)** tall   **d)** loyal

_____ 29. **notorious**   **a)** too bold   **b)** written   **c)** known widely but unfavorably   **d)** lacking skill

_____ 30. **mesmerize**   **a)** control   **b)** hypnotize   **c)** wipe out   **d)** slow down

_____ 31. **superfluous**   **a)** useful   **b)** unclear   **c)** extra   **d)** ahead

_____ 32. **provocative**   **a)** careful   **b)** arousing interest   **c)** inconsistent   **d)** able to improve

_____ 33. **metamorphosis**   **a)** secret plot   **b)** fantasy   **c)** journey   **d)** change

_____ 34. **sanction**   **a)** authorize   **b)** prepare   **c)** present   **d)** free from a difficulty

_____ 35. **sedentary**   **a)** excessive   **b)** sitting   **c)** repeated   **d)** harmless

_____ 36. **oblivious**   **a)** courageous   **b)** unaware   **c)** quiet   **d)** reliable

_____ 37. **lucid**   **a)** clear   **b)** generous in forgiving   **c)** careful   **d)** bold

_____ 38. **plight**   **a)** minor weakness   **b)** difficult situation   **c)** travel   **d)** environment

_____ 39. **inundate**   **a)** flood   **b)** delay   **c)** approve   **d)** swallow

_____ 40. **perfunctory**   **a)** unenthusiastic   **b)** on time   **c)** troubled   **d)** well-prepared

_____ 41. **grotesque**   **a)** harmless   **b)** unclear   **c)** dirty   **d)** distorted

_____ 42. **travesty**   **a)** campaign   **b)** ill will   **c)** mockery   **d)** copy

_____ 43. **tenet**   **a)** peculiarity   **b)** principle   **c)** disadvantage   **d)** apartment dweller

_____ 44. **symmetrical**   **a)** uniform   **b)** well-proportioned   **c)** extra   **d)** colorful

_____ 45. **indigenous**   **a)** native   **b)** underground   **c)** following established rules   **d)** distant

_____ 46. **germane**   **a)** evil   **b)** chief   **c)** relevant   **d)** growing

_____ 47. **cohesive**   **a)** sticking together   **b)** risky   **c)** separating   **d)** slippery

_____ 48. **incongruous**   **a)** not noticeable   **b)** gathered together   **c)** inconsistent   **d)** inborn

_____ 49. **replete**   **a)** empty   **b)** unclear   **c)** well-filled   **d)** finished

_____ 50. **vociferous**   **a)** busy   **b)** talented   **c)** noisy   **d)** vicious

SCORE: (Number correct) _____ × 2 = _____ %

Name: _____

Unit Three: *Pretest*

In the space provided, write the letter of the choice that is closest in meaning to the **boldfaced** word.

_____ 1. **encompass**   **a)** include   **b)** draw   **c)** separate   **d)** purchase

_____ 2. **stringent**   **a)** dry   **b)** strict   **c)** loose   **d)** long

_____ 3. **adept**   **a)** forceful   **b)** exact   **c)** balanced   **d)** skilled

_____ 4. **eradicate**   **a)** wipe out   **b)** scold   **c)** restore   **d)** hold onto

_____ 5. **sordid**   **a)** slow   **b)** unprepared   **c)** morally low   **d)** injured

_____ 6. **entrepreneur**   **a)** lawyer   **b)** business investor   **c)** college educator   **d)** police officer

_____ 7. **stint**   **a)** period of work   **b)** sequence of events   **c)** exercise   **d)** stunt

_____ 8. **presumptuous**   **a)** indecent   **b)** lacking standards of selection   **c)** nervous   **d)** too bold

_____ 9. **meticulous**   **a)** broken-down   **b)** curious   **c)** careful and exact   **d)** irregular

_____ 10. **repugnant**   **a)** scornful   **b)** offensive   **c)** harmful   **d)** impressive

_____ 11. **foible**   **a)** character flaw   **b)** ambition   **c)** noble quality   **d)** accident

_____ 12. **magnanimous**   **a)** nameless   **b)** proud   **c)** generous in forgiving   **d)** lacking standards

_____ 13. **exhort**   **a)** strongly urge   **b)** travel   **c)** escape   **d)** hint

_____ 14. **rancor**   **a)** pride   **b)** fear   **c)** strong desire   **d)** ill will

_____ 15. **innocuous**   **a)** delightful   **b)** harmless   **c)** dangerous   **d)** disappointing

_____ 16. **masochist**   **a)** one who likes to suffer   **b)** egotist   **c)** fan
   d) one who expects the worst

_____ 17. **deplore**   **a)** command   **b)** disapprove of   **c)** encourage   **d)** prevent

_____ 18. **atrophy**   **a)** weaken   **b)** reward   **c)** expand   **d)** strengthen

_____ 19. **unprecedented**   **a)** overly noticeable   **b)** without authority   **c)** unexpected
   d) having never happened before

_____ 20. **mitigate**   **a)** make worse   **b)** make less severe   **c)** remove   **d)** hide

_____ 21. **deprivation**   **a)** lack of a basic necessity   **b)** depth   **c)** disapproval   **d)** privacy

_____ 22. **imperative**   **a)** thoughtful   **b)** more harmful than at first evident   **c)** likely   **d)** necessary

_____ 23. **objective**   **a)** useful   **b)** poorly supported   **c)** based on facts   **d)** emotional

_____ 24. **exacerbate**   **a)** make worse   **b)** remove   **c)** bring closer   **d)** strengthen

_____ 25. **rejuvenate**   **a)** set free   **b)** grow   **c)** refresh   **d)** make easier

(Continues on next page)

_____ 26. **exorbitant**   **a)** absorbent   **b)** excessive   **c)** quarrelsome   **d)** well-timed

_____ 27. **decorum**   **a)** correctness in manners   **b)** talent   **c)** repayment   **d)** indirect remark

_____ 28. **facilitate**   **a)** approve   **b)** serve   **c)** make easier   **d)** clear from blame

_____ 29. **synchronize**   **a)** spread throughout   **b)** separate   **c)** reduce   **d)** cause to occur together

_____ 30. **espouse**   **a)** prolong   **b)** support   **c)** delay   **d)** marry

_____ 31. **extricate**   **a)** run away   **b)** confuse   **c)** free from difficulty   **d)** complicate

_____ 32. **exhilaration**   **a)** freedom   **b)** thirst   **c)** wisdom   **d)** gladness

_____ 33. **proficient**   **a)** proud   **b)** wise   **c)** skilled   **d)** well-known

_____ 34. **annihilate**   **a)** guide   **b)** misunderstand   **c)** carry out   **d)** destroy

_____ 35. **criterion**   **a)** philosophy   **b)** standard for judgment   **c)** political theory   **d)** state of mind

_____ 36. **vindicate**   **a)** clear from blame   **b)** ridicule   **c)** escape   **d)** formally question

_____ 37. **emanate**   **a)** go above   **b)** run through   **c)** go down   **d)** come forth

_____ 38. **holistic**   **a)** democratic   **b)** secretive   **c)** emphasizing the whole   **d)** little-known

_____ 39. **subversive**   **a)** being a servant   **b)** acting to overthrow   **c)** willing   **d)** planning to build

_____ 40. **analogy**   **a)** original   **b)** sample   **c)** summary   **d)** comparison

_____ 41. **standardize**   **a)** allow   **b)** simplify   **c)** limit   **d)** make uniform

_____ 42. **homogeneous**   **a)** pure   **b)** smooth   **c)** uniform   **d)** separate

_____ 43. **recrimination**   **a)** environment   **b)** ambition   **c)** robbery   **d)** countercharge

_____ 44. **flamboyant**   **a)** talkative   **b)** courageous   **c)** showy   **d)** exact

_____ 45. **panacea**   **a)** cure-all   **b)** state of uncertainty   **c)** reward   **d)** false medicine

_____ 46. **utilitarian**   **a)** useless   **b)** built-in   **c)** practical   **d)** beautiful

_____ 47. **orthodox**   **a)** firm   **b)** favorable   **c)** traditional   **d)** new

_____ 48. **tenuous**   **a)** weak   **b)** boring   **c)** showy   **d)** well-supported

_____ 49. **staunch**   **a)** loyal   **b)** in doubt   **c)** proud   **d)** easy to handle

_____ 50. **placebo**   **a)** standard   **b)** harmless substance used as medicine   **c)** wish   **d)** the whole

SCORE: (Number correct) _____ × 2 = _____ %

Unit Three: *Posttest*

In the space provided, write the letter of the choice that is closest in meaning to the **boldfaced** word.

____ 1. **decorum**   a) indirect remark   b) correctness in manners   c) repayment   d) talent

____ 2. **encompass**   a) separate   b) draw   c) include   d) purchase

____ 3. **vindicate**   a) ridicule   b) escape   c) clear from blame   d) formally question

____ 4. **analogy**   a) sample   b) original   c) comparison   d) summary

____ 5. **objective**   a) poorly supported   b) useful   c) emotional   d) based on facts

____ 6. **meticulous**   a) irregular   b) broken-down   c) curious   d) careful and exact

____ 7. **annihilate**   a) destroy   b) misunderstand   c) carry out   d) guide

____ 8. **repugnant**   a) impressive   b) harmful   c) offensive   d) scornful

____ 9. **exacerbate**   a) bring closer   b) strengthen   c) make worse   d) remove

____ 10. **emanate**   a) go above   b) come forth   c) go down   d) run through

____ 11. **foible**   a) noble quality   b) ambition   c) character flaw   d) accident

____ 12. **magnanimous**   a) nameless   b) generous in forgiving   c) proud   d) lacking standards

____ 13. **exhort**   a) hint   b) strongly urge   c) travel   d) escape

____ 14. **stringent**   a) long   b) loose   c) strict   d) dry

____ 15. **holistic**   a) emphasizing the whole   b) secretive   c) democratic   d) little-known

____ 16. **rancor**   a) ill will   b) fear   c) strong desire   d) pride

____ 17. **innocuous**   a) delightful   b) harmless   c) dangerous   d) disappointing

____ 18. **facilitate**   a) make easier   b) serve   c) approve   d) clear from blame

____ 19. **presumptuous**   a) indecent   b) lacking standards of selection   c) nervous   d) too bold

____ 20. **unprecedented**   a) overly noticeable   b) without authority   c) unexpected
d) having never happened before

____ 21. **mitigate**   a) make less severe   b) make worse   c) hide   d) remove

____ 22. **subversive**   a) being a servant   b) willing   c) planning to build   d) acting to overthrow

____ 23. **adept**   a) forceful   b) exact   c) skilled   d) balanced

____ 24. **atrophy**   a) strengthen   b) reward   c) expand   d) weaken

____ 25. **sordid**   a) slow   b) morally low   c) unprepared   d) injured

(Continues on next page)

_____ 26. **deprivation**   **a)** disapproval   **b)** depth   **c)** lack of a basic necessity   **d)** privacy

_____ 27. **imperative**   **a)** thoughtful   **b)** more harmful than at first evident   **c)** likely   **d)** necessary

_____ 28. **extricate**   **a)** run away   **b)** free from difficulty   **c)** confuse   **d)** complicate

_____ 29. **exhilaration**   **a)** gladness   **b)** freedom   **c)** thirst   **d)** wisdom

_____ 30. **masochist**   **a)** one who expects the worst   **b)** egotist   **c)** fan   **d)** one who likes to suffer

_____ 31. **rejuvenate**   **a)** set free   **b)** refresh   **c)** grow   **d)** make easier

_____ 32. **eradicate**   **a)** wipe out   **b)** scold   **c)** restore   **d)** hold onto

_____ 33. **exorbitant**   **a)** excessive   **b)** absorbent   **c)** quarrelsome   **d)** well-timed

_____ 34. **synchronize**   **a)** cause to occur together   **b)** separate   **c)** reduce   **d)** spread throughout

_____ 35. **deplore**   **a)** command   **b)** encourage   **c)** disapprove of   **d)** prevent

_____ 36. **stint**   **a)** stunt   **b)** sequence of events   **c)** exercise   **d)** period of work

_____ 37. **espouse**   **a)** prolong   **b)** support   **c)** delay   **d)** marry

_____ 38. **proficient**   **a)** wise   **b)** proud   **c)** well-known   **d)** skilled

_____ 39. **entrepreneur**   **a)** business investor   **b)** lawyer   **c)** college educator   **d)** police officer

_____ 40. **criterion**   **a)** philosophy   **b)** political theory   **c)** standard for judgment   **d)** state of mind

_____ 41. **staunch**   **a)** easy to handle   **b)** loyal   **c)** proud   **d)** in doubt

_____ 42. **flamboyant**   **a)** showy   **b)** exact   **c)** talkative   **d)** courageous

_____ 43. **orthodox**   **a)** new   **b)** favorable   **c)** traditional   **d)** firm

_____ 44. **placebo**   **a)** wish   **b)** harmless substance used as medicine   **c)** the whole   **d)** standard

_____ 45. **panacea**   **a)** reward   **b)** state of uncertainty   **c)** cure-all   **d)** false medicine

_____ 46. **utilitarian**   **a)** built-in   **b)** practical   **c)** useless   **d)** beautiful

_____ 47. **tenuous**   **a)** showy   **b)** boring   **c)** weak   **d)** well-supported

_____ 48. **homogeneous**   **a)** separate   **b)** uniform   **c)** smooth   **d)** pure

_____ 49. **recrimination**   **a)** environment   **b)** robbery   **c)** countercharge   **d)** ambition

_____ 50. **standardize**   **a)** make uniform   **b)** allow   **c)** simplify   **d)** limit

SCORE: (Number correct) _____ × 2 = _____ %

Unit Four: *Pretest*

In the space provided, write the letter of the choice that is closest in meaning to the **boldfaced** word.

_____ 1. **forestall**   a) prevent   b) predict   c) rent   d) hurry

_____ 2. **retribution**   a) donation   b) looking back   c) evil   d) punishment

_____ 3. **interrogate**   a) put into practice   b) invent   c) formally question   d) blame sharply

_____ 4. **obsequious**   a) too anxious to serve   b) harmful   c) overly ambitious   d) tactful

_____ 5. **insinuate**   a) demand   b) state   c) deny   d) hint

_____ 6. **disparity**   a) sadness   b) inequality   c) blemish   d) similarity

_____ 7. **omnipotent**   a) all-powerful   b) forgiving   c) altogether   d) cure-all

_____ 8. **opportune**   a) generous   b) more important   c) well-timed   d) belittling

_____ 9. **fastidious**   a) not planned   b) attentive to details   c) quick   d) inferior

_____ 10. **heinous**   a) evil   b) mischievous   c) stubborn   d) depressed

_____ 11. **intuition**   a) inequality   b) instinct   c) punishment   d) wish

_____ 12. **implement**   a) encourage   b) carry out   c) insult   d) prevent

_____ 13. **discreet**   a) tactful   b) intense   c) knowledgeable   d) open

_____ 14. **inference**   a) rumor   b) meeting   c) assumption   d) speech

_____ 15. **complement**   a) praise   b) sin   c) make fun of   d) add what is needed

_____ 16. **impromptu**   a) forceful   b) unplanned   c) delayed   d) on time

_____ 17. **transgress**   a) follow   b) round out   c) travel   d) sin

_____ 18. **extenuating**   a) excusing   b) inferior   c) forceful   d) overly noticeable

_____ 19. **fraudulent**   a) intense   b) dishonest   c) creative   d) dangerous

_____ 20. **redeem**   a) show to be true   b) restore to favor   c) select   d) ignore

_____ 21. **vehement**   a) forceful   b) wicked   c) rude   d) calm

_____ 22. **auspicious**   a) threatening   b) lazy   c) favorable   d) not trusting

_____ 23. **subordinate**   a) irritating   b) inferior   c) quiet   d) chief

_____ 24. **rebuke**   a) compromise   b) fix   c) scold   d) admire

_____ 25. **validate**   a) dislike   b) prove   c) discover   d) notice

(Continues on next page)

_____ 26. **macabre**   **a)** frightful   **b)** depressed   **c)** cheerful   **d)** common

_____ 27. **quandary**   **a)** wild disorder   **b)** peak   **c)** state of uncertainty   **d)** opposite

_____ 28. **fabricate**   **a)** misinterpret   **b)** put away   **c)** clothe   **d)** invent

_____ 29. **derogatory**   **a)** healthful   **b)** unable to be repaired   **c)** belittling   **d)** proud

_____ 30. **turbulent**   **a)** ambitious   **b)** wildly disturbed   **c)** mixed   **d)** fast

_____ 31. **impending**   **a)** about to happen   **b)** illegal   **c)** historical   **d)** usual

_____ 32. **paramount**   **a)** dramatic   **b)** disturbed   **c)** unknown   **d)** chief

_____ 33. **emulate**   **a)** be tardy   **b)** misunderstand   **c)** imitate   **d)** prepare

_____ 34. **abrasive**   **a)** rough   **b)** friendly   **c)** mild   **d)** foolish

_____ 35. **docile**   **a)** violent   **b)** early   **c)** easy to discipline   **d)** irritating

_____ 36. **antithesis**   **a)** disorder   **b)** theory   **c)** effect   **d)** opposite

_____ 37. **incapacitate**   **a)** disable   **b)** allow   **c)** increase   **d)** fight

_____ 38. **admonish**   **a)** imitate   **b)** scold   **c)** publicize   **d)** frighten

_____ 39. **prognosis**   **a)** hope   **b)** memory   **c)** opposite   **d)** prediction

_____ 40. **tumult**   **a)** series   **b)** uncertainty   **c)** uproar   **d)** scolding

_____ 41. **permeate**   **a)** imitate   **b)** spread throughout   **c)** pollute   **d)** deny the authority of

_____ 42. **insidious**   **a)** more harmful than at first evident   **b)** sly   **c)** more noticeable than desired   **d)** slow

_____ 43. **flout**   **a)** beat   **b)** surprise   **c)** suggest   **d)** make fun of

_____ 44. **obtrusive**   **a)** about to happen   **b)** too near   **c)** undesirably noticeable   **d)** shocking

_____ 45. **expedite**   **a)** speed up   **b)** explore   **c)** sadden   **d)** elect

_____ 46. **innuendo**   **a)** threat   **b)** challenge   **c)** impression   **d)** indirect remark

_____ 47. **deride**   **a)** repair   **b)** take   **c)** ridicule   **d)** ease

_____ 48. **misconstrue**   **a)** misunderstand   **b)** dislike   **c)** reject   **d)** admire

_____ 49. **culmination**   **a)** country   **b)** highest point   **c)** edge   **d)** bottom

_____ 50. **hierarchy**   **a)** theory   **b)** employment   **c)** ranking   **d)** highest point

---

SCORE: (Number correct) _____ × 2 = _____ %

Unit Four: *Posttest*

In the space provided, write the letter of the choice that is closest in meaning to the **boldfaced** word.

_____ 1. **redeem**   **a)** show to be true   **b)** restore to favor   **c)** select   **d)** ignore

_____ 2. **forestall**   **a)** rent   **b)** predict   **c)** prevent   **d)** hurry

_____ 3. **intuition**   **a)** inequality   **b)** punishment   **c)** instinct   **d)** wish

_____ 4. **complement**   **a)** sin   **b)** praise   **c)** add what is needed   **d)** make fun of

_____ 5. **interrogate**   **a)** put into practice   **b)** formally question   **c)** invent   **d)** blame sharply

_____ 6. **prognosis**   **a)** memory   **b)** hope   **c)** prediction   **d)** opposite

_____ 7. **vehement**   **a)** wicked   **b)** forceful   **c)** calm   **d)** rude

_____ 8. **auspicious**   **a)** threatening   **b)** lazy   **c)** not trusting   **d)** favorable

_____ 9. **disparity**   **a)** sadness   **b)** similarity   **c)** inequality   **d)** blemish

_____ 10. **heinous**   **a)** depressed   **b)** evil   **c)** mischievous   **d)** stubborn

_____ 11. **docile**   **a)** easy to discipline   **b)** early   **c)** violent   **d)** irritating

_____ 12. **impromptu**   **a)** forceful   **b)** on time   **c)** delayed   **d)** unplanned

_____ 13. **tumult**   **a)** scolding   **b)** uproar   **c)** uncertainty   **d)** series

_____ 14. **fraudulent**   **a)** intense   **b)** creative   **c)** dishonest   **d)** dangerous

_____ 15. **subordinate**   **a)** inferior   **b)** irritating   **c)** chief   **d)** quiet

_____ 16. **abrasive**   **a)** foolish   **b)** rough   **c)** friendly   **d)** mild

_____ 17. **obsequious**   **a)** overly ambitious   **b)** harmful   **c)** too anxious to serve   **d)** tactful

_____ 18. **antithesis**   **a)** disorder   **b)** theory   **c)** opposite   **d)** effect

_____ 19. **incapacitate**   **a)** allow   **b)** disable   **c)** increase   **d)** fight

_____ 20. **implement**   **a)** carry out   **b)** encourage   **c)** insult   **d)** prevent

_____ 21. **insinuate**   **a)** demand   **b)** state   **c)** deny   **d)** hint

_____ 22. **inference**   **a)** rumor   **b)** assumption   **c)** meeting   **d)** speech

_____ 23. **rebuke**   **a)** compromise   **b)** scold   **c)** fix   **d)** admire

_____ 24. **impending**   **a)** illegal   **b)** about to happen   **c)** historical   **d)** usual

_____ 25. **validate**   **a)** dislike   **b)** prove   **c)** discover   **d)** notice

(Continues on next page)

_____ 26. **omnipotent**   a) cure-all   b) forgiving   c) all-powerful   d) altogether

_____ 27. **admonish**   a) publicize   b) frighten   c) imitate   d) scold

_____ 28. **fastidious**   a) not planned   b) attentive to details   c) quick   d) inferior

_____ 29. **macabre**   a) depressed   b) frightful   c) common   d) cheerful

_____ 30. **discreet**   a) open   b) knowledgeable   c) intense   d) tactful

_____ 31. **quandary**   a) state of uncertainty   b) peak   c) wild disorder   d) opposite

_____ 32. **opportune**   a) well-timed   b) more important   c) generous   d) belittling

_____ 33. **derogatory**   a) healthful   b) unable to be repaired   c) belittling   d) proud

_____ 34. **turbulent**   a) wildly disturbed   b) ambitious   c) mixed   d) fast

_____ 35. **transgress**   a) round out   b) follow   c) sin   d) travel

_____ 36. **extenuating**   a) overly noticeable   b) excusing   c) inferior   d) forceful

_____ 37. **paramount**   a) disturbed   b) dramatic   c) chief   d) unknown

_____ 38. **fabricate**   a) put away   b) misinterpret   c) invent   d) clothe

_____ 39. **retribution**   a) looking back   b) donation   c) punishment   d) evil

_____ 40. **emulate**   a) be tardy   b) imitate   c) misunderstand   d) prepare

_____ 41. **hierarchy**   a) theory   b) employment   c) ranking   d) highest point

_____ 42. **culmination**   a) country   b) highest point   c) edge   d) bottom

_____ 43. **deride**   a) repair   b) take   c) ease   d) ridicule

_____ 44. **insidious**   a) sly   b) more harmful than at first evident   c) more noticeable than desired   d) slow

_____ 45. **innuendo**   a) impression   b) challenge   c) threat   d) indirect remark

_____ 46. **obtrusive**   a) shocking   b) too near   c) undesirably noticeable   d) about to happen

_____ 47. **permeate**   a) imitate   b) spread throughout   c) deny the authority of   d) pollute

_____ 48. **misconstrue**   a) dislike   b) misunderstand   c) reject   d) admire

_____ 49. **expedite**   a) elect   b) speed up   c) explore   d) sadden

_____ 50. **flout**   a) beat   b) surprise   c) make fun of   d) suggest

SCORE: (Number correct) _____ × 2 = _____ %

Pretest / Posttest

ANSWER SHEET

1. _____	26. _____	51. _____	76. _____
2. _____	27. _____	52. _____	77. _____
3. _____	28. _____	53. _____	78. _____
4. _____	29. _____	54. _____	79. _____
5. _____	30. _____	55. _____	80. _____
6. _____	31. _____	56. _____	81. _____
7. _____	32. _____	57. _____	82. _____
8. _____	33. _____	58. _____	83. _____
9. _____	34. _____	59. _____	84. _____
10. _____	35. _____	60. _____	85. _____
11. _____	36. _____	61. _____	86. _____
12. _____	37. _____	62. _____	87. _____
13. _____	38. _____	63. _____	88. _____
14. _____	39. _____	64. _____	89. _____
15. _____	40. _____	65. _____	90. _____
16. _____	41. _____	66. _____	91. _____
17. _____	42. _____	67. _____	92. _____
18. _____	43. _____	68. _____	93. _____
19. _____	44. _____	69. _____	94. _____
20. _____	45. _____	70. _____	95. _____
21. _____	46. _____	71. _____	96. _____
22. _____	47. _____	72. _____	97. _____
23. _____	48. _____	73. _____	98. _____
24. _____	49. _____	74. _____	99. _____
25. _____	50. _____	75. _____	100. _____

Pretest

ANSWER KEY

1. d	26. a	51. a	76. a
2. a	27. c	52. b	77. d
3. b	28. a	53. a	78. d
4. d	29. b	54. c	79. b
5. c	30. b	55. d	80. c
6. a	31. c	56. c	81. b
7. d	32. b	57. c	82. a
8. d	33. a	58. a	83. b
9. a	34. c	59. b	84. d
10. d	35. a	60. a	85. b
11. a	36. a	61. b	86. d
12. d	37. d	62. a	87. a
13. b	38. d	63. d	88. a
14. c	39. b	64. b	89. c
15. a	40. a	65. a	90. c
16. d	41. b	66. b	91. a
17. d	42. a	67. c	92. d
18. d	43. d	68. d	93. b
19. a	44. d	69. c	94. a
20. c	45. b	70. d	95. d
21. a	46. a	71. c	96. c
22. b	47. c	72. d	97. d
23. d	48. b	73. b	98. a
24. c	49. a	74. a	99. a
25. a	50. c	75. b	100. d

Posttest

ANSWER KEY

1. a	26. c	51. c	76. c
2. b	27. a	52. c	77. c
3. a	28. c	53. d	78. c
4. c	29. d	54. a	79. b
5. b	30. a	55. c	80. d
6. d	31. b	56. b	81. c
7. b	32. d	57. b	82. b
8. d	33. b	58. c	83. d
9. b	34. c	59. b	84. c
10. d	35. d	60. a	85. b
11. a	36. c	61. d	86. a
12. b	37. b	62. d	87. d
13. d	38. c	63. a	88. b
14. c	39. d	64. d	89. b
15. d	40. c	65. d	90. b
16. b	41. b	66. b	91. b
17. a	42. a	67. b	92. b
18. d	43. c	68. a	93. a
19. b	44. b	69. d	94. a
20. a	45. d	70. a	95. c
21. c	46. b	71. d	96. b
22. c	47. b	72. a	97. c
23. c	48. b	73. a	98. c
24. b	49. a	74. c	99. c
25. d	50. a	75. c	100. b

Answers to the Pretests and Posttests:

ADVANCING VOCABULARY SKILLS, SHORT VERSION

Unit One		Unit Two		Unit Three		Unit Four	
Pretest	*Posttest*	*Pretest*	*Posttest*	*Pretest*	*Posttest*	*Pretest*	*Posttest*
1. c	1. a	1. d	1. b	1. a	1. b	1. a	1. b
2. d	2. a	2. a	2. a	2. b	2. c	2. d	2. c
3. a	3. b	3. c	3. b	3. d	3. c	3. c	3. c
4. c	4. b	4. b	4. d	4. a	4. c	4. a	4. c
5. b	5. b	5. a	5. c	5. c	5. d	5. d	5. b
6. d	6. a	6. c	6. d	6. b	6. d	6. b	6. c
7. a	7. c	7. b	7. a	7. a	7. a	7. a	7. b
8. c	8. c	8. b	8. c	8. d	8. c	8. c	8. d
9. a	9. a	9. c	9. d	9. c	9. c	9. b	9. b
10. d	10. b	10. d	10. a	10. b	10. b	10. a	10. b
11. d	11. d	11. b	11. b	11. a	11. c	11. b	11. a
12. a	12. b	12. a	12. c	12. c	12. b	12. b	12. d
13. d	13. b	13. c	13. d	13. a	13. b	13. a	13. b
14. a	14. b	14. a	14. b	14. d	14. c	14. c	14. c
15. c	15. d	15. d	15. c	15. b	15. a	15. d	15. a
16. b	16. b	16. b	16. b	16. a	16. a	16. b	16. b
17. b	17. b	17. c	17. d	17. b	17. b	17. d	17. c
18. a	18. d	18. a	18. c	18. a	18. a	18. a	18. c
19. d	19. a	19. d	19. a	19. d	19. d	19. b	19. b
20. d	20. a	20. d	20. d	20. b	20. d	20. b	20. a
21. b	21. d	21. c	21. b	21. a	21. a	21. a	21. d
22. a	22. b	22. d	22. c	22. d	22. d	22. c	22. a
23. c	23. d	23. b	23. d	23. c	23. c	23. b	23. b
24. a	24. c	24. a	24. c	24. a	24. d	24. c	24. b
25. d	25. d	25. b	25. a	25. c	25. b	25. b	25. b
26. c	26. b	26. c	26. b	26. b	26. c	26. a	26. c
27. d	27. a	27. b	27. a	27. a	27. d	27. c	27. d
28. d	28. c	28. a	28. b	28. c	28. b	28. d	28. b
29. b	29. c	29. c	29. c	29. d	29. a	29. c	29. b
30. a	30. d	30. d	30. b	30. b	30. d	30. b	30. d
31. c	31. b	31. d	31. c	31. c	31. b	31. a	31. a
32. b	32. a	32. b	32. b	32. d	32. a	32. d	32. a
33. a	33. c	33. a	33. d	33. c	33. a	33. c	33. c
34. d	34. d	34. c	34. a	34. d	34. a	34. a	34. a
35. b	35. c	35. b	35. b	35. b	35. c	35. c	35. c
36. a	36. c	36. a	36. b	36. a	36. d	36. d	36. b
37. d	37. d	37. d	37. a	37. d	37. b	37. a	37. c
38. c	38. c	38. d	38. b	38. c	38. d	38. b	38. c
39. c	39. b	39. a	39. a	39. b	39. a	39. d	39. c
40. a	40. d	40. c	40. a	40. d	40. c	40. c	40. b
41. b	41. c	41. d	41. d	41. d	41. b	41. b	41. c
42. a	42. c	42. c	42. c	42. c	42. a	42. a	42. b
43. c	43. b	43. a	43. b	43. d	43. c	43. d	43. d
44. b	44. c	44. b	44. b	44. c	44. b	44. c	44. b
45. c	45. d	45. b	45. a	45. a	45. c	45. a	45. d
46. d	46. a	46. c	46. c	46. c	46. b	46. d	46. c
47. b	47. b	47. a	47. a	47. c	47. c	47. c	47. b
48. a	48. b	48. d	48. c	48. a	48. b	48. a	48. b
49. c	49. b	49. c	49. c	49. a	49. c	49. b	49. b
50. b	50. d	50. b	50. c	50. b	50. a	50. c	50. c

Answers to the Activities in
ADVANCING VOCABULARY SKILLS, SHORT VERSION

Chapter 1 (Apartment Problems)

Ten Words in Context		Matching Words/Defs		Sentence Check 1		Sentence Check 2	Final Check	
1. c	6. a	1. 4	6. 2	1. c	6. g	1–2. c, h	1. e	6. i
2. a	7. b	2. 7	7. 8	2. a	7. j	3–4. d, b	2. c	7. j
3. b	8. a	3. 6	8. 5	3. b	8. f	5–6. f, a	3. a	8. d
4. c	9. a	4. 1	9. 3	4. e	9. i	7–8. e, g	4. b	9. h
5. b	10. b	5. 10	10. 9	5. h	10. d	9–10. i, j	5. g	10. f

Chapter 2 (Hardly a Loser)

Ten Words in Context		Matching Words/Defs		Sentence Check 1		Sentence Check 2	Final Check	
1. c	6. a	1. 3	6. 8	1. f	6. g	1–2. f, a	1. c	6. d
2. b	7. a	2. 6	7. 9	2. b	7. a	3–4. g, d	2. f	7. a
3. c	8. b	3. 4	8. 2	3. c	8. h	5–6. i, b	3. g	8. j
4. c	9. b	4. 1	9. 5	4. j	9. e	7–8. c, e	4. h	9. i
5. a	10. a	5. 10	10. 7	5. i	10. d	9–10. h, j	5. b	10. e

Chapter 3 (Grandfather at the Art Museum)

Ten Words in Context		Matching Words/Defs		Sentence Check 1		Sentence Check 2	Final Check	
1. a	6. a	1. 7	6. 3	1. h	6. c	1–2. h, i	1. e	6. h
2. a	7. b	2. 8	7. 10	2. i	7. g	3–4. g, b	2. b	7. j
3. b	8. a	3. 1	8. 4	3. j	8. b	5–6. j, c	3. g	8. d
4. c	9. b	4. 6	9. 5	4. e	9. a	7–8. d, f	4. c	9. f
5. c	10. a	5. 2	10. 9	5. d	10. f	9–10. a, e	5. a	10. i

Chapter 4 (My Brother's Mental Illness)

Ten Words in Context		Matching Words/Defs		Sentence Check 1		Sentence Check 2	Final Check	
1. a	6. a	1. 7	6. 3	1. h	6. c	1–2. h, i	1. e	6. h
2. a	7. b	2. 8	7. 10	2. i	7. g	3–4. g, b	2. b	7. j
3. b	8. a	3. 1	8. 4	3. j	8. b	5–6. j, c	3. g	8. d
4. c	9. b	4. 6	9. 5	4. e	9. a	7–8. d, f	4. c	9. f
5. a	10. a	5. 2	10. 9	5. d	10. f	9–10. a, e	5. a	10. i

Chapter 5 (A Phony Friend)

Ten Words in Context		Matching Words/Defs		Sentence Check 1		Sentence Check 2	Final Check	
1. b	6. b	1. 6	6. 1	1. i	6. h	1–2. f, a	1. d	6. j
2. a	7. a	2. 7	7. 3	2. c	7. f	3–4. i, d	2. f	7. c
3. a	8. a	3. 2	8. 10	3. e	8. b	5–6. e, j	3. e	8. b
4. c	9. c	4. 9	9. 5	4. j	9. d	7–8. b, g	4. i	9. h
5. b	10. b	5. 4	10. 8	5. g	10. a	9–10. c, h	5. a	10. g

Chapter 6 (Coco the Gorilla)

Ten Words in Context		Matching Words/Defs		Sentence Check 1		Sentence Check 2	Final Check	
1. b	6. b	1. 9	6. 3	1. f	6. c	1–2. e, f	1. a	6. j
2. a	7. b	2. 5	7. 10	2. j	7. d	3–4. i, a	2. c	7. h
3. a	8. c	3. 2	8. 1	3. i	8. e	5–6. d, g	3. f	8. b
4. c	9. a	4. 7	9. 4	4. h	9. a	7–8. h, b	4. i	9. e
5. a	10. c	5. 8	10. 6	5. b	10. g	9–10. j, c	5. g	10. d

Chapter 7 (Our Annual Garage Sale)

Ten Words in Context		Matching Words/Defs		Sentence Check 1		Sentence Check 2	Final Check	
1. c	6. a	1. 2	6. 1	1. j	6. g	1–2. b, e	1. f	6. g
2. b	7. b	2. 3	7. 4	2. c	7. f	3–4. f, h	2. a	7. j
3. c	8. c	3. 8	8. 7	3. a	8. e	5–6. d, a	3. h	8. c
4. c	9. a	4. 9	9. 5	4. b	9. h	7–8. g, i	4. i	9. d
5. a	10. c	5. 10	10. 6	5. i	10. d	9–10. j, c	5. e	10. b

Chapter 8 (My Large Family)

Ten Words in Context		Matching Words/Defs		Sentence Check 1		Sentence Check 2	Final Check	
1. c	6. b	1. 7	6. 10	1. e	6. d	1–2. e, f	1. f	6. c
2. a	7. b	2. 1	7. 8	2. i	7. h	3–4. d, i	2. h	7. g
3. a	8. a	3. 5	8. 4	3. g	8. a	5–6. h, j	3. j	8. a
4. c	9. c	4. 2	9. 3	4. f	9. j	7–8. c, g	4. i	9. e
5. a	10. a	5. 6	10. 9	5. b	10. c	9–10. a, b	5. d	10. b

Chapter 9 (A Costume Party)

Ten Words in Context		Matching Words/Defs		Sentence Check 1		Sentence Check 2	Final Check	
1. b	6. a	1. 5	6. 9	1. j	6. b	1–2. d, j	1. h	6. e
2. a	7. a	2. 6	7. 3	2. g	7. e	3–4. g, a	2. a	7. b
3. c	8. a	3. 10	8. 2	3. i	8. h	5–6. i, e	3. i	8. f
4. a	9. c	4. 8	9. 1	4. d	9. a	7–8. h, f	4. c	9. j
5. b	10. a	5. 7	10. 4	5. c	10. f	9–10. c, b	5. g	10. d

Chapter 10 (The Missing Painting)

Ten Words in Context		Matching Words/Defs		Sentence Check 1		Sentence Check 2	Final Check	
1. b	6. a	1. 4	6. 3	1. c	6. b	1–2. d, b	1. d	6. i
2. a	7. c	2. 10	7. 9	2. g	7. e	3–4. a, h	2. a	7. h
3. c	8. b	3. 8	8. 1	3. i	8. d	5–6. c, g	3. f	8. b
4. a	9. c	4. 5	9. 7	4. a	9. f	7–8. e, i	4. g	9. e
5. b	10. b	5. 6	10. 2	5. j	10. h	9–10. j, f	5. j	10. c

Chapter 11 (An Ohio Girl in New York)

Ten Words in Context		Matching Words/Defs		Sentence Check 1		Sentence Check 2	Final Check	
1. a	6. a	1. 3	6. 10	1. f	6. e	1–2. c, a	1. i	6. c
2. c	7. b	2. 1	7. 8	2. a	7. b	3–4. i, j	2. g	7. f
3. a	8. a	3. 9	8. 2	3. g	8. j	5–6. d, g	3. e	8. h
4. c	9. a	4. 6	9. 5	4. i	9. c	7–8. f, b	4. j	9. b
5. b	10. c	5. 4	10. 7	5. d	10. h	9–10. h, e	5. a	10. d

Chapter 12 (How Neat Is Neat Enough)

Ten Words in Context		Matching Words/Defs		Sentence Check 1		Sentence Check 2	Final Check	
1. c	6. b	1. 8	6. 3	1. j	6. d	1–2. a, g	1. g	6. a
2. a	7. a	2. 4	7. 9	2. e	7. h	3–4. h, e	2. e	7. j
3. b	8. b	3. 10	8. 1	3. f	8. i	5–6. f, j	3. c	8. f
4. a	9. c	4. 6	9. 5	4. c	9. g	7–8. c, d	4. b	9. i
5. a	10. a	5. 2	10. 7	5. a	10. b	9–10. i, b	5. d	10. h

Chapter 13 (Thomas Dooley)

Ten Words in Context	Matching Words/Defs	Sentence Check 1	Sentence Check 2	Final Check
1. b 6. a	1. 4 6. 3	1. c 6. j	1–2. f, c	1. a 6. g
2. a 7. b	2. 6 7. 5	2. f 7. g	3–4. b, i	2. d 7. h
3. a 8. c	3. 9 8. 7	3. d 8. h	5–6. d, a	3. b 8. f
4. c 9. a	4. 8 9. 10	4. i 9. e	7–8. g, e	4. c 9. j
5. c 10. b	5. 1 10. 2	5. b 10. a	9–10. j, h	5. e 10. i

Chapter 14 (Twelve Grown Men in a Bug)

Ten Words in Context	Matching Words/Defs	Sentence Check 1	Sentence Check 2	Final Check
1. c 6. c	1. 3 6. 2	1. a 6. f	1–2. c, i	1. g 6. a
2. a 7. b	2. 5 7. 9	2. j 7. e	3–4. g, j	2. b 7. f
3. b 8. c	3. 10 8. 6	3. h 8. b	5–6. d, h	3. h 8. i
4. c 9. a	4. 1 9. 7	4. d 9. i	7–8. a, e	4. d 9. e
5. a 10. a	5. 8 10. 4	5. c 10. g	9–10. b, f	5. j 10. c

Chapter 15 (A Different Kind of Doctor)

Ten Words in Context	Matching Words/Defs	Sentence Check 1	Sentence Check 2	Final Check
1. b 6. a	1. 10 6. 3	1. i 6. e	1–2. d, b	1. e 6. b
2. c 7. a	2. 6 7. 9	2. b 7. d	3–4. c, g	2. a 7. j
3. a 8. c	3. 4 8. 8	3. h 8. a	5–6. j, i	3. d 8. g
4. b 9. b	4. 1 9. 5	4. c 9. j	7–8. e, a	4. i 9. h
5. b 10. a	5. 2 10. 7	5. g 10. f	9–10. h, f	5. f 10. c

Chapter 16 (My Devilish Older Sister)

Ten Words in Context	Matching Words/Defs	Sentence Check 1	Sentence Check 2	Final Check
1. b 6. b	1. 6 6. 9	1. i 6. a	1–2. a, d	1. a 6. d
2. a 7. c	2. 4 7. 8	2. b 7. c	3–4. c, i	2. g 7. i
3. b 8. a	3. 10 8. 2	3. h 8. g	5–6. j, h	3. f 8. e
4. a 9. b	4. 1 9. 7	4. e 9. d	7–8. g, b	4. b 9. c
5. a 10. c	5. 3 10. 5	5. j 10. f	9–10. e, f	5. h 10. j

Chapter 17 (Harriet Tubman)

Ten Words in Context	Matching Words/Defs	Sentence Check 1	Sentence Check 2	Final Check
1. a 6. b	1. 4 6. 7	1. c 6. j	1–2. i, c	1. e 6. f
2. b 7. a	2. 9 7. 5	2. d 7. c	3–4. a, g	2. j 7. g
3. c 8. b	3. 6 8. 8	3. e 8. a	5–6. b, h	3. a 8. b
4. a 9. c	4. 10 9. 1	4. g 9. h	7–8. f, e	4. i 9. h
5. a 10. a	5. 2 10. 3	5. b 10. j	9–10. d, j	5. c 10. d

Chapter 18 (Tony's Rehabilitation)

Ten Words in Context	Matching Words/Defs	Sentence Check 1	Sentence Check 2	Final Check
1. c 6. a	1. 5 6. 1	1. h 6. a	1–2. i, g	1. i 6. f
2. a 7. b	2. 2 7. 3	2. i 7. j	3–4. f, d	2. c 7. b
3. a 8. a	3. 6 8. 9	3. d 8. f	5–6. a, c	3. d 8. j
4. b 9. c	4. 10 9. 8	4. b 9. e	7–8. j, h	4. a 9. e
5. c 10. a	5. 4 10. 7	5. g 10. c	9–10. e, b	5. h 10. g

Chapter 19 (Rumors)

Ten Words in Context	Matching Words/Defs	Sentence Check 1	Sentence Check 2	Final Check
1. b 6. a	1. 9 6. 6	1. e 6. c	1–2. i, g	1. c 6. e
2. a 7. a	2. 5 7. 1	2. g 7. j	3–4. h, e	2. f 7. h
3. c 8. a	3. 8 8. 3	3. d 8. h	5–6. j, c	3. b 8. i
4. a 9. a	4. 2 9. 4	4. f 9. i	7–8. d, b	4. a 9. g
5. c 10. b	5. 10 10. 7	5. b 10. a	9–10. f, a	5. d 10. j

Chapter 20 (Firing Our Boss)

Ten Words in Context	Matching Words/Defs	Sentence Check 1	Sentence Check 2	Final Check
1. b 6. b	1. 10 6. 2	1. j 6. b	1–2. c, e	1. b 6. e
2. b 7. a	2. 8 7. 3	2. a 7. i	3–4. i, h	2. a 7. d
3. a 8. c	3. 5 8. 4	3. h 8. e	5–6. g, d	3. c 8. g
4. c 9. a	4. 1 9. 6	4. c 9. d	7–8. f, a	4. f 9. j
5. a 10. b	5. 9 10. 7	5. g 10. f	9–10. j, b	5. h 10. i

Name: _____

Mastery Test: *Chapter 1 (Apartment Problems)*

In the space provided, write the word from the box needed to complete each sentence. Then put the **letter** of that word in the column at the left. Use each word once.

a. **detriment**	b. **dexterous**	c. **discretion**	d. **facetious**	e. **gregarious**
f. **optimum**	g. **ostentatious**	h. **scrupulous**	i. **sensory**	j. **vicarious**

_____ 1. Babies benefit from a great deal of _____ stimulation: different textures to feel, shapes and colors to look at, and various sounds to hear.

_____ 2. The boys' club has made Hank more comfortable with others. In the past, he usually stayed by himself, but now he's much more _____.

_____ 3. Anita is _____ about not wasting her employer's time. Although she uses a computer all day, she never sends personal e-mail or plays computer games until she gets home.

_____ 4. When Brian said he spent all the money I had lent him on a new sports car, I wasn't sure if he was being serious or _____.

_____ 5. It will be many years before I can afford to travel much, but in the meantime, I get _____ pleasure from hearing about my friends' exciting vacations.

_____ 6. Not being able to read well is a(n) _____ to most careers.

_____ 7. To be great performers, piano players must be _____ with their hands.

_____ 8. Experts say that the _____ age for receiving the measles vaccine is 15 months. Children younger than that aren't well protected by the injection.

_____ 9. It's_____ of the Millers to build a huge fancy vacation home that they'll use only once or twice a year. Why must they make such a show of having money?

_____ 10. It's difficult to make a child understand the need for _____. What parent hasn't had the experience of hearing his child yell out some true, but embarrassing fact, such as "Look! That man doesn't have any hair on his head!"

SCORE: (Number correct) _____ × 10 = _____ %

Mastery Test: *Chapter 2 (Hardly a Loser)*

In the space provided, write the word from the box needed to complete each sentence. Then put the **letter** of that word in the column at the left. Use each word once.

a. **collaborate**	b. **despondent**	c. **instigate**	d. **resilient**	e. **retrospect**
f. **rudimentary**	g. **scoff**	h. **squelch**	i. **venerate**	j. **zealot**

_____ 1. In _____, Tim believes his marriage to Lily could have been saved. But at the time, he was convinced that they should split up.

_____ 2. The world _____s Isaac Newton for discovering the laws of gravity.

_____ 3. After breaking her hip, Mrs. Murphy was _____, but she became more hopeful and cheerful when she was discharged from the hospital.

_____ 4. Our neighbor is a _____ about keeping his yard neat. When a single leaf falls off a tree, he rushes out of his house to rake it up.

_____ 5. Winnie was a happy, fun-loving girl when she got married. But five years of living with her sour, serious husband has _____(e)d her bubbly personality.

_____ 6. Joan didn't take part in the snowball fight, but she _____(e)d it by giving the boys huge piles of snowballs.

_____ 7. John Lennon and Paul McCartney _____(e)d in writing many of the Beatles' hit songs, including "Yesterday" and "Yellow Submarine."

_____ 8. People with AIDS are much less _____ than others. A flu attack that most of us can easily shake off is life-threatening to them.

_____ 9. Anyone with even a(n) _____ understanding of electricity knows it's not a good idea to use a metal fork to take a piece of toast from the toaster.

_____ 10. My little sister's friends _____(e)d at her when she claimed she could do magic tricks. Their laughter stopped, however, when she made a pair of pigeons appear from nowhere.

SCORE: (Number correct) _____ × 10 = _____ %

Mastery Test: *Chapter 3 (Grandfather at the Art Museum)*

In the space provided, write the word from the box needed to complete each sentence. Then put the **letter** of that word in the column at the left. Use each word once.

a. **ambiguous**	b. **dissident**	c. **embellish**	d. **fritter**	e. **inadvertent**
f. **inane**	g. **juxtapose**	h. **lethargy**	i. **sporadic**	j. **subsidize**

_____ 1. Nita allows her son to _____ away his weekly allowance on junk. She says he'll soon learn that it's better to save his money for something he really wants.

_____ 2. We watched in wonder as the baker _____(e)d the wedding cake with colorful flowers, hearts, and birds.

_____ 3. Dr. Green was disturbed to see such _____ in young Lisa. Usually, children her age have a great amount of energy.

_____ 4. Here's one of the _____ excuses people have given on insurance forms for accidents: "Coming home, I drove into the wrong driveway and hit a tree I don't have."

_____ 5. Every member of the school board but one voted to hire the new teacher. The _____ kept saying, "There's something about him that I just don't like."

_____ 6. The laundry soap ad _____(e)d an ugly, stained shirt with a beautiful, bright shirt that had supposedly been washed in the soap.

_____ 7. The town business association has established a scholarship to _____ a needy business student each year at the local college.

_____ 8. Instead of having a steady job, Lila stays home with her children and makes a little extra money now and then by doing _____ sewing for friends.

_____ 9. Cora's failure to send Rachel a wedding invitation was entirely _____. As soon as Cora realized her mistake, she telephoned Rachel to invite her.

_____ 10. One famous psychological test involves showing people inkblots in shapes purposely made _____ enough so that a variety of different things can be "seen" in each design.

SCORE: (Number correct) _____ × 10 = _____ %

Mastery Test: *Chapter 4 (My Brother's Mental Illness)*

In the space provided, write the word from the box needed to complete each sentence. Then put the **letter** of that word in the column at the left. Use each word once.

a. **berate**	b. **estrange**	c. **euphoric**	d. **impetuous**	e. **infallible**
f. **maudlin**	g. **regress**	h. **relinquish**	i. **ubiquitous**	j. **zenith**

_____ 1. McDonald's is certainly a(n) _____ restaurant chain. It's almost impossible to find a city that doesn't contain a set of the "golden arches."

_____ 2. "Don't _____ the child so," Mrs. Lopez told her husband. "He'll learn more if you just explain what he's done wrong instead of scolding him so harshly."

_____ 3. My older brother seems to believe he's really _____. Whenever someone disagrees with him, he won't even consider the possibility that he's mistaken.

_____ 4. Since so many people who diet eventually _____ to their old weights, wouldn't it make more sense simply to eat sensibly than to diet constantly?

_____ 5. The young woman _____(e)d custody of her baby to adoptive parents because she wanted the child to have a good home, and she knew she wasn't able to provide one.

_____ 6. Timmy was _____ when his parents, at last, agreed to let him have the puppy he'd been begging for. He walked around singing and smiling all day.

_____ 7. Some child stars reached the _____ of their careers at a very young age and later felt like failures because they couldn't stay at the top.

_____ 8. Last Friday night, my sister and I popped popcorn, put on our pajamas, and cried together over a silly, sentimental movie. Then we laughed at ourselves for being so _____.

_____ 9. Harry's relationship with his two sisters had always been poor, but he completely _____(e)d them when, without their knowledge, he took several of their mother's belongings from her home the day she died.

_____ 10. Phyllis stole a tube of mascara just because she felt like it. She later discovered that her _____ act wasn't worth the humiliation and grief that resulted when she was caught.

SCORE: (Number correct) _____ × 10 = _____ %

Mastery Test: *Chapter 5 (A Phony Friend)*

In the space provided, write the word from the box needed to complete each sentence. Then put the **letter** of that word in the column at the left. Use each word once.

a. **equivocate**	b. **fortuitous**	c. **impeccable**	d. **liaison**	e. **predisposed**
f. **propensity**	g. **reprehensible**	h. **sham**	i. **solace**	j. **solicitous**

_____ 1. Alice knows she has a(n) _____ to overspend on clothes, so she has put herself on a clothing budget.

_____ 2. Because my grandmother is _____ to pneumonia, I make sure she stays warm and healthy during the flu season.

_____ 3. Teenagers often _____ about their plans. When asked where they're going, they say "Out," and when asked what they'll be doing, they say "Nothing much."

_____ 4. Because Julie speaks both Vietnamese and English well, she acts as a(n) _____ between various Vietnamese immigrants and the telephone company, banks, and so on.

_____ 5. Children traveling alone on airplanes generally get very _____ attention from the flight attendants, who keep them well supplied with coloring books, snacks, and pillows.

_____ 6. Stealing money is bad enough, but stealing from a charity is really _____.

_____ 7. Bob and Tina's meeting was unusually _____: intending to visit someone else, Bob knocked on Tina's apartment door by mistake.

_____ 8. I used to envy my neighbor's _____ housekeeping until I realized how much time she spends cleaning. I live a messier but more balanced life.

_____ 9. Mrs. Walker has been lonely since all her children moved to other areas. Her children hope that their frequent e-mails and photographs provide her with some _____.

_____ 10. After Billy spent ten of his hard-earned dollars on an autographed picture of his baseball hero, he was heartbroken to learn that the player's signature was a(n) _____.

SCORE: (Number correct) _____ × 10 = _____ %

Mastery Test: *Chapter 6 (Coco the Gorilla)*

In the space provided, write the word from the box needed to complete each sentence. Then put the **letter** of that word in the column at the left. Use each word once.

a. **attrition**	b. **circumvent**	c. **cohesive**	d. **grievous**	e. **inundate**
f. **oblivious**	g. **reticent**	h. **robust**	i. **sanction**	j. **vociferous**

_____ 1. Our house was so _____(e)d by carpenter ants that we finally were forced to call an exterminator.

_____ 2. The baseball player's protest was _____—he stamped his feet and screamed at the umpire.

_____ 3. There are many possible explanations as to why some families fall apart and have little contact while others are so much more _____.

_____ 4. The rate of _____ in William's high school class was terrible. Of the 104 students who entered ninth grade with him, only 47 graduated.

_____ 5. After the car accident, Rodrigo wandered around in a daze, _____ to the blood that was running down his face and soaking his shirt.

_____ 6. The pilot _____(e)d the storm by flying above it.

_____ 7. Many actors are quite happy to talk about their film careers, but _____about their private lives.

_____ 8. The earthquake was especially _____ for those victims who lost friends and family as well as possessions.

_____ 9. The principal wouldn't _____ the use of the gym for an after-school dance club, even though one of the teachers agreed to be in charge of it.

_____ 10. It's hard to believe that Ana and Tomas's baby, who was so tiny and weak when she was born prematurely, has grown into such a _____ one-year-old.

SCORE: (Number correct) _____ × 10 = _____ %

Mastery Test: *Chapter 7 (Our Annual Garage Sale)*

In the space provided, write the word from the box needed to complete each sentence. Then put the **letter** of that word in the column at the left. Use each word once.

a. **bolster**	b. **depreciate**	c. **indiscriminate**	d. **inquisitive**	e. **nebulous**
f. **relegate**	g. **replete**	h. **sedentary**	i. **tenet**	j. **terse**

_____ 1. A flaw in a diamond will _____ the gem's market value.

_____ 2. Being accepted to two good schools _____(e)d Amy's confidence in her ability to do well in college.

_____ 3. If the tax laws sometimes seem _____ to IRS agents, how is the average person supposed to make sense of them?

_____ 4. My sister's_____ shopping has resulted in a closet full of clothes that don't go together and that she doesn't even especially like.

_____ 5. Scott was such a(n) _____ child that his father teased him by saying, "You ask so many questions that you'll probably be a game show host when you grow up."

_____ 6. One _____ of the Ben & Jerry's ice cream company is that a percentage of their profits will be donated to peace efforts.

_____ 7. Our car was too old and broken-down to trade in. It could only be _____(e)d to the junk pile.

_____ 8. Since Carla is a receptionist, her work is very _____. As a result, she makes a special effort to exercise every day.

_____ 9. One expensive kennel guarantees that your dog will be well cared for during your vacation. It offers cages _____ with such luxuries as air conditioning and pillows.

_____ 10. Writer Dorothy Parker was well-known for her brief, witty statements. She once suggested this _____ sentence for her own gravestone: "Excuse my dust."

SCORE: (Number correct) _____ × 10 = _____ %

Mastery Test: *Chapter 8 (My Large Family)*

In the space provided, write the word from the box needed to complete each sentence. Then put the **letter** of that word in the column at the left. Use each word once.

a. **clandestine**	b. **contingency**	c. **egocentric**	d. **exonerate**	e. **incongruous**
f. **indigenous**	g. **liability**	h. **prolific**	i. **reinstate**	j. **superfluous**

_____ 1. Mint is _____ to the town of North Judson, Indiana. Each summer, the town hosts a "Mint Festival" to celebrate its favorite native crop.

_____ 2. _____ people do not necessarily feel good about themselves. Sometimes people focus on themselves too much because of self-doubt and insecurity.

_____ 3. To prepare everyone for the _____ of a car accident, many states require drivers to buy accident insurance.

_____ 4. After spending 45 minutes cramming our belongings into the back of our station wagon, Dad said, "The next time we go camping, we take only the necessities. All this _____ junk stays home!"

_____ 5. Johann Sebastian Bach was _____ as both a composer and a parent. In addition to writing numerous pieces of music, he fathered twenty children.

_____ 6. People who oppose the death penalty point out that occasionally, a person who has been put to death has later been _____(e)d of the crime.

_____ 7. The fireplace in my aunt's old house has a(n) _____ closet next to it. The closet is concealed because it was once used to hide escaped slaves on their way North.

_____ 8. My brother's shyness is a great _____. Whenever he meets someone who interests him, he's usually too embarrassed to speak.

_____ 9. Madeline's boss _____(e)d her in her old job as shop manager when she returned to work after maternity leave.

_____ 10. Hal and Lisa spent so much on their new house that they had almost no money left to furnish it. It seems _____ to have this lovely, expensive home filled with cast-off sofas and chairs from thrift shops and garage sales.

> **SCORE:** (Number correct) _____ × 10 = _____ %

Mastery Test: *Chapter 9 (A Costume Party)*

In the space provided, write the word from the box needed to complete each sentence. Then put the **letter** of that word in the column at the left. Use each word once.

a. **austere**	b. **esoteric**	c. **facsimile**	d. **grotesque**	e. **mesmerize**
f. **metamorphosis**	g. **notorious**	h. **perfunctory**	i. **provocative**	j. **travesty**

_____ 1. Hitler is so _____ that his name has come to represent evil to most people.

_____ 2. A native of Kansas, Randy was _____(e)d by the towering skyline of New York City.

_____ 3. My brother's major—nuclear physics—is so _____ that he finds it difficult to discuss it at length with most people.

_____ 4. Quaker meeting houses tend to be very _____ because the worshippers don't want to be distracted by a lot of decoration.

_____ 5. I spend a little more money by buying my clothes at Bloom's, but it's worth it. The salespeople there give me sincere personal attention, instead of the _____ treatment I've experienced at other stores.

_____ 6. Common ways to make ads _____ are the use of humor and famous singers.

_____ 7. Numerous bee stings caused Levi's face to swell in such a _____ manner that he was barely recognizable.

_____ 8. In the front window of a local French restaurant is a _____ of the Eiffel Tower— in miniature, of course.

_____ 9. With its violence and phony drama, most so-called "professional" wrestling is really a _____ of the sport.

_____ 10. Panicked by his wife's leaving him, Travis immediately promised to undergo a complete _____: from a cold workaholic to a warm person who makes time for his family. To do so, he's even willing to go into therapy.

SCORE: (Number correct) _____ × 10 = _____ %

Mastery Test: *Chapter 10 (The Missing Painting)*

In the space provided, write the word from the box needed to complete each sentence. Then put the **letter** of that word in the column at the left. Use each word once.

a. **connoisseur**	b. **conspiracy**	c. **contrite**	d. **distraught**	e. **germane**
f. **lucid**	g. **plight**	h. **superficially**	i. **symmetrical**	j. **verbose**

_____ 1. Someone who admires all things French—food, art, wine, and literature—is called a Francophile, while a _____ of everything English is called an Anglophile.

_____ 2. To argue fairly, stick to the topic. Don't bring up old sore points that aren't _____ to the issue at hand.

_____ 3. The suspenseful movie *Gaslight* concerns an evil husband's _____ to make his wife believe she's going insane.

_____ 4. When the young mother first missed her little boy in the park, she wasn't too disturbed, but after ten minutes of searching without success, she became _____.

_____ 5. The day-care teacher was disturbed to see Emily's father's reaction to the birthday card Emily had so carefully made for him. He glanced at it only _____ and said, "That's nice. Now get in the car."

_____ 6. Wendy's financial _____ is severe. She's out of work and has barely enough money for the bus fare to interview for a new job.

_____ 7. Because humans are basically _____—their left and right sides are mirror images of each other—they have a well-balanced appearance.

_____ 8. When my dog is scolded for some misdeed, her drooping tail and saddened eyes make it seem that she's _____.

_____ 9. If your essay is _____, it doesn't necessarily mean you're naturally wordier than other students. You just haven't taken the time to edit out repetitions and unnecessary words.

_____ 10. Cheryl was so helpless with laughter that she couldn't provide a _____ explanation of what had happened. She could only gasp out fragments of sentences, such as "And then the chair. . . . But Thomas was trying. . . . And the *noise!*"

SCORE: (Number correct) _____ × 10 = _____ %

Mastery Test: *Chapter 11 (An Ohio Girl in New York)*

In the space provided, write the word from the box needed to complete each sentence. Then put the **letter** of that word in the column at the left. Use each word once.

a. **adept**	b. **encompass**	c. **entrepreneur**	d. **eradicate**	e. **homogeneous**
f. **presumptuous**	g. **sordid**	h. **standardize**	i. **stint**	j. **stringent**

_____ 1. The principal called a special meeting to address the _____ problem of drug use in the school system.

_____ 2. Nancy has tried to _____ the ants in her kitchen, but no matter how often she sprays, they soon reappear.

_____ 3. The two-week survival course _____(e)d all we would need to know, from starting a campfire to building a shelter to finding food in the wilderness.

_____ 4. Some people would like all countries to adopt the metric system in order to _____ the system of weights and measures worldwide.

_____ 5. When Helen needed a kidney transplant, several of her friends insisted she take one of theirs. They didn't realize there are _____ guidelines determining who can be a successful donor.

_____ 6. When we were young, our grandfather would tell us colorful stories about his _____ as a circus clown.

_____ 7. I was annoyed with Eileen yesterday. I felt it was _____ of her to try to sell me magazine subscriptions since I had invited her over for a social visit.

_____ 8. An excellent public speaker with a likable personality, Jim is _____ at getting others to see things from his point of view.

_____ 9. On hot summer days in our small town, you can see many young _____s operating their own lemonade or iced-tea stands.

_____ 10. When we decided to get rid of our chickens, I offered our three white hens to a neighboring egg farmer, but he refused them. He wanted to keep his all-brown flock _____.

SCORE: (Number correct) _____ × 10 = _____ %

Mastery Test: *Chapter 12 (How Neat Is Neat Enough?)*

In the space provided, write the word from the box needed to complete each sentence. Then put the **letter** of that word in the column at the left. Use each word once.

a. **exhort**	b. **flamboyant**	c. **foible**	d. **innocuous**	e. **magnanimous**
f. **masochist**	g. **meticulous**	h. **rancor**	i. **recrimination**	j. **repugnant**

_____ 1. Determined that the casting director would notice her, the would-be actress wore a _____ costume—featuring feathers, pearls, and spangles—to the audition.

_____ 2. Elizabeth is so kind and good-natured that her friends cheerfully overlook her _____ of talking too much.

_____ 3. The scratch on our car's fender seemed _____ at first, but it soon began to rust. We ended up paying $185 to have it fixed.

_____ 4. Because he'd had so much difficulty with his studies, Oscar's parents _____(e)d him to go to summer school.

_____ 5. It's amazing how _____ a formerly appetizing dish can become after it's spent a few weeks forgotten in the back of the refrigerator.

_____ 6. It certainly was _____ of Charlie to forgive Eric for losing Charlie's winning lottery ticket worth $500.

_____ 7. Karen's friends called her a _____ when they learned that she planned to run in two marathons in one weekend.

_____ 8. The home-team fans felt such _____ for the visiting team that they began booing and shouting insults before the game even began.

_____ 9. Henry is _____ about his car. He washes it by hand every Saturday, changes the oil four times a year, and won't allow anyone to eat in it.

_____ 10. The warring couple spent their first session with the marriage counselor trading _____s such as "You're never home at night!" and "Well, if you weren't so grouchy, I might stay home more!"

SCORE: (Number correct) _____ × 10 = _____ %

Mastery Test: *Chapter 13 (Thomas Dooley)*

In the space provided, write the word from the box needed to complete each sentence. Then put the **letter** of that word in the column at the left. Use each word once.

a. **atrophy**	b. **deplore**	c. **deprivation**	d. **exacerbate**	e. **imperative**
f. **mitigate**	g. **objective**	h. **panacea**	i. **unprecedented**	j. **utilitarian**

_____ 1. You can _____ the stress of preparing for finals by studying carefully throughout the semester.

_____ 2. David's mother left an urgent message on his answering machine: "It's _____ that you call me before Thursday!"

_____ 3. The doctors explained that Uncle Tim's muscles will gradually _____, making it increasingly more difficult for him to walk.

_____ 4. My brother's dorm room is strictly _____. The room is empty except for the necessities: a desk, chair, bed, dresser, and bookcase.

_____ 5. Marie wished her husband would be more _____ and consider the facts instead of always judging things by his own narrow point of view, without even thinking.

_____ 6. Karen believes that moving away from home would be a(n) _____ for her problems, but I think it will take more than that to cure all her difficulties.

_____ 7. People who suffer a(n) _____ of foods containing vitamin C develop a disease called scurvy.

_____ 8. Luis doesn't simply _____ the evils in the world; he tries to work to make the world better.

_____ 9. The high-school band has won the state competition for a(n) _____ six straight years. The previous record was five years in a row.

_____ 10. Bonnie thought ice water would cool the burning in her mouth from the Chinese mustard, but a drink did just the opposite—the water _____(e)d her discomfort.

SCORE: (Number correct) _____ × 10 = _____ %

Mastery Test: *Chapter 14 (Twelve Grown Men in a Bug)*

In the space provided, write the word from the box needed to complete each sentence. Then put the **letter** of that word in the column at the left. Use each word once.

a. **decorum**	b. **espouse**	c. **exhilaration**	d. **exorbitant**	e. **extricate**
f. **facilitate**	g. **orthodox**	h. **rejuvenate**	i. **synchronize**	j. **tenuous**

_____ 1. A man on the street corner handed out pamphlets that _____(e)d the cause of the homeless.

_____ 2. The injured deer carefully _____(e)d itself from the thorny brush by the side of the road.

_____ 3. The ski trip was worthwhile just to see the _____ on Joanne's face the first time she made it down the hill without falling.

_____ 4. People hired for the staff of the elegant new hotel must have a strong sense of _____. Guests there will expect to be treated with formal politeness.

_____ 5. Dawn's boyfriend sometimes shows poor judgment. Although he makes a very low salary, he spends a(n) _____ amount of money on fancy sneakers and leather jackets.

_____ 6. Uncle Richard loves his power tools because they _____ tasks he finds difficult because of his arthritis.

_____ 7. "A cup of warm cocoa will _____ you," said Mom. And sure enough, I soon felt as good as new.

_____ 8. My friendship with Debby is _____. If it were subjected to the least bit of conflict, I don't think it would survive.

_____ 9. The differing times on the clocks in the living room, kitchen, and bedroom drive me crazy. Before going to bed tonight, I'm going to _____ them.

_____ 10. _____ standards of dress vary from culture to culture. While men in the United States are expected to wear pants, men in other countries often wear long robes.

SCORE: (Number correct) _____ × 10 = _____ %	

Mastery Test: *Chapter 15 (A Different Kind of Doctor)*

In the space provided, write the word from the box needed to complete each sentence. Then put the **letter** of that word in the column at the left. Use each word once.

a. **analogy**	b. **annihilate**	c. **criterion**	d. **emanate**	e. **holistic**
f. **placebo**	g. **proficient**	h. **staunch**	i. **subversive**	j. **vindicate**

_____ 1. To _____ himself, Joe produced evidence that he had been out of town the day that green paint was sprayed all over school.

_____ 2. One widely used _____ is the comparison of the pastor of a congregation to the shepherd of a flock of sheep.

_____ 3. A delicious aroma of baking bread _____(e)d from the kitchen.

_____ 4. It made me angry when my parents judged my boyfriends only by the _____ of the length of their hair.

_____ 5. I feel sorry for ants when they work so hard to construct an anthill, only to have a child come along and _____ it with one blow of his foot.

_____ 6. Dr. Wyatt is a _____ practitioner. She considers the health of the entire body when attempting to heal one of its parts.

_____ 7. The sports fans in our town are _____ supporters of the home team. They're loyal even during a losing season.

_____ 8. Zamil used to be a _____ secretary, but since she hadn't worked in a while, she decided to brush up on her office skills before going back to work.

_____ 9. The old movie was about a _____ plot that failed to overthrow a powerful, cruel dictator.

_____ 10. Carl was furious when he realized his doctor had been treating his headaches with _____s. He felt this treatment meant the doctor believed Carl was only imagining his headaches.

SCORE: (Number correct) _____ × 10 = _____ %	

Mastery Test: *Chapter 16 (My Devilish Older Sister)*

In the space provided, write the word from the box needed to complete each sentence. Then put the **letter** of that word in the column at the left. Use each word once.

a. **disparity**	b. **forestall**	c. **insidious**	d. **insinuate**	e. **interrogate**
f. **obsequious**	g. **omnipotent**	h. **opportune**	i. **permeate**	j. **retribution**

_____ 1. To _____ any chance of the chicken salad spoiling, do not let it sit outside all afternoon at the picnic.

_____ 2. As _____ for starting a rebellion against the government, the leaders of the uprising were jailed.

_____ 3. Don't tell Jasmin that her new striped dress makes her look slender. She'll think you mean to _____ that she's overweight.

_____ 4. Lead poisoning may not be immediately apparent. It can be _____, eventually leading to effects as harmful as brain damage.

_____ 5. My grandfather believes his 22-year-old fiancée loves him, but the _____ in their ages makes it seem more likely that she loves his money.

_____ 6. In describing a(n) _____ coworker, Elizabeth explained, "If a superior says 'Jump like a frog!' her only response is 'How high?' "

_____ 7. Quicksand is formed when water _____s loose sand and makes its surface so soft that it cannot support weight.

_____ 8. In a democracy, no single person is _____. Even the President has to get approval from Congress in order to carry out his policies.

_____ 9. Since my parents were so pleased with my grades, I thought it was a(n) _____ time to ask if I could borrow the car.

_____ 10. When rumors began about steroids in the weight room, the principal kept all members of the weightlifting club after school to _____ them about drugs.

SCORE: (Number correct) _____ × 10 = _____ %	

Mastery Test: *Chapter 17 (Harriet Tubman)*

In the space provided, write the word from the box needed to complete each sentence. Then put the **letter** of that word in the column at the left. Use each word once.

a. **complement**	b. **discreet**	c. **fastidious**	d. **flout**	e. **heinous**
f. **implement**	g. **impromptu**	h. **inference**	i. **intuition**	j. **obtrusive**

_____ 1. Cynthia's all-white living room is a little dull. If it were my house, I'd _____ it with some colorful pillows and pictures.

_____ 2. Bookkeepers and accountants must be _____. Overlooking even one little detail can cause problems in their work.

_____ 3. The new people next door seem to actually want to create bad feelings with their neighbors. They _____ neighborhood standards by never cutting the grass, leaving an abandoned car in the yard, and dumping trash everywhere.

_____ 4. When our school _____ s the reduced budget, there will no longer be money to support extracurricular activities.

_____ 5. Politicians must be _____ about their personal lives because revealing sensitive information can give other candidates something to use against them in an election campaign.

_____ 6. Leila's bright red dress was certainly _____ at the funeral.

_____ 7. My parents haven't said what they think of my new boyfriend, but since they are silent, my _____ is that they dislike him.

_____ 8. Obviously, some people enjoy reading about _____ crimes. Books about murders are often best-sellers, and the more gruesome the crime, the better the book sells.

_____ 9. One group that had no time to rehearse a skit gave a(n) _____ performance so funny and lively that it may even have benefited from the lack of practice.

_____ 10. I just knew Emil's business partner would let him down, but he wouldn't believe me until it happened. Now Emil says he should have trusted my "feminine _____."

SCORE: (Number correct) _____ × 10 = _____ %

Mastery Test: *Chapter 18 (Tony's Rehabilitation)*

In the space provided, write the word from the box needed to complete each sentence. Then put the **letter** of that word in the column at the left. Use each word once.

a. **auspicious**	b. **expedite**	c. **extenuating**	d. **fraudulent**	e. **innuendo**
f. **rebuke**	g. **redeem**	h. **subordinate**	i. **transgress**	j. **vehement**

_____ 1. People who believe in astrology often plan important events for days that the stars "say" are _____.

_____ 2. Any ad for a product that promises to help you lose weight without dieting or exercising must be _____.

_____ 3. Needing his order soon, a customer spoke to the manager, who promised to _____ a rapid delivery.

_____ 4. I'll never forgive myself for gossiping so cruelly about our new neighbor. Now that I know and like her, I've _____(e)d myself for my behavior a hundred times.

_____ 5. "It's true I lied to you about being out of town last weekend," Jan admitted to Brian, "but there were _____ circumstances. I had promised your mother that I wouldn't see you over the weekend so that you could concentrate on studying for Monday's exam."

_____ 6. Turning away from a life of crime, the robber _____(e)d himself by teaching citizens how to protect themselves against theft.

_____ 7. Malik reports to his boss—the vice president of the company. She, in turn, is _____ to the executive vice president.

_____ 8. Joey's parents had laid down so many rules for him that it was impossible for the little boy not to _____ once in a while.

_____ 9. My uncle is so _____ in his opinions on politics that it's impossible to have a casual conversation with him on the topic. He gets too carried away by his passion.

_____ 10. Richard listened politely to the information about where to buy a hairpiece, but he resented the _____ that his baldness made him unattractive.

> ***SCORE:*** (Number correct) _____ × 10 = _____ %

Mastery Test: *Chapter 19 (Rumors)*

In the space provided, write the word from the box needed to complete each sentence. Then put the **letter** of that word in the column at the left. Use each word once.

a. **deride**	b. **derogatory**	c. **fabricate**	d. **impending**	e. **macabre**
f. **misconstrue**	g. **paramount**	h. **quandary**	i. **turbulent**	j. **validate**

_____ 1. Children like to frighten each other at slumber parties by telling _____ stories about demons, ghosts, and vampires.

_____ 2. Being with Fred can be depressing because of all his _____ remarks. Just once, I'd like to hear him say something good about someone else.

_____ 3. When the staff heard that a huge snowstorm was on its way, everyone in the office left for home early, hoping to miss the _____ bad weather.

_____ 4. You may get some laughs when you _____ someone's appearance, but some of us find your scornful remarks more in bad taste than amusing.

_____ 5. Gina was so anxious to impress her college friends that she pretended to have a boyfriend at Harvard. The guy she _____(e)d was rich, intelligent, and spoke five foreign languages.

_____ 6. My low opinion of Brian was _____(e)d when I learned he had faked an auto accident in order to file a dishonest insurance claim.

_____ 7. I enjoy sailing when the water is calm, but if the lake becomes _____, I promptly become "seasick."

_____ 8. Vicky always _____s my compliments, somehow finding an insult in every comment I intend to be encouraging.

_____ 9. When your boss says a job is _____, you should consider it more important than any other project you're working on.

_____ 10. Linda's adoptive parents were in a _____ about what to tell her regarding her birth. Should she be told the truth, or would it be too painful to know that she'd been left at the entrance of a hospital emergency room the day she was born?

SCORE: (Number correct) _____ × 10 = _____ %

Mastery Test: *Chapter 20 (Firing Our Boss)*

In the space provided, write the word from the box needed to complete each sentence. Then put the **letter** of that word in the column at the left. Use each word once.

a. **abrasive**	b. **admonish**	c. **antithesis**	d. **culmination**	e. **docile**
f. **emulate**	g. **hierarchy**	h. **incapacitate**	i. **prognosis**	j. **tumult**

_____ 1. Dee's parrot is so _____ that you can hand-feed it without fear of getting bitten.

_____ 2. Sandpaper comes in different degrees of roughness. The most _____ type has large pieces of sand.

_____ 3. When it comes to work, Marco is the _____ of Lee. Marco is ambitious and finds work challenging, while Lee tries to wriggle out of work whenever possible.

_____ 4. It's appropriate to _____ a worker who forgets to punch the timecard only once or twice, but a stronger reaction is needed for someone who forgets almost every day.

_____ 5. The Fourth of July show begins with a band concert. Next, there's a sing-along. The _____ of the evening is a fifteen-minute display of spectacular fireworks.

_____ 6. There's no way I'll be able to give a speech tomorrow. I've just begun to lose my voice, and the doctor's _____ is that it'll get even weaker for at least two more days.

_____ 7. What is the point of having a band play at that restaurant? The _____ from the diners is so great that you can't possibly appreciate the music.

_____ 8. My broken arm was beneficial in that it _____(e)d me for most household chores.

_____ 9. My brother quit smoking the day he saw his six-year-old pick up one of his cigarettes and put it in her own mouth. "I want my daughter to _____ my good behaviors, not my bad ones," he said.

_____ 10. If I ever entered the military service, I'd have to learn the _____ of ranks. I have no idea if a major is higher than a lieutenant or vice versa.

SCORE: (Number correct) _____ × 10 = _____ %

Answers to the Mastery Tests:
ADVANCING VOCABULARY SKILLS, SHORT VERSION

Chapter 1 (Apartment Problems)

1. i
2. e
3. h
4. d
5. j
6. a
7. b
8. f
9. g
10. c

Chapter 2 (Hardly a Loser)

1. e
2. i
3. b
4. j
5. h
6. c
7. a
8. d
9. f
10. g

Chapter 3 (Grandfather at the Art Museum)

1. d
2. c
3. h
4. f
5. b
6. g
7. h
8. i
9. e
10. a

Chapter 4 (My Brother's Mental Illness)

1. i
2. a
3. e
4. g
5. h
6. c
7. j
8. f
9. b
10. d

Chapter 5 (A Phony Friend)

1. f
2. e
3. a
4. d
5. j
6. g
7. b
8. c
9. i
10. h

Chapter 6 (Coco the Gorilla)

1. e
2. j
3. c
4. a
5. f
6. b
7. g
8. d
9. i
10. h

Chapter 7 (Our Annual Garage Sale)

1. b
2. a
3. e
4. c
5. d
6. i
7. f
8. h
9. g
10. j

Chapter 8 (My Large Family)

1. f
2. c
3. b
4. j
5. h
6. d
7. a
8. g
9. i
10. c

Chapter 9 (A Costume Party)

1. g
2. e
3. b
4. a
5. h
6. i
7. d
8. c
9. j
10. f

Chapter 10 (The Missing Painting)

1. a
2. e
3. b
4. d
5. h
6. g
7. i
8. c
9. j
10. f

Chapter 11 (An Ohio Girl in New York)

1. g
2. d
3. b
4. h
5. j
6. i
7. f
8. a
9. c
10. e

Chapter 12 (How Neat Is Neat Enough?)

1. b
2. c
3. d
4. a
5. j
6. e
7. f
8. h
9. g
10. i

Chapter 13 (Thomas Dooley)

1. f
2. e
3. a
4. j
5. g

6. h
7. c
8. b
9. i
10. d

Chapter 14 (Twelve Grown Men in a Bug)

1. b
2. e
3. c
4. a
5. d

6. f
7. h
8. j
9. i
10. g

Chapter 15 (A Different Kind of Doctor)

1. j
2. a
3. d
4. c
5. b

6. e
7. h
8. g
9. i
10. f

Chapter 16 (My Devilish Older Sister)

1. b
2. j
3. d
4. c
5. a

6. f
7. i
8. g
9. h
10. e

Chapter 17 (Harriet Tubman)

1. a
2. c
3. d
4. f
5. b

6. j
7. h
8. e
9. g
10. i

Chapter 18 (Tony's Rehabilitation)

1. a
2. d
3. b
4. f
5. c

6. g
7. h
8. i
9. j
10. e

Chapter 19 (Rumors)

1. e
2. b
3. d
4. a
5. c

6. j
7. i
8. f
9. g
10. h

Chapter 20 (Firing Our Boss)

1. e
2. a
3. c
4. b
5. d

6. i
7. j
8. h
9. f
10. g

Mastery Test: *Unit One*

PART A
Complete each sentence in a way that clearly shows you understand the meaning of the **boldfaced** word.
Take a minute to plan your answer before you write.

Example: I was being **facetious** when I said that ___*my parrot can tell the future. In fact, he's always wrong*___ .

1. I would be **euphoric** if _____

_____ .

2. I have a **propensity** to _____ . For example, _____

_____ .

3. Rhetta **frittered** away her money on _____

_____ .

4. A **zealot** in the environmental movement would never _____

_____ .

5. Being **gregarious**, Marisol wants to celebrate her birthday by _____

_____ .

6. I was **despondent** because _____

_____ .

7. An **inane** way to study for final exams is to _____

_____ .

8. At the mall, my **impetuous** friend _____

_____ .

9. The mayor **estranged** many voters when he _____

_____ .

10. In **retrospect**, I realized that _____

_____ .

(Continues on next page)

PART B

Use each of the following ten words in sentences of your own. Make it clear that you know the meaning of the word you use. Feel free to use the past tense or plural form of a word.

a. **ambiguous**	b. **embellish**	c. **infallible**	d. **ostentatious**	e. **scoff**
f. **scrupulous**	g. **sensory**	h. **sham**	i. **vicarious**	j. **zenith**

11. _____

_____

12. _____

_____

13. _____

_____

14. _____

_____

15. _____

_____

16. _____

_____

17. _____

_____

18. _____

_____

19. _____

_____

20. _____

_____

SCORE: (Number correct) _____ × 5 = _____ %

Mastery Test: *Unit Two*

PART A

Complete each sentence in a way that clearly shows you understand the meaning of the **boldfaced** word. Take a minute to plan your answer before you write.

Example: On our picnic, we carried a basket **replete** with ___*a complete meal and plenty of snacks*___.

1. A very **terse** answer to the question "Did you have fun at the dentist's office?" is "_____

   _____."

2. A loud voice would probably be a **liability** in _____

   _____.

3. One good way to **bolster** a friend's spirits is to _____

   _____.

4. One **verbose** way of saying no is "_____

   _____."

5. Reverend Patterson's appearance is **incongruous** with my image of a minister. He wears _____

   _____.

6. As a child, I was **contrite** after _____

   _____.

7. Vanessa is so **egocentric** that _____

   _____.

8. I was **distraught** when _____

   _____.

9. One way to **circumvent** rush-hour traffic is to _____

   _____.

10. One of the most **notorious** people I've ever heard of is _____, who became notorious

    because _____.

(Continues on next page)

PART B

Use each of the following ten words in sentences of your own. Make it clear that you know the meaning of the word you use. Feel free to use the past tense or plural form of a word.

| a. **clandestine** | b. **depreciate** | c. **exonerate** | d. **inquisitive** | e. **mesmerize** |
| f. **metamorphosis** | g. **plight** | h. **relegate** | i. **sedentary** | j. **superficially** |

11. _____

_____

12. _____

_____

13. _____

_____

14. _____

_____

15. _____

_____

16. _____

_____

17. _____

_____

18. _____

_____

19. _____

_____

20. _____

_____

SCORE: (Number correct) _____ × 5 = _____ %

Name: _____

Mastery Test: *Unit Three*

PART A
Complete each sentence in a way that clearly shows you understand the meaning of the **boldfaced** word. Take a minute to plan your answer before you write.

Example: Kim must be an **adept** manager because _____*she was just promoted again*_____.

1. My parents often **exhort** me to _____

   _____.

2. A good way to **exacerbate** a sore throat is to _____

   _____.

3. My best friend has an odd **foible**: _____

   _____.

4. The **magnanimous** boss _____

   _____.

5. Usual classroom **decorum** forbids _____

   _____.

6. The singer's **flamboyant** outfit consisted of _____

   _____.

7. I **deplore** _____ because _____

   _____.

8. I can count on _____ to **rejuvenate** me because

   _____.

9. **Emanating** from the kitchen was _____

   _____.

10. I am quite **proficient** at _____. For example, _____

    _____.

(Continues on next page)

PART B

Use each of the following ten words in sentences of your own. Make it clear that you know the meaning of the word you use. Feel free to use the past tense or plural form of a word.

a. **analogy**	b. **criterion**	c. **eradicate**	d. **exorbitant**	e. **imperative**
f. **meticulous**	g. **objective**	h. **repugnant**	i. **stint**	j. **synchronize**

11. _____

_____

12. _____

_____

13. _____

_____

14. _____

_____

15. _____

_____

16. _____

_____

17. _____

_____

18. _____

_____

19. _____

_____

20. _____

_____

SCORE: (Number correct) _____ × 5 = _____ %

Mastery Test: *Unit Four*

PART A
Complete each sentence in a way that clearly shows you understand the meaning of the **boldfaced** word. Take a minute to plan your answer before you write.

Example: Jeff should be **discreet** about the party because _____ *it's meant to be a surprise* _____.

1. The **docile** dog _____

   _____.

2. Ted **flouted** the traffic laws by _____

   _____.

3. There was a huge **tumult** when _____

   _____.

4. An **obsequious** secretary, Agnes often _____

   _____.

5. Charles **misconstrued** my dinner invitation. He _____ _____

   _____.

6. Maureen obviously had **fabricated** her excuse. She told the teacher, "_____

   _____."

7. To **implement** her vacation plans, Ruth started to _____

   _____.

8. After getting a D in chemistry, I tried to **redeem** myself by _____

   _____.

9. You can tell that my sister is **fastidious** by looking at her bedroom, where _____

   _____.

10. When Len said that his brother wouldn't even give him the time of day, he meant to **insinuate** that _____

   _____

   _____.

(Continues on next page)

PART B

Use each of the following ten words in sentences of your own. Make it clear that you know the meaning of the word you use. Feel free to use the past tense or plural form of a word.

a. **antithesis**	b. **complement**	c. **derogatory**	d. **emulate**	e. **inference**
f. **intuition**	g. **paramount**	h. **prognosis**	i. **quandary**	j. **rebuke**

11. _____

_____

12. _____

_____

13. _____

_____

14. _____

_____

15. _____

_____

16. _____

_____

17. _____

_____

18. _____

_____

19. _____

_____

20. _____

_____

SCORE: (Number correct) _____ × 5 = _____ %

Vocabulary Placement Test

NAME: _____

SECTION: _____ DATE: _____

SCORE: _____

> This test contains 100 items. You have 30 minutes to take the test. In the space provided, write the letter of the choice that is closest in meaning to the **boldfaced** word.
>
> *Important:* Keep in mind that this test is for placement purposes only. **If you do not know a word, leave the space blank rather than guess at it.**

_____ 1. to **deceive** a) prove b) mislead c) reach d) get back

_____ 2. **earnest** a) serious and sincere b) illegal c) wealthy d) hidden

_____ 3. **inferior** a) not proper b) clear c) poor in quality d) inside

_____ 4. to **comprehend** a) describe b) understand c) make use of d) prepare

_____ 5. **unanimous** a) alone b) animal-like c) unfriendly d) in full agreement

_____ 6. the **vicinity** a) area nearby b) city c) enemy d) information

_____ 7. **current** a) healthy b) modern c) well-known d) necessary

_____ 8. **internal** a) forever b) inside c) outside d) brief

_____ 9. **maximum** a) least b) expensive c) cheap d) greatest

_____ 10. an **objective** a) goal b) puzzle c) cause d) supply

_____ 11. a **potential** a) favorite b) possibility c) refusal d) desire

_____ 12. to **detect** a) discover b) make c) follow d) commit a crime

_____ 13. to **establish** a) receive b) delay c) set up d) attract

_____ 14. to **pursue** a) follow b) run from c) suggest d) create

_____ 15. **vague** a) missing b) unclear c) kind d) necessary

_____ 16. **suitable** a) simple b) needed c) profitable d) proper

_____ 17. a **category** a) kindness b) horror c) type d) question

_____ 18. **reluctant** a) unwilling b) lost c) unhappy d) well-known

_____ 19. to **coincide** a) pay b) decide c) get in the way d) happen together

_____ 20. to **inhabit** a) enter b) live in c) get used to d) understand

_____ 21. **apparent** a) together b) obvious c) motherly d) welcome

_____ 22. **accustomed** a) in the habit b) specially made c) necessary d) extra

_____ 23. to **revise** a) give advice b) go back c) change d) awaken

_____ 24. a **contrast** a) purpose b) choice c) agreement d) difference

_____ 25. **awkward** a) forward b) boring c) clumsy d) clever

(Continues on next page)

_____ 26. **urban** a) of a city b) circular c) not allowed d) large

_____ 27. **lenient** a) light b) not strict c) delayed d) not biased

_____ 28. to **endorse** a) suggest b) stop c) support d) start

_____ 29. a **novice** a) book b) false impression c) beginner d) servant

_____ 30. to **deter** a) prevent b) make last longer c) refuse d) damage

_____ 31. to **verify** a) imagine b) prove c) keep going d) cancel

_____ 32. **moderate** a) generous b) not final c) medium d) bright

_____ 33. a **diversity** a) separation b) conclusion c) enthusiasm d) variety

_____ 34. **accessible** a) easily reached b) itchy c) difficult d) folded

_____ 35. **lethal** a) sweet-smelling b) ancient c) deadly d) healthy

_____ 36. **vivid** a) brightly colored b) local c) large d) very talkative

_____ 37. to **convey** a) allow b) communicate c) invent d) approve

_____ 38. **inevitable** a) unavoidable b) dangerous c) spiteful d) doubtful

_____ 39. a **ritual** a) business deal b) war c) ceremony d) show

_____ 40. **elaborate** a) large b) complex c) expensive d) boring

_____ 41. the **essence** a) fundamental characteristic b) tiny part c) much later d) rule

_____ 42. to **coerce** a) attract b) refuse c) remove d) force

_____ 43. **skeptical** a) stubborn b) forceful c) generous d) doubting

_____ 44. **vital** a) weak b) stiff c) necessary d) unimportant

_____ 45. **innate** a) learned b) underneath c) inborn d) clever

_____ 46. a **vocation** a) hobby b) trip c) report d) profession

_____ 47. to **defy** a) send for b) resist c) improve d) approve

_____ 48. **adverse** a) strict b) profitable c) rhyming d) harmful

_____ 49. **consecutive** a) late b) following one after another c) able d) at the same time

_____ 50. **audible** a) able to be heard b) believable c) willing d) nearby

(Continues on next page)

_____ 51. to **encounter**   **a)** come upon   **b)** count up   **c)** depart from   **d)** attack

_____ 52. **obsolete**   **a)** modern   **b)** difficult to believe   **c)** out-of-date   **d)** not sold

_____ 53. to **terminate**   **a)** stop   **b)** continue   **c)** begin   **d)** approach

_____ 54. **altruistic**   **a)** honest   **b)** lying   **c)** proud   **d)** unselfish

_____ 55. to **enhance**   **a)** reject   **b)** get   **c)** improve   **d)** free

_____ 56. **nocturnal**   **a)** supposed   **b)** not logical   **c)** complex   **d)** active at night

_____ 57. to **suffice**   **a)** think up   **b)** be good enough   **c)** allow   **d)** reject

_____ 58. to **retaliate**   **a)** repair   **b)** repeat   **c)** renew   **d)** pay back

_____ 59. to **incorporate**   **a)** combine   **b)** anger   **c)** separate   **d)** calm

_____ 60. an **incentive**   **a)** fear   **b)** pride   **c)** concern   **d)** encouragement

_____ 61. **covert**   **a)** distant   **b)** hidden   **c)** changed   **d)** adjusted

_____ 62. to **alleviate**   **a)** make anxious   **b)** depart   **c)** infect   **d)** relieve

_____ 63. to **aspire**   **a)** dislike   **b)** strongly desire   **c)** impress   **d)** respect

_____ 64. an **extrovert**   **a)** shy person   **b)** magnet   **c)** main point   **d)** outgoing person

_____ 65. **prone**   **a)** disliked   **b)** tending   **c)** active   **d)** rested

_____ 66. **ominous**   **a)** happy   **b)** threatening   **c)** depressed   **d)** friendly

_____ 67. **complacent**   **a)** workable   **b)** lazy   **c)** self-satisfied   **d)** healthy

_____ 68. a **consensus**   **a)** majority opinion   **b)** total   **c)** study   **d)** approval

_____ 69. to **condone**   **a)** forgive   **b)** represent   **c)** arrest   **d)** appoint

_____ 70. **deficient**   **a)** forgotten   **b)** lacking   **c)** complete   **d)** well-known

_____ 71. **fallible**   **a)** capable of error   **b)** complete   **c)** incomplete   **d)** simple

_____ 72. **pragmatic**   **a)** ordinary   **b)** slow   **c)** wise   **d)** practical

_____ 73. **avid**   **a)** bored   **b)** disliked   **c)** enthusiastic   **d)** plentiful

_____ 74. **explicit**   **a)** everyday   **b)** distant   **c)** permanent   **d)** stated exactly

_____ 75. **ambivalent**   **a)** unknown   **b)** having mixed feelings   **c)** temporary   **d)** able to be done

(Continues on next page)

_____ 76. **vicarious**   a) experienced indirectly   b) lively   c) inactive   d) occasional

_____ 77. **rudimentary**   a) rude   b) planned   c) partial   d) elementary

_____ 78. to **collaborate**   a) respect   b) work hard   c) work together   d) search

_____ 79. to **venerate**   a) protect   b) create   c) make unfriendly   d) respect

_____ 80. **inadvertent**   a) unintentional   b) not for sale   c) distant   d) near

_____ 81. **predisposed**   a) against   b) unwilling to speak   c) undecided   d) tending beforehand

_____ 82. **robust**   a) extremely careful   b) healthy and strong   c) tall   d) loyal

_____ 83. **sedentary**   a) sitting   b) excessive   c) harmless   d) repeated

_____ 84. **clandestine**   a) well-lit   b) secret   c) noble   d) harmless

_____ 85. **austere**   a) wealthy   b) complex   c) plain   d) far

_____ 86. **notorious**   a) too bold   b) written   c) known widely but unfavorably   d) lacking skill

_____ 87. **lucid**   a) clear   b) generous in forgiving   c) careful   d) bold

_____ 88. to **encompass**   a) include   b) draw   c) separate   d) purchase

_____ 89. **meticulous**   a) broken-down   b) curious   c) careful and exact   d) irregular

_____ 90. **innocuous**   a) delightful   b) harmless   c) dangerous   d) disappointing

_____ 91. to **rejuvenate**   a) set free   b) grow   c) refresh   d) make easier

_____ 92. to **facilitate**   a) approve   b) make easier   c) serve   d) clear from blame

_____ 93. **proficient**   a) proud   b) wise   c) skilled   d) well-known

_____ 94. to **emanate**   a) go above   b) run through   c) go down   d) come forth

_____ 95. to **implement**   a) encourage   b) carry out   c) insult   d) prevent

_____ 96. to **fabricate**   a) misinterpret   b) put away   c) clothe   d) invent

_____ 97. to **emulate**   a) be tardy   b) misunderstand   c) imitate   d) prepare

_____ 98. a **prognosis**   a) hope   b) prediction   c) opposite   d) memory

_____ 99. a **tumult**   a) uproar   b) uncertainty   c) series   d) scolding

_____ 100. to **insinuate**   a) demand   b) state   c) deny   d) hint

STOP. This is the end of the test. If there is time remaining, you may go back and recheck your answers. When the time is up, hand in both your answer sheet and this test booklet to your instructor.

To the Instructor: Use these guidelines to match your students with the appropriate TP vocabulary book.						
Score	0–9	10–24	25–49	50–74	75–90	91–100
Recommended Book	VB	GBV	BVS	IVS	AVS	AWP

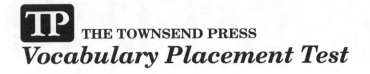

THE TOWNSEND PRESS

Vocabulary Placement Test

NAME: _____

SECTION: _____ DATE: _____

SCORE: _____

ANSWER SHEET

1. _____	26. _____	51. _____	76. _____
2. _____	27. _____	52. _____	77. _____
3. _____	28. _____	53. _____	78. _____
4. _____	29. _____	54. _____	79. _____
5. _____	30. _____	55. _____	80. _____
6. _____	31. _____	56. _____	81. _____
7. _____	32. _____	57. _____	82. _____
8. _____	33. _____	58. _____	83. _____
9. _____	34. _____	59. _____	84. _____
10. _____	35. _____	60. _____	85. _____
11. _____	36. _____	61. _____	86. _____
12. _____	37. _____	62. _____	87. _____
13. _____	38. _____	63. _____	88. _____
14. _____	39. _____	64. _____	89. _____
15. _____	40. _____	65. _____	90. _____
16. _____	41. _____	66. _____	91. _____
17. _____	42. _____	67. _____	92. _____
18. _____	43. _____	68. _____	93. _____
19. _____	44. _____	69. _____	94. _____
20. _____	45. _____	70. _____	95. _____
21. _____	46. _____	71. _____	96. _____
22. _____	47. _____	72. _____	97. _____
23. _____	48. _____	73. _____	98. _____
24. _____	49. _____	74. _____	99. _____
25. _____	50. _____	75. _____	100. _____

ANSWER KEY

1. b	26. a	51. a	76. a
2. a	27. b	52. c	77. d
3. c	28. c	53. a	78. c
4. b	29. c	54. d	79. d
5. d	30. a	55. c	80. a
6. a	31. b	56. d	81. d
7. b	32. c	57. b	82. b
8. b	33. d	58. d	83. a
9. d	34. a	59. a	84. b
10. a	35. c	60. d	85. c
11. b	36. a	61. b	86. c
12. a	37. b	62. d	87. a
13. c	38. a	63. b	88. a
14. a	39. c	64. d	89. c
15. b	40. b	65. b	90. b
16. d	41. a	66. b	91. c
17. c	42. a	67. c	92. b
18. a	43. d	68. a	93. c
19. d	44. c	69. a	94. d
20. b	45. c	70. b	95. b
21. b	46. d	71. a	96. d
22. a	47. b	72. d	97. c
23. c	48. d	73. c	98. b
24. d	49. b	74. d	99. a
25. c	50. a	75. b	100. d

To the Instructor: Use these guidelines to match your students with the appropriate TP vocabulary book.

Score	0–9	10–24	25–49	50–74	75–90	91–100
Recommended Book	VB	GBV	BVS	IVS	AVS	AWP

Words in BUILDING VOCABULARY SKILLS, SHORT VERSION

accelerate
accessible
acknowledge
acute
adapt
adverse
advocate
affirm
alleged
allude
alternative
anecdote
anonymous
apprehensive
appropriate
arrogant
audible
avert
awe
bestow
candid
cite
coerce
coherent
comparable
compatible
compel
compensate
competent
comply
concede
conceive
concise
confirm
consecutive
consequence
conservative
conspicuous
contrary
convey

data
deceptive
defer
defy
delete
delusion
denounce
derive
destiny
detain
deter
deteriorate
devise
dialog
diminish
disclose
discriminate
dismal
dismay
dispense
diversity
donor
drastic
elaborate
elapse
elite
emerge
endeavor
endorse
equate
erode
erratic
essence
evasive
exempt
exile
exotic
extensive
fluent
forfeit

fortify
frugal
futile
gesture
gruesome
harass
hypocrite
idealistic
illuminate
illusion
immunity
impact
impair
impartial
imply
impose
impulsive
indifferent
indignant
indulgent
inept
inevitable
infer
inhibit
innate
integrity
intervene
isolate
lament
legitimate
lenient
lethal
liberal
malicious
mediocre
menace
moderate
morale
morbid
naive

notable
novice
obsession
obstacle
obstinate
option
ordeal
overt
parallel
passive
patron
perceptive
persistent
phobia
plausible
prevail
procrastinate
profound
prominent
propel
provoke
prudent
query
rational
recede
recipient
reciprocate
recur
refuge
refute
reminisce
reprimand
restrain
retain
retort
retrieve
revert
revoke
ridicule
ritual

sadistic
savor
scapegoat
seclusion
sedate
severity
shrewd
simultaneous
site
skeptical
stereotype
stimulate
strategy
submit
subside
subtle
summon
superficial
supplement
surpass
susceptible
sustain
tactic
tedious
tentative
theoretical
transaction
transition
transmit
undermine
unique
universal
urban
valid
verify
versatile
vigorous
vital
vivid
vocation

Words in IMPROVING VOCABULARY SKILLS, SHORT VERSION

absolve	constitute	enhance	intermittent	prompt
abstain	constrict	enigma	intricate	prone
acclaim	contemplate	epitome	intrinsic	proponent
adamant	contemporary	escalate	ironic	punitive
adjacent	contend	esteem	legacy	qualm
affiliate	contrive	euphemism	longevity	quest
agnostic	conventional	evoke	lucrative	rapport
alleviate	conversely	exemplify	magnitude	rationale
allusion	covert	exhaustive	malign	recession
aloof	cryptic	explicit	mandatory	reconcile
altruistic	curtail	exploit	mediate	rehabilitate
ambivalent	cynic	expulsion	menial	relentless
amiable	decipher	extrovert	mercenary	render
amoral	default	fallible	methodical	reprisal
animosity	deficient	feasible	mobile	retaliate
antagonist	deficit	feign	mortify	revulsion
appease	degenerate	fiscal	mundane	rigor
arbitrary	demise	flagrant	muted	rupture
aspire	depict	flippant	niche	sanctuary
assail	deplete	fluctuate	nocturnal	saturate
attest	detract	formulate	nominal	scrutiny
attribute	detrimental	furtive	nullify	sinister
augment	devastate	gape	nurture	speculate
averse	digress	garble	obscure	squander
avid	diligent	gaunt	obsolete	succumb
banal	discern	genial	ominous	suffice
benefactor	disdain	gloat	orient	syndrome
benevolent	dispatch	habitat	pacify	taint
blatant	dispel	hypothetical	pathetic	tangible
blight	dissent	immaculate	perception	terminate
calamity	diversion	impasse	persevere	transcend
charisma	divulge	implausible	plagiarism	transient
commemorate	dwindle	implicit	poignant	traumatic
complacent	eccentric	incentive	ponder	turmoil
comprehensive	elation	incoherent	pragmatic	venture
concurrent	elicit	incorporate	precedent	vile
condone	empathy	indispensable	predominant	vindictive
confiscate	encounter	infamous	prerequisite	virile
congenial	endow	inhibition	pretentious	vulnerable
consensus	engross	intercede	prevalent	waive

Words in ADVANCING VOCABULARY SKILLS, SHORT VERSION

abrasive
adept
admonish
ambiguous
analogy
annihilate
antithesis
attrition
atrophy
auspicious
austere
berate
bolster
circumvent
clandestine
cohesive
collaborate
complement
connoisseur
conspiracy
contingency
contrite
criterion
culmination
decorum
deplore
depreciate
deprivation
deride
derogatory
despondent
detriment
dexterous
discreet
discretion
disparity
dissident
distraught
docile
egocentric

emanate
embellish
emulate
encompass
entrepreneur
equivocate
eradicate
esoteric
espouse
estrange
euphoric
exacerbate
exhilaration
exhort
exonerate
exorbitant
expedite
extenuating
extricate
fabricate
facetious
facilitate
facsimile
fastidious
flamboyant
flout
foible
forestall
fortuitous
fraudulent
fritter
germane
gregarious
grievous
grotesque
heinous
hierarchy
holistic
homogeneous
impeccable

impending
imperative
impetuous
implement
impromptu
inadvertent
inane
incapacitate
incongruous
indigenous
indiscriminate
infallible
inference
innocuous
innuendo
inquisitive
insidious
insinuate
instigate
interrogate
intuition
inundate
juxtapose
lethargy
liability
liaison
lucid
macabre
magnanimous
masochist
maudlin
mesmerize
metamorphosis
meticulous
misconstrue
mitigate
nebulous
notorious
objective
oblivious

obsequious
obtrusive
omnipotent
opportune
optimum
orthodox
ostentatious
panacea
paramount
perfunctory
permeate
placebo
plight
predisposed
presumptuous
proficient
prognosis
prolific
propensity
provocative
quandary
rancor
rebuke
recrimination
redeem
regress
reinstate
rejuvenate
relegate
relinquish
replete
reprehensible
repugnant
resilient
reticent
retribution
retrospect
robust
rudimentary
sanction

scoff
scrupulous
sedentary
sensory
sham
solace
solicitous
sordid
sporadic
squelch
standardize
staunch
stint
stringent
subordinate
subsidize
subversive
superficially
superfluous
symmetrical
synchronize
tenet
tenuous
terse
transgress
travesty
tumult
turbulent
ubiquitous
unprecedented
utilitarian
validate
vehement
venerate
verbose
vicarious
vindicate
vociferous
zealot
zenith

Notes